Mothering in East Asian Communities: Politics and Practices

Mothering in East Asian Communities

Politics and Practices

Edited by

Patti Duncan and Gina Wong

Demeter Press logo based on the sculpture "Demeter" by Maria-Luise Bodirsky
<www.keramik-atelier.bodirsky.de>

Cover Print by Shu-Ju Wang, "(Asleep in the Chamber of Mirrors) Moonlight
Becomes Frost Becomes Apple Pie Becomes Moon Cake Becomes Moonlight,"
from Red Bean Paste and Apple Pie, 2012, www.fingerstothebone.com Printed
and Bound in Canada.

Library and Archives Canada Cataloguing in Publication

Mothering in East Asian communities : politics and practices / edited by
Patti Duncan and Gina Wong.
Includes bibliographical references.

ISBN 978-1-927335-24-6 (pbk.)

1. Motherhood–Political aspects–Canada. 2. Motherhood– Social aspects–
Canada. 3. Motherhood–Political aspects–United States. 4. Motherhood–Social
aspects–United States. 5. Mothers– Canada. 6. Mothers–United States. 7. East
Asians–Canada. 8. East Asians–United States. I. Duncan, Patti, 1970-, editor II.
Wong, Gina, 1971-, editor

HQ759.M88398 2014   306.874'308995071   C2014-905837-3

Demeter Press
140 Holland Street West
P. O. Box 13022
Bradford, ON L3Z 2Y5
Tel: (905) 775-9089
Email: info@demeterpress.org
Website: www.demeterpress.org

Table of Contents

TABLE OF CONTENTS

Dedications

Dedicated to our children—Chance, Cassie, Iris, and Kieran.

Acknowledgements

We are grateful to Andrea O'Reilly whose tireless work in motherhood scholarship has had no bounds in giving voice and affirmation to the experiences of motherhood and mothering across cultures and communities. We greatly appreciate her support and encouragement of our passion and experiences as mothers within East Asian communities. We also want to acknowledge and thank all the contributors to the volume, who worked with us for over two years to see it to its completion. We appreciate your powerful approaches to this subject, and are inspired by your commitment to thinking through the politics and practices of mothering in East Asian communities. We especially want to thank Shu-Ju Wang, for generously offering her art for the cover of the book. We also thank Lyndsay Kirkham at Demeter Press, for her work to get this collection out into the world. And for support in completing this project, we thank Susan Shaw, Karen Mills, and the School of Language, Culture, and Society, at Oregon State University.

As well, we acknowledge mothers of East Asian descent living within the complex, diverse realities of North America. Each day, your pride and dedication to your children, families, and communities are integral to the fabric of these communities, and to the cultures in which we exist. It's our hope that this book honors as well as gives voice and legitimacy to all of our experiences.

I (Patti) thank my partner, Skye, for supporting this work, and my son, Chance, for inspiring it. I'm also grateful to Gina, friend and collaborator, for envisioning this project with me.

My (Gina) deepest gratitude goes to Patti for her work in seeing this collection through and for her great leadership, collaboration, and brilliance.

I also thank my partner Tom and my children — Iris, Cassie, and Kieran. Bringing this collection to fruition led me to reflect on my parent's (Wai Kiang and Grace Wong) experience of emigration to Canada and what it may have been like; and the hardships they encountered to create a better life in Canada. For that, I am particularly thankful.

ACKNOWLEDGEMENTS OF REPRINTED CHAPTERS

Hosu Kim and Grace M. Cho, "The Kinship of Violence," from *Journal of Korean Adoption Studies*, vol. 1, no. 3 (Summer 2012) edited by Jennifer Kwon Dobbs. Copyright 2012 by Global Overseas Adoptees Link. Reprinted by permission of Global Overseas Adoptees Link.

Fiona Tinwei Lam, "Chrysanthemum," "Kite," and "Snowman," from *Enter the Chrysanthemum* (Caitlin Press, 2009). Reprinted with permission of Vici Johnston, Caitlin Press.

Rita Wong, "a wandering daughter's grammar," from *Monkeypuzzle* (Press Gang, 1998). Reprinted with permission of Rita Wong.

Fiona Tinwei Lam, "Tiger in the Hornet's Nest: The Furor over Amy Chua's Battle Hymn of the Tiger Mother" reprinted with permission of both author and publisher from The Tyee online news magazine, January 20, 2011: http://thetyee.ca/Life/2011/01/20/TigerMother/.

Introduction

Contextualizing and Politicizing Mothering in East Asian Communities

PATTI DUNCAN AND GINA WONG

The cover of *Mothering in East Asian Communities* features a recent painting by Asian American artist, Shu-Ju Wang, entitled "(Asleep in the Chamber of Mirrors) Moonlight Becomes Frost Becomes Apple Pie Becomes Moon Cake Becomes Moonlight." This polyptych of four panels, painted in gouache and acrylic, is part of a series by the artist, "Red Bean Paste and Apple Pie," and engages themes of food as commentary on social and political meanings of East Asian experiences. It represents, in Wang's words, "a personal exploration of my story of immigration and a broader look at what it means to be an American." [1] As mothers of East Asian descent, living and working in North America, this painting captures what we desire to convey through this collection. The image at the center of this painting indicates both a beating heart and a small giraffe, evoking feelings about pregnancy, childhood, and the work associated with caring for children. Food and flowers surround this center, with depictions of apple pies and moon cakes, suggestive of nurturance within the context of Asian immigrant families and communities. We strongly identify with the circularity suggested by the painting's title, implying a search for place, a politicization of "home," and a persistent sense of movement. To be "asleep in the chamber of mirrors" signals a sense of rest and caregiving, and simultaneously a process of conscious self-reflection, structured by and through multiple looking relations. To us, Wang's piece delineates the complexities illustrated within the

I

chapters of this collection, revolving around politics and practices of motherhood and mothering in East Asian communities.

In this introduction, we contextualize motherhood/mothering among East Asian women, discussing central themes and current challenges and possibilities that contribute to this discourse. We raise critical questions about the social, cultural, and political meanings of race, class, gender, nation, sexual orientation, and mothering, for Asian women. And we discuss the unique contributions of this volume, which includes writings by scholars, artists, activists, and East Asian mothers, in genres ranging from academic papers representing multiple disciplines and intersecting politics to creative reflections and poetry.

To ground our discussion and make clear our own stakes in this discourse, we briefly contextualize our relationships to motherhood within East Asian communities. We do so with the hope of engaging feminist principles of standpoint theory and situated knowledges, making clear how our lived, daily experiences are connected to larger social and political processes. We are committed to thinking through the intersections of race, ethnicity, gender, class, sexuality, culture, and national belonging that shape the experiences of East Asian mothers, both in our home countries and in diasporic communities, and we situate ourselves to highlight the ways in which our personal experiences are grounded in larger, social/structural processes. Patti Duncan is an Asian Pacific American feminist scholar and mother, of Korean and Scottish descent. She identifies as mixed race, keenly attentive to the distinct cultural meanings this marker carries in the U.S. and South Korea. As the child of a Korean immigrant mother and a white U.S. former army serviceman, Patti grew up with the stigma associated with both Korean camptown workers and Asian "military brides" in the U.S. Now, as the mother of a mixed race son, she is interested in exploring the ways our reproductive labor—as East Asian feminist mothers—may offset the multiple systems of oppression that our children encounter in an increasingly globalized world. Gina Wong is a Chinese Canadian psychologist, feminist writer, researcher, and academic who is passionate about understanding mothering and motherhood from scholarly and academic perspectives. She was born and lived in Montreal, Quebec until the age of nine years old with her two older sisters and Chinese immigrant parents. At the age of ten, her family moved to Edmonton, Alberta and her younger sister was born. In her girlhood, Gina experienced discrimination and racism from her peers. As well, her parents experienced issues of acculturation, which affected the family dynamics in deeply entrenched ways. As a mother of two young mixed race daughters, and as a psychologist who works with Asian girls and women, Gina is keenly motivated to understand, give voice to, and engender sensitivity around experiences of East Asian girls, women, and mothers.

THE POLITICS OF TERMINOLOGY

In this project, we have been concerned about the inclusiveness of the term, "East Asian," often assumed to refer only to those of Chinese, Japanese, and Korean backgrounds. We use the term as inclusively as possible, including Southeast Asian communities. We also use the term interchangeably with other terms, for example, "Asian North American," "Asian Pacific Islander," and, at times, "Asian." However, we realize the limitations associated with these politics of terminology. While Asian North American is frequently used to denote communities of Asian descent in both the U.S. and Canada—the primary areas of focus for this volume—some critics have argued that this designation also risks subsuming Canadian writings and experiences under an assumed U.S. "American" context. Also, while within U.S. cultural politics, the terms "Asian Pacific American," "Asian and Pacific Islander," and "Asian American" (or "Asian/American") are commonly used within our communities, these terms do not carry the same political meaning or resonance in Canadian and other contexts. Even within each context, these commonly used terms risk rendering invisible the communities often most marginalized.

Demeter Press recently published *South Asian Mothering: Negotiating Culture, Family and Selfhood*, edited by Jasjit K. Sangha and Tahira Gonsalves, and our book is imagined as a complementary collection with our explicit focus on the experiences of East Asian mothers and motherhood, particularly in relation to Canadian and U.S. contexts. When we employ the term "East Asian" we hope to make explicit both the specificities of East Asian women's experiences of mothering and motherhood, and the significant relationships our communities have with other communities of color. We make an effort to use "Asian American" and "Asian Canadian" to refer to these distinct contexts, with full realization that our experiences in these different national contexts inform our understandings of racialization and the naming practices that go along with it. And when speaking about Asians more generally, including within or in relation to various homelands, we attempt to clarify and situate within specific geographical contexts as much as possible, noting also the problems and limitations with such associations, particularly for those of us who have experienced physical and/or cultural forms of displacement and resettlement.

HISTORICIZING EAST ASIAN MOTHERING

Scholars who explore motherhood in communities of color in North America draw attention to the ways in which race, class, gender, and other categories intersect in experiences of mothering, emphasizing the ways in which women of color have been excluded from an idealized white, middle-class, heteronormative model of motherhood. Historically, like other people of color in North America, Asian immigrants have been exploited for their labor and rarely treated as members of families. In the late nineteenth century and early twentieth century, nearly a million Asian immigrants entered the U.S., many of whom sought work or were recruited as contract laborers to build the transcontinental railroad and work on plantations, and were subsequently stigmatized as "coolies." In Canada, Asian immigrants were similarly recruited to work on the Canadian Pacific Railway, and perform other types of hard labor. The majority of these workers were men, leading to "bachelor societies" in which male workers were physically separated from their families left behind in the home countries.

Anti-Asian U.S. immigration laws included the Chinese Exclusion Act of 1882. As well, known as "humiliation day" in Canada, July 1, 1923, the Canadian Chinese Exclusion Act came into effect and a Head Tax for immigrants to enter Canada was invoked, increasing from fifty dollars to five hundred dollars. For nearly a quarter of a century, Chinese immigration to Canada was thwarted. Such laws promoted labor exploitation and resulted in split-family households (Amott and Matthaei; Takaki). The deliberate fracturing of Asian families served the economic interests of white, middle- and upper-class landowners, who could pay Asian male workers less than a "family wage" and house them in dormitory style bunks. During this period, Asian women faced severe restrictions in entering the U.S. and Canada, and comprised only a small percentage of Asian immigrant communities (Chan; Takaki). Some women entered the countries as "picture brides," a result of the restrictive "Gentleman's Agreement" of 1907, which prohibited the entry of Japanese laborers to the U.S., but granted access to wives and children of those already in the country. Given the presence of anti-miscegenation laws and sentiments, many Asian immigrant men were unable to partner with other women in the U.S., and thus arranged marriages from afar through letters and photographs (L. Kim). Hence, Asian

North American experiences of motherhood were forged from this period on within transnational contexts, shaped by anti-Asian immigrant laws and sentiments. In fact, as Laura Hyun-Yi Kang suggests, "[a]rrangements such as 'split households,' 'paper sons,' and 'picture brides' reveal the geographically scattered and situationally invented modes of marriage and family formation for early Asian immigrant communities" (142).

More recently, Asian immigrant women have been constructed as cheap labor, often within service industries and domestic work. Factors associated with globalization have resulted in economic disparities among various Asian communities in Canada and the U.S., as well as an increase in Asian women as migrant laborers in "care work," including domestic work, childcare, nursing, and the sex industry. These forces affect Asian North American women's experiences of motherhood and contribute to the global displacement of women and the racialized division of mothering and reproductive labor. When Asian immigrant women and other women from the global South migrate to perform care work as domestic workers and nannies for children in the North, they experience what Pierrette Hondagneu-Sotelo and Ernestine Avila refer to as "transnational motherhood," in which women with few economic options are compelled to leave their own children behind to care for the children of those with greater economic options and resources. This framework suggests more elastic definitions of motherhood, "shaped by economic insecurity and processes of racialized gender, in which some mothers may not have the option to be physically present with their own children but nevertheless are still actively engaged in the experience of motherhood and/or the process of mothering" (Duncan, "Teaching the Politics of Transnational Motherhood" 71).

THEORETICAL FRAMEWORKS

Our understanding of the politics and practices of motherhood/mothering within East Asian communities is influenced by the general scholarship of motherhood studies, shaped by such thinkers as Adrienne Rich, Sara Ruddick, Evelyn Nakano Glenn, Patricia Hill Collins, and Andrea O'Reilly. One of the foundational concepts within motherhood studies has been the critical distinction between *motherhood*—as institution—and *mothering*—to refer to women's lived experiences of having and/or raising children. This framework draws attention to the ways in which motherhood is socially and culturally constructed, shaped by race, class, culture, sexuality, and other social categories. It rejects any easy formation of a "universal" experience of motherhood, and allows for an understanding of the ways that motherhood as an institution has often been oppressive for many groups of women, even while the act of mothering may provide a space for resistance, empowerment, and joy. Another critical framework that informs and shapes the scholarship on East Asian mothering is that of intersectionality. This feminist framework, originally delineated by Kimberlé Crenshaw to analyze the experiences of Black women, is a theoretical and methodological approach that suggests that all forms of oppression intersect with one another, creating a matrix of oppression. Gender, race, class, sexuality, nation, ability, and other categories intersect, shaping our experiences and social interactions.

Also central to the study of mothering in East Asian communities is a transnational feminist theoretical framework, attentive to global contexts, histories of colonialism and war, and relations between nation-states, as well as our specific histories of immigration and migration. This framework, invoking Chandra Mohanty's discussion in "Genealogies of Community, Home, and Nation," takes into account the ways in which East Asian women engaged in mothering practices currently live within diasporic and transnational networks, rooted in specific homelands while also creating communities in Canada, the U.S., and many other countries. East Asian women in North America may identify as immigrants or refugees, as migrant or temporary workers, as transnational adoptees, and/or as second, third, or fourth generation Asian Americans or Canadians, and U.S. or Canadian citizens, for example. Many of us are mixed race or multiracial. Some of us are not aware of the specifics of our racial, ethnic backgrounds. Some of us may experience specific issues related to war and resettlement. As Linda Trinh Vo and Sucheng Chan suggest, many first-generation Vietnamese, Cambodian, and Hmong women resettled in North America after experiencing war and trauma and living as refugees. And while many of us may speak multiple languages, others have not had access to our so-called "mother tongues"—the languages of our "home" countries—or we were never taught to speak these languages. Important to note is that East Asians in North America experience various levels of access to resources. Contrary to the myth of the "model minority," not all East Asians are materially successful, middle-class, heterosexual, able-bodied, members of nuclear families. In fact, the geopolitics that structure our (lack of) belonging actually delegitimize some members of our communities who do not meet the norms associated with citizenship status, upward mobility, and family.

Finally, the scholarship on mothering within East Asian communities is also informed by epistemological frameworks within women's and gender studies (particularly women of color studies) and Asian (North) American studies, both of which critique traditional methodological approaches, arguing instead for alternative frameworks attentive to the voices and experiences of marginalized communities. These scholarly frameworks, illustrated within many of the chapters of this volume, are rooted in movements for social justice that emphasize structural, rather than individual or interpersonal analyses of power relations. Such approaches recognize the value of lived experience and frequently rely on standpoint theory, a concept noted earlier, which recognizes that our perspectives are shaped by our social locations.

CENTRAL THEMES WITHIN THE SCHOLARSHIP ON MOTHERHOOD IN EAST ASIAN CONTEXTS

While there are numerous themes relevant to the scholarship on mothering within East Asian communities, we focus on several issues that influence the current discourse, including mothering within—and despite—legacies of imperialism, colonization, war, and militarism; mothering across borders (related to the effects of globalization and the labor exploitation of Asian migrant workers); transnational adoption; and mothering in the welfare state within increasingly neoliberal contexts. In recent years, all of these themes have been central to the scholarly work, activism, and community organizing of Asian North American women and mothers.

East Asian perspectives on motherhood/mothering must acknowledge the significant impact of histories of colonialism and war on our communities. Early patterns of immigration to North America were heavily influenced by these forces, and more recent migration patterns reflect the ways in which nation states within Asia continue to experience militarization and grapple with multiple legacies of colonialism. For example, some scholars have explored the experiences of Korean *kijich'on* (military camptown) women who associated with U.S. soldiers stationed in South Korea. As several researchers have demonstrated, a highly regulated system of militarized prostitution exists wherever U.S. army bases are established, as has been documented in South Korea, the Philippines, Okinawa, and Vietnam (Moon; Enloe; Yuh; Okazawa-Rey; Sturdevant and Stoltzfus). Social interactions within these military camptowns emblematize extreme disparities between U.S. military personnel and local communities, as discussed by Hosu Kim and Grace Cho in this volume. Wherever the camptowns exist, locals report not only an organized sex industry but also significant increases in poverty and violence against women and children. As Katharine Moon has demonstrated, militarized prostitution in South Korea is highly systematized, sponsored, and regulated by both the U.S. military and the Korean government. Local women who associate with U.S. soldiers are often stigmatized within their communities and families, and as Margo Okazawa-Rey and others suggest, their children are subsequently stigmatized. One reason for the stigmatization is that Korean women and children associated with U.S. military personnel signify the unequal neoimperialist relationship between the U.S. and Korea, and become physical embodiments of war, loss, and the subjugation of Korea by the U.S. (Duncan, "Genealogies of Unbelonging").

Similarly, Melinda de Jesús, in *Pinay Power: Theorizing the Filipina/American Experience*, suggests that Filipino Americans "suffer from the effects of colonial mentality: our complicated relationship with the United States and its imperialist legacy has had a tremendous impact upon our sense of history and identity" (3). In addition, Filipinas, she argues, remain "contingently visible: as nameless, faceless overseas contract workers, sex workers, and mail-order brides scattered across the globe" (3). This historical invisibility of Filipinas within the diaspora also renders invisible the experiences of Filipina mothers, particularly those whose work is already invisible within an international division of labor.

This point leads to another critical theme within the scholarship on mothering in East Asian communities, namely the practice of mothering from afar as noted in our earlier section. Sau-ling Wong uses the term "diverted mothering" to define a process in which "time and energy available for mothering are diverted from those who, by kinship or communal ties, are their more rightful recipients" (69). She focuses on the "hidden power differential" that structures diverted mothering, to emphasize the ways in which mothering responsibilities may be distributed among groups marked by racialized gender. While Wong focuses on the reproductive labor of women of color in the U.S. in cinematic representations, her point is echoed by other scholars who locate this phenomenon within the material effects of globalization and structural adjustment policies, compelling some women to engage in mothering and care work within an international division of reproductive labor (Nakano Glenn; Parreñas; Chang).

Transnational adoption represents another central theme in the scholarship on mothering within East Asian communities. Also referred to as international adoption or intercountry adoption, transnational adoption has been heavily shaped by relationships between sending and receiving nations, for example South Korea, one of the largest "sending" nations, and the U.S., one of the most prominent "receiving" nations (Trenka, Oparah, and Shin). According to recent reports, there are up to 200,000 Korean adoptees in the U.S., Canada, and other western countries, and thousands of adoptees from China, Vietnam, Thailand, Cambodia, the Philippines, Taiwan, Indonesia, and other Asian countries. This unidirectional movement of children from Asia and the Pacific to western countries also highlights colonial relations between nations, as Kim and Cho argue in their chapter in this collection, "The Kinship of Violence," and results in large communities of East Asians in North America who were adopted by predominantly white parents. In addition, western military invasions and occupations within Asian countries have resulted in transnational adoptions from those countries, leading Karen Dubinsky to suggest that transnational adoption is integral to foreign policy for countries like the U.S. Largely invisible in the discourse on transnational adoption are the birth mothers, including thousands of Asian women compelled to give up their children by a variety of complex factors, often shaped by war and militarism, sexual violence, association with the sex industry, stigma of mixed race children (especially those fathered by U.S. servicemen in some countries, as noted earlier), the stigma of single motherhood, and economic necessity, among other reasons. Rupa Bagga-Raoulx discusses the narratives and experience of birth mothers in her chapter in this collection. Also, as Jennifer Katz and Emily Hunt suggest, ideas about "good mothers" have often been associated with white, middle-class, heterosexual norms, resulting in a privileging of adoptive mothers over birth mothers.

Mothering is differentially constructed for women, shaping women's experiences of motherhood based on race, class, sexuality, age, ability, and other social categories. Notions of "good" and "bad," or "fit" and "unfit" mothers are often informed by these categories, resulting in some mothers being valued *as* mothers, while others are devalued and face serious obstacles to mothering their children. As one example, Timothy Gitzen, in his chapter in this collection, analyzes how mothers of gay sons are cast as "bad" mothers within contemporary South Korean society. Furthermore, as we discuss in the next section, popular assumptions of Asian Pacific Islanders as "model minorities" contrast profoundly with the realities for many Asian immigrant and refugee women in the U.S. welfare state.

ADDITIONAL CHALLENGES FOR EAST ASIAN MOTHERS

"Where are you from? (When are you going back?)" This question, so common and frequently cited by Asian North American writers, raises a number of critical challenges for East Asian mothers. First, the common follow-up: "where are you *really* from?" asked of those whose responses fail to satisfy the curiosity of the interrogators, implies that Asians can never claim full citizenship or national belonging within Canada or the U.S. Second, as the parenthetical note above suggests, the question always implies an expected "return" to the homeland. Our presence here is anticipated to be temporary, illuminating the physical, ideological, and geopolitical borders between nation-states, and suggesting a lack of national belonging. And finally, the assumption that we do not belong subsequently implies that our children, too, cannot belong. Integral to these challenges are the intersections of racism, xenophobia, and the pressure to assimilate to (white) mainstream society. When we—or our children—are mixed race with light skin, this pressure may be more complex, as there may be an additional pressure to "pass." In fact, the potential challenges of raising mixed race sons are taken up in this volume in a chapter by Melinda de Jesús, Patti Duncan, Reshmi Dutt-Ballerstadt, and Linda Pierce Allen.

Another contemporary challenge for mothers and families of East Asian descent involves the experience of transnational motherhood mentioned earlier. Processes associated with globalization and structural adjustment politics affect Asian women's access to employment, resulting in their over-representation in migrant "care work" and reproductive labor, often requiring that they leave their own children behind in countries of origin, to travel abroad in order to find employment as nannies, domestic workers, and/or in the sex industry. Their experience of mothering their own children from afar may be comprised of phone calls and remittances, while their actual physical mothering labor is transferred to the children of their employers. This process has had a particularly devastating effect on Filipino families, as Rhacel Salazar Parrenas points out, although this formation of transnational households is also documented among women and families of many other sending countries. As Charlene Tung suggests, Asian women and other migrant women engage in transformative redefinitions of motherhood and mothering through their increasingly complex gendered, racialized negotiations with the demands of work and motherhood, particularly through transnational mothering. Their experiences illustrate structural and institutionalized forms of oppression, as well as creative modes of resistance and survival. In her chapter in this collection, Valerie Francisco analyzes the politicization and activism among a group of Filipino migrant mothers in New York.

At the same time, mothering practices among Asian North American women are also constrained by an overarching set of stereotypes and controlling images, including the myth of the model minority, an assumption that Asians as a group are middle- or upper-class, highly educated, successful in math and science, and extremely competitive. Along with the stereotype of the model minority—a trope engaged by several authors in this collection—East Asian women are frequently depicted within a binary representation consisting of the hypersexual, morally depraved "dragon lady" and the submissive, passive, and docile "lotus blossom" (Tajima). Such representations are common in mainstream cinema and popular culture, and contribute to what Sumi Cho calls "racialized sexual harassment," as well as other forms of racialized, sexualized violence. A more recent controlling image of East Asian mothers, specifically, is that of the Asian "Tiger Mother," revolving around Amy Chua's controversial memoir, *Battle Hymn of the Tiger Mother*. In her book, Chua proudly describes raising her two daughters in an extremely strict, middle-class environment, in which they were required to earn all As in school, practice the piano and violin for hours each day, and never attend play-dates or sleepovers. In Chua's argument, strict "Chinese parenting" is superior to lackadaisical and overly accommodating "Western parenting," and results in greater success among Asians. Her essentialist argument—and generalizations about "Chinese" and "Western" parenting—have been critiqued by many readers, but the overwhelming success of the book indicates the power and allure of this stereotype, an issue addressed by several authors of this volume. Taken together, the controlling images and stereotypes of East Asians contribute to the invisibility of the needs and experiences of working-class and poor members of our communities, particularly those who are immigrants and refugees. They also further marginalize all East Asian women, especially those who are not heterosexual, cisgender, and able-bodied. Like other stereotypes, these representations create rigid norms for East Asian women and mothers, making it difficult to recognize the complex realities of our communities.

Within Asian North American literature and literary criticism, a great deal has been written about motherhood in relation to conflicted mother-daughter relationships, particularly between Asian immigrant mothers and their U.S. or Canadian born daughters. The conflicts that often structure these relationships have been explored in well known writings such as Maxine Hong Kingston's *The Woman Warrior: A Memoir of a Girlhood Among Ghosts*, Amy Tan's *The Joy Luck Club*, Fae Myenne Ng's *Bone*, and Nora Okja Keller's *Comfort Woman*, as well as critical analyses by Leslie Bow, Wendy Ho, Erin Khue Ninh, and others. While the conflicts are sometimes portrayed as the result of cultural differences between first and second generation Asians, some critics have pointed out the ways that such conflicts are actually deepened and reinforced by racism and anti-immigrant sentiments in North America, economic insecurity, cultural displacement, and the pressure to assimilate. These experiences are also influenced by the stereotypes of Asian women and girls mentioned above. In her chapter in this collection, Pamela Thoma explores some of these themes, revealing the ways neoliberal maternal discourse is reinforced through particular narratives.

Other challenges for East Asian mothers include a simultaneous invisibility and hypervisibility, as evidenced by the multitude of stereotypes, particularly about Asian women, mothers, and family norms; increased poverty for many recent immigrants and refugees; barriers to citizenship and language; labor exploitation; lack of access to health care, including reproductive health and justice; and multiple forms of violence, including domestic violence, sexual violence, and the forms of systematized state violence that bolster oppression in our communities. These challenges are compounded by the intersections of racism, sexism, classism, heterosexism and homophobia, and other systems of oppression.

As noted earlier, mothering is differentially constructed for women, structured by race, ethnicity, class, culture, national belonging, sexuality, and ability, and other social categories. These processes result in some mothers being valued for their work as mothers, while others are devalued, and their children are subsequently devalued. For example, in the current welfare state, prevailing cultural narratives of Asian Pacific Americans as model minorities contrast sharply with the construction of Asian immigrant and refugee women as abusing the U.S. welfare system and squandering public resources. As Lynn Fujiwara has argued, the dismantling of federally mandated social programs, including the 1996 Personal Responsibility Work Opportunity Reconciliation Act (PRWORA) signed by President Bill Clinton, which targeted immigrant mothers and their children, has had a devastating effect on Asian immigrant families in the U.S., particularly within the Southeast Asian community. Fujiwara notes: "The pervasiveness of the 'model minority' myth concealed the depth of poverty among some Asian immigrant and refugee groups, and the increasing need for public assistance among Asian immigrants and refugees, thus veiling the obstacles that these individuals and families negotiate as they operate in a system that defines them as outsiders and undeserving of public support" (xvi). In addition, neoliberal economic policies and globalization that result in cutting welfare entitlements and public services result in what Evelyn Nakano Glenn refers to as racialized gendered servitude, structured by unequal relationships in care work, as well as the transnational family arrangements mentioned earlier. Thus, poor Asian immigrant women, like many other groups of women of color, have encountered serious obstacles in mothering their children.

SITES OF RESISTANCE AND EMPOWERMENT

Despite the many challenges delineated above, East Asian women remain committed to caring for their children and families, and work to resist multiple, intersecting systems of oppression. In doing so, they create an empowering vision for Asian American and Asian Canadian mothers and families. For example, in Merle Woo's well-known 1981 poem, "Letter to Ma," she writes, "…my life has been formed by your life. Together we have lived one hundred and eleven years in this country as yellow women…" (141). Acknowledging the many sacrifices the narrator's mother made, she continues, "[w]orking all your life as a maid, waitress, salesclerk, office worker, mother. But throughout there is an image of you as strong and courageous, and persevering…" (141). And because of her mother's strength and perseverance, she writes, "I saw myself as having worth; now I begin to love myself more, see our potential, and fight for just that kind of social change that will affirm me, my race, my sex, my heritage. And while I affirm myself, Ma, I affirm you" (142). Indeed, affirming East Asian women and mothers by honoring their stories and experiences of struggle, invisibility, marginalization, pain, and resistance is one of the goals of this collection. By doing so, we challenge notions that East Asians have to assimilate to North American standards to fit in and that we do not have a place of belonging in the U.S. and Canada. We include accounts of how we make our lives as East Asian daughters and mothers amid the myth of the model minority and the tiger mother stereotype. And against a backdrop of militarism, government and media propaganda, and gendered, racialized sociopolitical contexts, authors in this collection explore and critique politics and practices that impinge on East Asian mothers' roles and opportunities.

While the oppression of East Asian mothers is patently told in this volume, so too are their strength and courage delineated as authors raise questions about how we challenge and resist the multiple barriers experienced by East Asian mothers. Through interrogating the social, cultural, and political meanings of race, class, gender, sexual orientation, nation, and mothering, we hope to identify and resist oppression. Also, acknowledging and giving voice to our unique and distinct experiences may validate, legitimize, and empower Asian women and mothers.

An example of such validation and empowerment is the "Mama's Day Our Way" campaign by Strong Families, a national initiative in the U.S. working for social justice for all families, including immigrant families, low-income families, and LGBTQ families. Strong Families is a program of Forward Together, discussed in this volume by Kryn Freehling-Burton and Eveline Shen. Recognizing that the majority of families do not fit the white, middle-class, heterosexual norms often comprising "ideal" notions of family, this campaign works to change attitudes and shape policy on behalf of all kinds of mothers and families. The organization also works for reproductive justice, emphasizing the ways in which communities of color are often targeted by structural forms of oppression. Their "Mama's Day Our Way" campaign includes a number of original, creative mother's day cards celebrating experiences of mothers and forms of mothering often overlooked in mainstream media and society. In particular, they include powerful artistic images of women of color, immigrant women, queer mothers, single mothers, disabled mothers, and fathers, all engaged in mothering their children. Such images counter the negative representations that dominate our society, and offer new possibilities for East Asian mothers.

Mothers in East Asian communities also work to resist and challenge forms of oppression through maintaining ties to their ethnic and cultural backgrounds, and teaching their children to be proud of their racial, ethnic, and cultural identities. In her research with Korean "military brides" raising children in the U.S., Ji-Yeon Yuh discusses respondents' determination to mother their children despite lacking the "Korean-style" maternal authority they desired (and would have had access to, in different circumstances). Korean mothers raising mixed race children in the U.S. recounted experiences of watching their children as they were subjected to racial slurs and racist abuse. Many of these women took action on behalf their children; and Yuh describes their maternal advocacy as "acts of resistance toward racism and institutional and social authority" (104). In addition, some women reported raising their children to eat Korean food, speak Korea, and understand Korean culture as a significant aspect of their mothering, and as an implicit act of resistance to the racism they experienced in the U.S. (Yuh 105-106). Similarly, authors in this volume suggest complex forms of resistance to oppression, including Merose Hwang's discussion of Korean women in the 1920s and 1930s who found ways to circumnavigate dominant narratives of motherhood, childcare, and health practices propagated by the Japanese colonial press.

Additionally, because many Asian North American women participate in work outside the home, they challenge both the stereotype of a financially dependent "stay at home" wife and mother within a conventional western nuclear family, as well as assumptions about white patriarchal motherhood. To raise their children, like other women of color in North America, Asian Pacific women have developed more collective approaches to mothering, relying on both extended family and community members—what Patricia Hill Collins refers to as "fictive kin" in her discussion of Black women's experiences of motherhood. Such arrangements, like the experience of transnational motherhood discussed earlier, involve complex gendered, racialized negotiations of work and motherhood and engage transformative and potentially empowering redefinitions of mothering and motherhood. The ways in which such subjectivities may be mobilized is a central theme of Francisco's discussion in her chapter about Filipina migrant mothers' activism.

Earlier, we highlighted our own experiences and backgrounds, not only for context but also as a conscious attempt to link our daily, material realities as mothers of East Asian descent to the larger social, political, and global processes that structure our experiences. In doing so, we link our work to the struggles of other mothers of East Asian descent, both in North America and globally, as do many of the authors in this volume. Situating ourselves within multiple, intersecting systems of oppression and privilege enables us to identify and acknowledge multiple sites of resistance and empowerment. Despite the many obstacles East Asian women have encountered in North America, many continue to resist multiple forms of oppression and to actively engage motherhood/mothering as an act of empowerment. In fact, as Yen Le Espiritu suggests, the very act of forming and maintaining strong families in a hostile environment is itself a form of resistance (140).

ORGANIZATION OF THE BOOK

Part I of our anthology, "Remembering/Historicizing," offers both historicization of specific contexts that have shaped East Asian mothers' experiences, as well as personal narratives and theoretical musings invested in memory and the processes of remembering. We begin with Hosu Kim and Grace Cho's "The Kinship of Violence," which historicizes and analyzes Korean transnational adoption through contextualizing the adoption of approximately 200,000 children from Korea. Kim and Cho emphasize the role of U.S. militarism in shaping adoption from South Korea, as well as the neocolonial relationship between the U.S. and South Korea. In particular, they reframe the "war orphan"—"not as the child who has lost her parents to war, but more broadly, as the child who was born out of the social and material conditions of U.S. militarism in Korea and South Korean nationalism." These authors explicitly link transnational adoption from Korea to U.S. military presence and camptown prostitution, referring to the military camptown as "the space of U.S. occupation and unresolved war," and underscoring the roles of both biopolitical and geopolitical interests of South Korea and the U.S. The lack of social welfare programs coupled with intense shame attributed to unwed "bad" mothers led to the invisibility of birthmothers, which depicts a violent suppression of history. We begin with this chapter as a way to both mark this violent suppression of history and critically disrupt it.

With "Kinship of Violence" as context, we move into "Cheeseburger Season," a personal narrative in which Grace Cho uses food to narrate her relationship with her mother, who struggled with schizophrenia and agoraphobia, entangled with the legacies of war and militarism in South Korea. "My mother's love of cheeseburgers went way back to the U.S. military occupation of Korea," Cho writes. "As a bargirl at a U.S. naval base, she had access to luxurious American foods that most Koreans could only dream of—it was sort of a fringe benefit of serving American soldiers. Before that, she was like any other Korean, whose first taste of American food probably came from scavenging in the dumpsters outside U.S. Army mess halls." Through her narrative, Cho links food and culture, poverty and the U.S. military occupation, and all the anguish and pain experienced by East Asian mothers and daughters who struggle to survive despite histories of war, militarism, and violence. In fact, Cho's evocative remembering/retelling signals a deliberate act of resistance to the complex forms of oppression that shaped her mother's life.

Merose Hwang, in "The Asian Motherhood Stigma: A Historical Glance at Embedded Women's Practices in Korean Colonial Media," discusses the ways that Korean print media in the 1920s and 1930s reconceptualized women and mothers within a new global standard of capitalist modernity which rejected and stigmatized traditional shamanic practices in favor of consumerism and professionalization (through westernization) of the medical field. Hwang examines how Japanese colonial government and the media depicted rural Korean women as poor, unfit wives and mothers in an effort to control and force them into submission. Meanwhile, idealized womanhood and motherhood became commercially driven, as middleclass women were pressured to purchase products and food items in order to provide "proper" hygiene and nutrition for their children. Elite motherhood was normalized, while popular media stigmatized traditional childbirth practices involving midwives and herbalists, as well as the experiential knowledge and local, alternative healthcare and childrearing practices often used by poor, rural mothers. Despite the pressures to fulfill "good mothering" practices, Hwang describes how women resisted by continuing to seek out local female healthcare providers, unlicensed by the colonial government, even when it meant breaking the law.

Fiona Tinwei Lam and Dmae Roberts approach the subject of East Asian mothering creatively, and from positions of longing and regret, as they explore the chasms that so often exist between mother and child. Lam's poem, "Chrysanthemum," denotes a sense of grieving within the East Asian mother-daughter relationship, as the narrator reflects on her mother's painting—so careful, slow, and precise, turning empty page into a beautiful masterpiece. The narrator's longing is captured: "If only I had been paper / a delicate, upturned face stroked / with such precise tenderness." And Roberts, in "The Purpose of This Life," reflects on growing up mixed race in America with a Taiwanese immigrant mother who was filled with "emptiness." She explores Buddhist notions of suffering as she narrates her mother's final days, writing, "We didn't know each other's language well enough. Rarely could we talk with any kind of understanding, and even after her death, I'm still trying to understand." Roberts' process of remembering, like Cho's, indicates a desire to affirm her mother's strength even while she narrates the complex forms of oppression she encountered. And, concluding the first section, Rita Wong's poem, "a wandering daughter's grammar," addresses roles imposed on daughters—constraints, the silencing of self, and repression—all quietly threaded with possibilities, potential, and hope as felt through Wong's words, "sisterhood: towards including mother if possible."

In the second section, "Negotiating Constructions of (East Asian) Motherhood," authors engage specific discourses, debates, and areas of contestation. In her personal essay, "Tiger in the Hornets' Nest: The Furor Over Amy Chua's *Battle Hymn of the Tiger Mother*," Fiona Tinwei Lam addresses the image of the "tiger mother" in relation to her experience as an Asian Canadian mother. She resists and "roars back" to the tiger mother as reinforcing stereotypes about Asians as model minorities, and as promoting and cultivating elitism. Lam underscores the significance of gleaning knowledge in spaces outside formal learning environments. Also, she discusses her hope to instill values like compassion, kindness, and self-awareness in her child, writing, "Like Chua, I want to prepare my child for the future—but in a different way."

Pamela Thoma revisits Chua's "tiger mother" in the next chapter, "Neoliberal Maternal Discourse, Tiger Mothers, and American Mother-Daughter Narrative," to discuss what she terms "neoliberal maternal discourse" (NMD)—a dialogue about neoliberal cultural citizenship and the practices associated with reproducing the American citizen-subject. Thoma suggests that the labor of mothering deemed most acceptable is the labor that enables and endorses consumption. And, as she writes, "the mother-daughter narrative of Asian American women writers has been important both in affirming the cultural citizenship of Asian American women and in articulating its racialized limits," suggesting the ways in which Asian American women's maternal labor has been appropriated by neoliberalism. Through a critical reading of Chua's memoir, Thoma demonstrates the ways in which the text centers bourgeois motherhood comprised of "consumer-based affective and material practices associated with the white, middle-class nuclear family," in effect producing a new trope, that of the *maternal model minority*.

In line with exploring pressure exerted upon East Asian subjects, the next chapter details a research study focused on Korean American college students' experiences in relation to "model minority" expectations. In "Korean American Mothering and Model Minority Children," June H. Sun and Hyojoung Kim present their findings after surveying nearly two hundred Korean American students regarding their perceptions of the ways their mothers parent them. While they found that mothering practices do not necessarily have a significant relationship to model minority expectations—that is, the expectation to live up to the myth of the model minority—they do suggest that participants' experiences of striving for material success are shaped by immigration experience and socioeconomic status. On the whole, the authors determine that pressure to live up to the myth of the model minority creates an excessive burden and stigma for Asian American college students.

In "Bad Mothers and 'Abominable Lovers': Goodness and Gayness in Korea," Timothy Gitzen raises questions about sexuality and motherhood in relation to mothering gay sons. Based on ethnographic research, Gitzen explores what happens when Korean sons "come out" to their mothers. In particular, he is interested in how women who had previously positioned themselves as "good mothers" must come to terms with their sons' sexual identities. "Goodness," Gitzen writes, "is both a discursive formation and a material or affective reality—the circulation of certain discourses and experiences garner affective value and are thus deemed 'good.' A Korean mother's goodness is wrapped up in her child's goodness (associated with heterosexual marriage and procreation, as well as certain ideals of masculinity and femininity), perpetuating heterosexism and homophobia in a goodness and gayness duality. Gitzen problematizes both "goodness" and "gayness," and suggests an ambivalence that illustrates the ways that "good mothers and gay sons…in fact are working both within and outside these rules and desires to allow for their inclusion."

Talia Esnard discusses maternal thinking and practices of mothers as entrepreneurs in her chapter, "Ideology, Gender, and Entrepreneurship: Implications for Perceptions and Experiences for Mothers in Taipei, Taiwan." Based on a phenomenological method of inquiry, Esnard's study exposes some of the key themes and conflicts that arise for mothers who are also entrepreneurs in Taiwan, including the struggle to balance work and motherhood in a patriarchal society with few resources for working mothers. She argues, "women who attempt to integrate mothering and entrepreneurship in Taiwan remain locked within, troubled by, and resistant to traditional ideals and practices of patriarchy, passivity and morality and the related intricacies of fusing ideologies." Esnard's study examines gender based ideologies, and the often conflicting realities influencing and controlling Asian mothers as entrepreneurs. The "good" wife and mother tenets predicated on filial honor, deference, and homemaking stand in opposition to the demands of owning and running a business. As Esnard suggests, her participants articulate opposition to the patriarchal ideologies of Taiwanese society, and resist and reshape how these ideologies affect their expected roles as mothers and entrepreneurs.

In her chapter, "Mothering Across Borders: South Korean Birthmothers' Perspectives," Rupa Bagga-Raoulx explores transnational adoption through an analysis of writings by Korean birth mothers. Situating her discussion within the larger context of transracial and transnational adoption, she explores the often invisible experiences of Korean birth mothers through field work with adoption workers, returning adoptees, and young mothers currently housed in maternity homes in South Korea. Bagga-Raoulx's discussion revolves around three volumes of letters written by birth mothers to the children they gave up for adoption. She explores recurring themes within these birth mothers' narratives, and discusses the complex reasons many women gave up or lost custody of their children.

The final section of *Mothering in East Asian Communities*, engages movements for social justice. The chapters in this section depict multiple ways that East Asian mothers, activists, and community members move toward personal transformation and social change and justice. Kryn Freehling-Burton and Eveline Shen, in their chapter, "Reproductive Justice and Mothering: API Activists Redefine a Movement," describe the impact of Forward Together, formerly known as Asian Communities for Reproductive Justice, situating the struggle for reproductive justice within anti-Asian immigration restrictions and multiple, intersecting forms of oppression. In this chapter, readers learn about some of the innovative programs offered by Forward Together, including their focus on sex education for youth, immigration reform, and their "Mamas Day Our Way" campaign, all of which detail the significance of reproductive justice for East Asian mothers and families, and other communities of color. Freehling-Burton and Shen demonstrate why a movement for reproductive justice—not framed simply as reproductive rights—is critical for East Asian communities and other communities of color, elucidating the ways in which such a movement works to address the needs of the most marginalized mothers (e.g., young mothers, immigrant mothers, queer and trans mothers, disabled mothers, and other mothers often excluded from mainstream discussions about motherhood).

In "For the Family: Filipina Migrant Mothers' Activism and their Transnational Families," Valerie Francisco describes the death of a Filipina migrant worker in New York in 2007, and the subsequent response by Kabalikat Domestic Workers Support Network, an organizing program comprised of Filipina domestic workers. Based on her fieldwork and interviews with Filipina domestic workers in New York and Manila, Francisco explores "the different political subjectivities migrant domestic workers use as resources for political mobilization in their migrant destinations," and suggests that their activism is shaped not only by their experiences as migrant and domestic workers but also their identities as women and mothers. She highlights the role of neoliberal globalization in producing transnational families and exploitative working conditions for migrant women, and argues that the mothers in her study actively engage a critique of the state and the political economy of migration. Discussing the ways in which migrant mothers draw on their experiences to work for social justice, Francisco writes: "Even if their families are absent from their daily lives, migrant mothers claim their redefined motherhood to inform a politics of collective opposition."

In the following chapter, Melinda de Jesús, Patti Duncan, Reshmi Dutt-Ballerstadt, and Linda Pierce Allen offer four meditations about their experiences as mothers of mixed race sons, "Asian Pacific American Mothering as Feminist Decolonizing Reproductive Labor: Four Meditations on Raising Hapa Boys." This chapter, based on a presentation at the 2013 Association for Asian American Studies Conference, opens up a space to theorize the work of feminist mothers and represents a collective effort to explore intersections of Asian Pacific American feminist mothering and activism. The authors ask how the work of Asian American feminist mothers may contribute to the process of decolonization, and how raising hapa boys in hegemonic heteropatriarchal white America can be figured as a political act. De Jesús, Duncan, Dutt-Ballerstadt, and Allen describe the complexities of raising mixed race sons within an increasingly multiracial society, and engage themes of racialization, white privilege, language, and masculinity.

Fiona Lam narrates a mother's experience flying a kite with her son in her poem, "Kite," remembering how just a year earlier, "he brimmed / sky and sunlight, first kite / soaring." Things are different now. "How I want that back…" she writes, describing a mother's changing relationship to her child as they grow up, and the increasing separation between them. Likewise, Lam's poem "Snowman," in which the narrator realizes her son must separate himself from her, offers a poignant reflection of the losses—and gains—associated with East Asian mothering. As with earlier pieces by Cho and Roberts, describing the processes associated with letting go of their mothers, Lam's narrator must let go of her son. In "Snowman," she writes, "Only / when it crumbled away / could he create again, / without me."

In "Bringing Visibility to East Asian Mothers in Prison," Anita Harker Armstrong and Victoria Law examine how race and gender impact East Asian mothers' experiences in the prison system and in the reentry process. Their chapter, which includes excerpts from a letter written by SoSon, an Asian American incarcerated mother, demonstrates the complexity of motherhood behind bars as well as the invisibility of East Asian women in prison, often affected by the myth of the model minority. Armstrong and Law also discuss the impact of detention and deportation on immigrant mothers who lack citizenship status in the U.S., suggesting that these issues may be more complex for mothers "who more often were the primary caretakers of their children prior to their incarceration, as they are forced to choose between bringing their children back into what may be very unstable or dangerous situations in their home country, or essentially *leaving* their children in the United States, which they will not be able to reenter."

Finally, in "Motherhood and the Race for Sustainability," Marie Lo returns to the controversy surrounding the "tiger mother," suggesting that it results in competing narratives of parenting, race, and nation, animated by class differences as well as conflicting responses to the effects of globalization on the environment. To expand the binary construction between an authoritarian Chinese-style of mothering versus a lax, indulgent western-style, Lo engages another point of reference—the "Femivore," or "radical homemaker"—in order to demonstrate how mothering becomes a racialized site for competing narratives of sustainability. She argues that "the racialization of motherhood privileges a particular vision of sustainability, political action and environmental consciousness aligned with white liberalism, implicitly designating Asians and Asian Americans as model minorities apathetic to environmentalism at best or environmentally destructive at worst." Through her analysis of "sustaining acts" within writings by Asian North American women, she suggests that the white liberal discourse of sustainability privileges a definition of "choice" that erases the sustainability acts—often figured as necessary acts of survival—by Asian women. Lo shifts the focus of sustainability to underscore the structural conditions that shape mothering in East Asian communities, allowing us to recognize the political acts of Asian American motherhood as "sustaining acts."

CONCLUSION

I left for you.
I came here for you.
I work for you.
I sing for you.
For you. For you. For you.

My mother sang songs that still echo in my head.
> *...I speak this language for you. I tell stories for you.*

My mother used to tell me stories of how it was.
> *For you. For you. For you...*

> ...through jungle leaves and killing fields, her stories stitched in my head for lost memories.

And so my mother reminds me of our story, left behind in a land I will never call my home.

And so my mother carries with her new dreams, in a land that drowns dreams in sweat reality.

My back aches for you.
I sacrifice for you.
I cry for you.
I hurt for you...
For you. For you. For you...

I return to my mother, who never left my side.
I see you, Mother...

I Was Born With Two Tongues

We conclude with this excerpt from "Mother," by Asian Pacific American spoken word artists I Was Born With Two Tongues. In their evocative piece, they suggest both the losses and sacrifices of a first generation Asian immigrant mother, and a daughter's longing and regret for the "home" she will never know. In this way, "Mother" addresses several key themes and challenges for mothers and mothering practices in East Asian communities, particularly with regard to the multiple negative stereotypes and controlling images of Asian Pacific women, the structural forms of oppression associated with economic injustice, labor exploitation, and Asian women migrant workers, and the lack of a sense of belonging experienced by so many women of East Asian descent in North America.

Yet this piece, while centering these politics of home and belonging, also suggests a daughter's decision to "return" to her mother. "I see you, Mother," the narrator states, suggesting a challenge to the invisibility of Asian Pacific women and mothers, and a refusal to be reduced to one-dimensional representations and stereotypes. In addition, the daughter/narrator's return invokes a reclaiming of both her mother and her racial, ethnic, cultural identity. In this volume, we echo such sentiments, as the authors illustrate the complex lived realities of mothering and motherhood within East Asian communities, and explore not only the multiple forms of oppression experienced by East Asian mothers but also potential sites of resistance and empowerment. The writings in *Mothering in East Asian Communities* richly engage the politics and practices of mothering in East Asian contexts. By raising critical questions about the social, cultural, and political meanings of race, gender, class, nation, sexual orientation, and mothering, these chapters contribute to the existing scholarship on motherhood and mothering and invite more discussion about the unique, heterogeneous experiences of East Asian mothers.

WORKS CITED

Amott, Teresa L. and Julie A. Matthaei. *Race, Gender, and Work: A Multicultural Economic History of Women in the United States.* Boston: South End Press, 1991. Print.

Briggs, Laura. *Somebody's Children: The Politics of Transracial and Transnational Adoption.* Durham and London: Duke University Press, 2012. Print.

Chan, Sucheng. *Asian Americans: An Interpretive History.* Boston: Twayne Publishers, 1991. Print.

Chan, Sucheng. *Survivors: Cambodian Refugees in the United States.* Bloomington: University of Illinois Press, 2004. Print.

Chua, Amy. *Battle Hymn of the Tiger Mother.* New York: Penguin, 2011. Print.

de Jesús, Melinda. Ed. *Pinay Power: Theorizing the Filipina/American Experience.* New York and London: Routledge, 2005. Print.

Dubinsky, Karen. *Babies Without Borders: Adoption and Migration Across the Americas.* New York: New York University Press, 2010. Print.

Duncan, Patti. "Genealogies of Unbelonging: Amerasians and Transnational Adoptees as Legacies of U.S. Militarism in South Korea." *Militarized Currents: Toward a Decolonized Future in Asia and the Pacific.* Ed. Setsu Shigematsu and Keith L. Camacho. Minneapolis: University of Minnesota Press, 2010. 277–307. Print.

—. "Teaching the Politics of Transnational Motherhood." *Journal of the Motherhood Initiative for Research and Community Involvement* 4.1

(2013): 67–80. Print.

Espiritu, Yen Le. "Race, Class, and Gender in Asian America." *Making More Waves: New Writing by Asian American Women.* Ed., Elaine H. Kim, Lilia V. Villanueva, and Asian Women United of California. Boston: Beacon Press, 1997. 135–141. Print.

Fujiwara, Lynn. *Mothers Without Citizenship: Asian Immigrant Families and the Consequences of Welfare Reform.* Minneapolis: University of Minnesota Press, 2008. Print.

Glenn, Evelyn Nakano, Grace Chang, and Linda Rennie Forcey, eds. *Mothering: Ideology, Experience, and Agency.* New York: Routledge, 1994. Print.

Glenn, Evelyn Nakano. *Forced to Care: Coercion and Caregiving in America.* Cambridge, MA: Harvard University Press, 2010. Print.

Ho, Wendy. *In Her Mother's House: The Politics of Asian American Mother-Daughter Writing.* New York: Altamira Press. 2000. Print.

Hondagneu-Sotelo, Pierrette and Ernestine Avila. " 'I'm Here, but I'm There': The Meanings of Latina Transnational Motherhood." *Women and Migration in the U.S.-Mexico Borderlands.* Ed. Denise A. Segura and Patricia Zavella. Durham: Duke University Press, 2007. 388–412. Print.

Hong, Grace Kyungwon. *The Ruptures of American Capital: Women of Color Feminism and the Culture of Immigrant Labor.* Minneapolis and London: University of Minnesota Press. 2006. Print.

Hune, Shirley and Gail M. Nomura, Eds. *Asian/Pacific Islander American Women: A Historical Anthology.* New York and London: New York University Press, 2003. Print.

Kang, Laura Hyun Yi. *Compositional Subjects: Enfiguring Asian/American Women.* Durham and London: Duke University Press, 2002. Print.

Katz, Jennifer and Emily Hunt. "Adoptive Mothers-Mothering." *Mothers, Mothering, and Motherhood Across Cultural Differences: A Reader.* Ed. Andrea O'Reilly. Bradford, ON: Demeter Press, 2014. 41–63. Print.

Kim, Lili M. "Redefining the Boundaries of Traditional Gender Roles: Korean Picture Brides, Pioneer Korean Immigrant Women, and Their Benevolent Nationalism in Hawai'i." *Asian/Pacific Islander American Women: A Historical Anthology.* Ed. Shirley Hune and Gail M. Nomura. New York: New York University Press, 2003. 106–119.

Mohanty, Chandra Talpade. *Feminism Without Borders: Decolonizing Theory, Practicing Solidarity.* Durham and London: Duke University

Press, 2003. Print.

Moon, Katharine H.S. *Sex Among Allies: Military Prostitution in U.S.-Korea Relations.* New York: Columbia University Press, 1997. Print.

Ninh, Erin Khue. *Ingratitude: The Debt-Bound Daughter in Asian American Literature.* New York: New York University Press, 2011. Print.

Okazawa-Rey, Margo. "Amerasian Children of GI Town: A Legacy of U.S. Militarism in South Korea." *Asian Journal of Women's Studies* 3.1 (1997). 71-102. Print.

O'Reilly, Andrea, Ed. *Maternal Theory: Essential Readings.* Bradford, ON: Demeter Press, 2007. Print.

Parreñas, Rhacel Salazar. *Servants of Globalization: Women, Migration, and Domestic Work.* Stanford, CA: Stanford University Press, 2001. Print.

Sangha, Jasjit K. and Tahira Gonsalves, eds. *South Asian Mothering: Negotiating Culture, Family and Selfhood.* Toronto: Demeter Press, 2013.

Schultermandl, Silvia. *Transnational Matrilineage: Mother-Daughter Conflicts in Asian American Literature.* Berlin: LIT Verlag, 2009. Print.

Sturdevant, Saundra Pollock, and Brenda Stoltzfus. *Let the Good Times Roll: Prostitution and the U.S. Military in Asia.* New York: The New Press, 1992. Print.

Tajima, Renee E. "Lotus Blossoms Don't Bleed: Images of Asian Women." *Making Waves: An Anthology of Writings By and About Asian American Women.* Ed. Asian Women United. Boston: Beacon Press, 1989. 308-317. Print.

Takaki, Ronald. *Strangers from a Different Shore: A History of Asian Americans.* New York: Penguin, 1989. Print.

Trenka, Jane Jeong, Julia Chinyere Oparah, and Sun Yung Shin, eds. *Outsiders Within: Writings on Transracial Adoption.* Cambridge, MA: South End Press, 2006. Print.

Vo, Linda Trinh. "Managing Survival: Economic Realities for Vietnamese American Women." *Asian/Pacific Islander American Women: A Historical Anthology.* Ed. Shirley Hune and Gail M. Nomura, New York: New York University Press, 2003. 237–52. Print.

Wang, Q. "Chinese Socialization and Emotion Talk between Mothers and Children in Native and Immigrant Chinese Families. *Asian American Journal of Psychology.* 2012. Advance online publication. doi:10.1037/a0030868

Wong, Gina. "Matroreform: Toward Collapsing the Mother's Panopticon." *Moms Gone Mad: Motherhood and Madness, Oppression and Resistance,* Ed. Gina Wong. Bradford, ON: Demeter Press, 2012. 95-107. Print.

Wong-Wylie, Gina. "Images and Echoes in Matroreform: A Cultural Feminism Perspective." *Journal of the Association for Research on Mothering,* 8.1-2 (2006), 135–146. Print.

—. "Matroreform: Reforming Mothering/Reforming Motherhood." *What Do Mothers Need? Motherhood Activists and Scholars Speak Out on Maternal Empowerment for the 21st Century.* Ed. Andrea O'Reilly. Bradford, ON: Demeter Press, 2012. 81–92. Print.

Wong, Sau-ling C. "Diverted Mothering: Representations of Caregivers of Color in the Age of 'Multiculturalism'." *Mothering: Ideology, Experience, and Agency.* Ed. Evelyn Nakano Glenn, Grace Chang, and Linda Rennie Forcey. New York: Routledge, 1994. 67–91. Print.

Woo, Merle. "Letter to Ma." *This Bridge Called My Back: Writings by Radical Women of Color,* Ed. Cherríe Moraga and Gloria Anzaldúa. New York: Kitchen Table Press, 1981. 140–147. Print.

Yuh, Ji-Yeon. *Beyond the Shadow of Camptown: Korean Military Brides in America.* New York: New York University Press, 2002. Print.

I: Remembering/Historicizing

1.

The Kinship of Violence

HOSU KIM AND GRACE M. CHO

In 1950, the Korean peninsula was the first theater of the Cold War. Though the Korean War garnered relatively little public attention, and was later dubbed "The Forgotten War" by Americans, it was a stunning spectacle for those who witnessed it. The United States' indiscriminate use of a new weapon of mass destruction—napalm—resulted in a physical landscape that had literally burned to the ground and a collateral damage rate unparalleled in modern history.

The three years of fighting resulted in a catastrophic loss for the Korean people—in terms of both the material destruction of civilian institutions and the fracturing of family ties. Three million civilians were reported dead, and another two million missing or wounded. Furthermore, when the border between North and South was closed in 1953, 10 million families became permanently separated. To put this in perspective, over half of the civilian population had suffered the irrecoverable loss of a family member.

The war resulted in a staggering number of children who had lost one or both parents, and this fact became the impetus for the emergence of transnational adoption. Widespread devastation and misery in the aftermath of war provided the rationale to send children to the U.S. and later, to other wealthy countries, so that they could have "a better life." A profound belief that children could have a better future in the adoptive country, engendered by the prevalence of the myth of the American dream in postwar Korea, encouraged birthmothers to give up their children. During the 1950s in the U.S., the adoption of Korean babies and children formed the basis of a new kind of kinship, and thus, war torn Korea became fertile ground for American couples looking to build a global American family.

However, critics of Korea's transnational adoption program have repeatedly asked some urgent questions: If conceived as a temporary solution to post-war poverty, how did transnational adoption turn into a permanent and widespread practice, sending some 200,000 Korean children abroad. Why is South Korea still a sending country when its economic profile now resembles that of a typical receiving country? Many of the explanations focus on South Korea's lack of social welfare programs and the societal stigmas attached to both unwed mothers and families that have adopted children.[2] While we agree that both of these factors are crucial to understanding the unidirectional movement of children westward from Korea, we would like to contextualize them through a different lens.

We locate ourselves among the scholars who have analyzed the phenomenon of Korean adoption within the history of U.S. militarism in Korea—a history that reaches back before the inception of South Korea itself. SooJin Pate, in her groundbreaking work on the making of the Korean orphan through militarized humanitarianism, asserts that: "...rather than a natural consequence of war, Korean adoption emerged from the neocolonial relations between the U.S. and Korea. And this relationship did not begin in 1950 with the formal start of the Korean War but in 1945" when the U.S. occupied the southern half of the Korean peninsula (14). We also want to remember the Korean War, not as a conflict that started in 1950 and ended in 1953, but as an unfolding event that began when the peninsula was divided in 1945 and has not yet ended.[3] In this context, we consider the "war orphan" not as the child who has lost her parents to war, but more broadly, as the child who was born out of the social and material conditions of U.S. militarism in Korea and South Korean nationalism.

If we were to flesh out this figure, we might find a tangle of other bodies—dead parents, living parents made socially dead, birthmothers seeking reunification on television, birthmothers who were never allowed any airtime because of their degraded social status, and American GI fathers who were not held accountable for the children they fathered in Korea. U.S. military presence created the conditions under which Korean women and American men came into sexual contact and thus, gave birth to the first group of Korean children to be sent abroad.[4] Although women working in U.S. camptowns, or *kijich'on*, made up the first generation of adoptees' birthmothers, this fact tends to be forgotten. When remembered, it is understood as something of the past, rather than as a history that haunts the present.

In Korean diaspora studies of the past 15 years, significant literatures have emerged about both transnational adoption and militarized prostitution in Korea as after-effects of the Cold War and U.S. neo-imperialism. While there is clearly a relationship between the two sets of practices, as scholars in each of these respective fields, we have noticed that there is little analysis that has attended to the intersection between adoption and military prostitution, with the exception of a few recent works.[5] In the proliferation of cultural production about search and reunion efforts between birthmothers and their children, for example, we do not hear about sex work as a circumstance that leads women to have children out of wedlock and then relinquish them. We hope not only to make these hidden contours of adoption visible, but also to notice the ways in which some bodies carry the imprints of those that have been erased. In doing so, we perform a kind of search and reunion that lays bare the Korean adoption industry's kinship to camptown prostitution.

This paper seeks to locate the roots of transnational adoption in the camptown—the space of U.S. occupation and unresolved war—where American soldiers fathered children born to Korean women who were either their girlfriends or paid sex workers. Critically engaging the issue of biracial children and their mothers, we argue that these bodies laid the foundation for transnational adoption, which enabled the biopolitical and geopolitical interests of South Korea and the U.S.

THE BODIES OF WAR

There was a popular image of a Korean child that circulated in the American press during the Korean War. His face is dirty and his clothes are tattered. He looks pitifully into the camera. To highlight his solitude, he stands alone in the middle of a desolate street. In another picture he is hunched over a bowl, devouring its contents and focused only on quelling his hunger.

Flash forward to 1955. Take the destitute Korean child out of Korea and picture him in a happy American family. Picture him in a good Christian home with seven adopted Korean siblings. They are smiling, free of hunger, well-groomed and surrounded by family. Their physical features indicate that they are the mixed race offspring of American soldiers. Although they were not in fact the first Korean children to come to the U.S., they are often cited as such, perhaps because they were adopted by the man who fathered the Korean adoption industry himself—Harry Holt. In this iconic family portrait of the Holts, the smiling Amerasian children represent the proto-type of the transnational Korean adoptee.

These images tell a partial story about the origins of transnational adoption and present themselves as evidence of America's familial supe-riority and benevolence. They also point to the camptown. The story of the Holts and their eight biracial Korean children—a legend among the adoptee community—invites us to consider the material conditions and kinship ties from which biracial children were extracted.

In our previous work, we have written at length about the figure of the *yanggongju* or the "western princess"—the Korean woman who has sexual relations with American soldiers—and the way in which this figure arose from the conditions of war and U.S. occupation, and later came to embody Korean society's ambivalent relationship to the U.S. (Cho). She was simul-taneously envied and despised because she represented access to the priv-ileges enjoyed by Americans, on one hand, and Korea's subordination to the U.S., on the other. Many of the women labeled as *yanggongju* came into contact with American soldiers through their work at the bars and clubs around the camptowns, and thus the stigma of prostitution was attached to all Korean women who consorted with American men.

While the origins of military prostitution are often located in the war and early post-war period, we contend that their roots can be traced back to the beginning of U.S. occupation in 1945 when the Japanese comfort sta-tions in Korea were turned over to the American occupation government. Informal exchange sex with Americans proliferated during the Korean War and by 1954, there were an estimated 350,000 prostitutes in Korea, 60% of whom serviced the American military forces. Through the 1960s and 70s military prostitution developed into a major institution for bolstering national security and became an important but unacknowledged part of South Korea's nation-building project (Moon). Because of the failure to re-solve the Korean War, U.S. troops have remained in South Korea and so has the rationale for militarized prostitution. As a result of this incipient system of militarized prostitution, combined with a high incidence of rape during the war as well as consensual forms of intimate contact between Korean fe-males and American men around the military bases, Korea witnessed the birth of a mixed race population that literally embodied the ties between the U.S. and Korea.

As our previous research has discussed, war has a double effect of be-ing paradoxically destructive and creative. While the Korean War resulted in overwhelming destruction and loss, it was precisely that destruction that laid the ground for new bodies, such as the *yanggongju* to emerge. These bodies constitute what Patti Duncan refers to as the "collateral excess bio-product of 'military necessity' " (296). We would like to make another distinction among these "excess bioproducts." In one sense, there is the biopolitical excess that is a direct result of collateral damage. Because of the indiscriminate bombing of civilian targets, the war created new categories of persons that required care—orphans, widows, the disabled, the homeless. In another sense, "excess bioproduct" refers to the new bodies that are born of militarized practices instituted as a result of long-term occupation and war, such as that of camptown prostitution. Camptown sex workers and biracial children who were fathered and abandoned by American soldiers, as an unintended military consequence, presented a very special kind of population problem for South Korea.

TRANSNATIONAL ADOPTION AND THE BIOPOLITICAL EXCESS OF THE CAMPTOWN

> The Holt agency figured out that I had a child and asked me to give up my child for adoption. So I did, for my child's future. That was a good decision. I see another mixed race child around here. I feel sorry for him. There is nothing they [mixed race people] can do in this country. So we should send them. Over there, they must be doing at least some sort of sports.... [Here] they can't go to military service. There is no use for them [in this society]. [The other child] is around 10 or 11 years old. To be adopted, he should not exceed 13 years old. I don't know the mother. But she should take this last chance for him. There are more days to come in the child's life. [We should] send him to his own country. (*From an oral history with a former camptown worker who relinquished her child.*)

Patti Duncan opens her essay, "Genealogies of Unbelonging: Amerasians and Transnational Adoptees as Legacies of U.S. Militarism in South Korea" with a scene from a classroom of biracial children in Korea at an alternative missionary school run by former camptown worker Kim Yeonja. Duncan explains, "Because discrimination against mixed-race people prevents them from attending public schools, Kim founded the True Love Mission, which she runs out of her home" (277). In this scene, Kim asks the children a telling question: "Which is better, Korea or America?" The children enthusiastically answer, "America." Duncan points out the irony that these kids are taught that America is superior even as they are severely stigmatized for being Amerasian. Perhaps more importantly, the message that these children belong to America is articulated through the message that they do not belong to Korea. It is typical for camptown women to be viewed as "Korean in birth but no longer Korean in body or spirit" (Moon 3). Their children, by virtue of having been fathered by American men, are automatically deemed "not Korean," with no possibility of a livable future in Korea. The U.S. is framed as the only nation that has the capacity to care for this population. Indeed, even in the birthmother's testimony above, she situates the U.S. as the rightful place for a biracial child ("his own country"). If the U.S. is "his own country" it is not because of any meaningful ties to the U.S. but by the force of exclusion from Korea. The scene from Kim Yeonja's missionary school is set in 1995, but the exclusionary beliefs and practices that have constructed biracial Koreans as foreigners in their country of birth can be traced back to the 1950s when the South Korean media began reporting on the new population that proliferated around U.S. camptowns as a "social problem." Dealing with "yankee wives" and "mixed race children" was perhaps the first major biopolitical project for the budding South Korean nation. Just a few years after its inception, a number of social policies were designed to eliminate the "problem."

Although the earliest adoptions were by American military personnel who adopted the "military mascot" children they had met around the bases, "it was the appearance of mixed-race children as a social welfare problem that spurred the Korean government to pursue international adoption as an emergency measure..." (E. Kim, "Origins" 4). As a social problem, this one was especially conspicuous because it was embodied in the form of a new population that symbolized the inherent contradiction of the nation-building project. Syngman Rhee, the first president of South Korea (1946 - 1960), envisioned South Korea as an uncontaminated and pure ethnic group as well as an anti-communism state, both of which Kwon In Sook in her book, *Korea is Military*, cogently recognizes as the two most important tenets underlying a modern Korea. If U.S. military presence was the condition under which a mixed race population was born in Korea, then the presence of military sex workers and their biracial children was an uncomfortable reminder of South Korea's dependence on the U.S. to carry out its anti-communist mission. It also revealed the two tenets to be paradoxical.

From the very beginning, the South Korean government consistently made efforts to eradicate or segregate biracial children, while their mothers were removed from "normal" society. According to Eleana Kim, mixed blood children "were being constructed as a category of concern and scientific knowledge production…In 1952, for example, it was reported in the *Dong-A Daily* that the Ministry of Social Affairs was compiling a census of mixed race children with the intention to arrange for their 'separate accommodations' " (Adopted Territory 61). With humanitarian funds from abroad, the Child Placement Service (아동 양호회) was established under a 1954 presidential order, for the purpose of providing international adoption of mixed race children to the U.S. and other Western countries (Hübinette, "Korean Adoption History"). The South Korean media told a concerned public: "Now, Mixed Race Children in Korea can go to the U.S." (The Chosun-Ilbo).

In an appeal to the UN ambassador to South Korea, President Syngman Rhee stated, "We are most anxious to send as many orphans to the States as possible. In particular we desire to have adopted those children of Western fathers and Korean mothers who can never hope to make a place for themselves in Korean society" (E. Kim, *Adopted Territory*, 62). In a personal plea to a prospective American adoptive family, he reiterated this belief in recommending that they adopt a "UN baby" rather than a fullblooded Korean child. "It is these children and not the Koreans who will find it difficult to make a happy life for themselves in our country." (As quoted in E. Kim, *Adopted Territory*, 66)

The rationale of the government's removal policy assumed Korean people's discrimination against mixed race children to be constant and unchanging and the children's maladjustment to Korean society to be a natural consequence, but at the time that President Rhee was making these claims, the children in question were only a few years old, as was the South Korean nation. The decisions were not based on any previous experience that the children would be unable to weather the effects of prejudice or that the society would be unable to adjust to and accommodate racial diversity. Instead, the eradication measures taken by the Rhee administration reflected the government's own prejudice, and enforced societal stigmas against the very children for whom social welfare was a purported concern. Even if South Korea's transnational adoption program was, in part, a matter of child social welfare, the irrational emphasis on sending away biracial children surely had more to do with the ideological underpinnings of South Korea's nation-building project. Biracial children were living proof of South Korea's compromised sovereignty for having established itself as a dependent of the U.S. military.

The discourse that developed throughout the 1950s about the mixed race population further constructed the biracial child as always already marginal, with no rightful place in South Korea (Hurh). In early statistics of Ministry of Health and Social Services, the category of mixed race children and of handicapped children is conflated in their adoption figures (Park). This means that mixed race children were interchangeable with the disabled, both of whom occupied the most marginal social positions and therefore were "justifiably" put up for transnational adoption. Not only were biracial children given the highest priority when placing Korean children with overseas adoptive families, adoption agency workers actively recruited in the camptowns. As a means of reinforcing their policy of eradicating the mixed race population, mothers working in the camptowns were the targets of campaigns to send their children to America.

These measures to convince camptown women to relinquish their children and Americans to take South Korea's "UN babies" were effective. Soo-Jin Pate estimates that between 1955 and 1957, 90% of Korean adoptees were biracial "despite the fact that mixed race children made up less than 1% of the entire war orphan population..." (8). Park further demonstrates the success of South Korea's policies in his sociological study, Minority Groups in South Korea in which he examined Ministry of Health and Welfare figures and estimated that at least ten percent and as much as forty percent of biracial children born to Korean women and American men were placed in adoption between the 1950s and 1980s (208-209). These disproportionate figures illuminate the significance of biracial children in Korean adoption history.

The Sunlit Sister Center, an advocacy organization for former camptown sex workers, reveals similarly striking figures. Their 2008 research report suggests that many camptown women wished to keep their children but made the difficult decision to relinquish them after realizing that the children's fathers had permanently abandoned them, and oftentimes, when urged to do so by adoption agency officials who reminded them that South Korea was a hopeless place for a mixed race child. Among the women they surveyed, most said that their pregnancies ended in abortions, which were facilitated by club owners who then required them to return to work immediately after the procedure.[6] However, almost 37% chose to give birth. About 25% of these women raised their biracial children as single mothers, while 40% placed their children in foreign adoption (Shin and Kim 61). The oral histories conducted with the birthmothers indicate that the women were attached to their children and waited for several years before deciding to give them up. Ultimately the decision was motivated by the belief that the U.S. could offer a life full of opportunity and free of racism. In one woman's words:

> …[my children] were mocked because of their mixed physical features. One time my older one came home with his trousers soaked and frozen with his own pee. Children bullied him by saying "You must have a big penis. Let me see." By the time my older one was around eight and the younger around seven, I decided…I talked to them for about a month and said, "we have been waiting a long time for your father who has never come. If you stay here [in Korea], you will face constant discrimination. However, in the U.S. there is no such thing." (*Sunlit Sister's Center* 58)

The effect of South Korea's national ideology towards biracial people resulted in exactly what Syngman Rhee predicted—a class of people for whom a normal life in Korea was foreclosed. Women who chose to keep their children had to contend with the knowledge that neither they nor their children would ever have the possibility of citizenship or a future free of discrimination. As Duncan explains:

> Since many kijich'on women are removed from their family registries, both they and their children are treated as noncitizens, and the children in such cases can claim no legal Korean citizenship. To claim U.S. citizenship, Amerasians in Korea require documentation from their fathers, many of whom abandoned their mothers when their tours of duty ended. Thus, Amerasian children often experience extreme stigma and discrimination within their home countires, while hoping to someday find their American fathers and live in the United States. Many Amerasians in Korea are, in effect, stateless (285).

To complicate matters further for these families, the Status of Forces Agreement between the U.S. and South Korea protects the privacy rights of American soldiers, so that U.S. military officials are under no obligation to cooperate with Korean women who are trying to locate their children's fathers (Okazawa-Rey). In this unequal gendered power dynamic, the rights

of American men are reinforced as the rights of Korean women are denied. Meanwhile, their children are suspended in a condition of stateless-
ness in which no rights at all can be claimed. Biracial children have only
the slimmest possibility of obtaining citizenship through their biological
fathers, and this fact often made adoption the only viable alternative.

THE COLD WAR'S NEW AMERICAN FAMILY

Although transnational adoption served the nascent South Korean government as a form of "purifying the population, through the regulation of
mixed-race children as well as the illicit sexuality of their Korean mothers,"
it was mutually beneficial to the United States' nation-building efforts (E.
Kim, "Origins" 15). There were just as many policies enacted on the U.S. side
that facilitated transnational adoption. Starting in 1953 a series of laws were
passed addressing the "problem" of Amerasian children, who were viewed
as a "national disgrace" for which Americans needed to make amends[7]. The
legislation pertaining to Amerasians, however, allowed for the immigration
of Amerasian children but not their mothers, while at the same time providing protection for the men who fathered them. What this amounted to was
a system of immigration that encouraged Amerasian children to come to
the U.S. only by means of adoption into an American family. Furthermore,
the prevailing ideology of 1950s America viewed the rearing of children as a
patriotic duty. If the children were Asian, Americans were taking their pa-
triotism one step further by inculcating American ideals into the hearts and
minds of foreign children, and serving a diplomatic function through their
parenting.

Christina Klein, in her groundbreaking work, *Cold War Orientalism*,
notes that U.S. private citizens' participation in transnational adoption
served U.S. foreign policy goals during the Cold War. Reflecting the high
stakes of U.S. geopolitical interests over the Asian region and the soaring
number of children who had been orphaned due to war, many faith-based
humanitarian organizations such as Christian Children's Funds actively ran
a series of campaigns to appeal to the U.S. public to save Asian orphans.
During the Korean War and its subsequent years, a barrage of popular
media and newsreels in the U.S. constantly portrayed Korean orphans as
the potential victims of North Korean communism. "The logic undergird-
ing…much of the CCF's promotional material, is that…hungry children
are susceptible to communist promises of a better future; thus hungry children threaten the security of Americans" (Klein 154).

Biracial children posed even more of a threat, because not only were they vulnerable to becoming communists themselves, their very presence in Korea could be used as evidence by communists that American intervention was the root of social ills such as "the mixed race problem." Pearl Buck, one of the main American proponents of transnational adoption, suggested that "hybrid Asian and American families created through adoption could eventually facilitate better political relations between the United States and Asia...in her view, the mixed-race children available for adoption were 'key children' who could facilitate relations between the U.S. and Asia and perhaps prevent further losses of Asian nations to communism" (Klein 144). Klein observes how such mixed race family formation through adoption "offered an imaginative justification for the permanent extension of U.S. power, figured as responsibility and leadership, beyond the nation's borders" and also allowed these families to imagine themselves as international American citizens (146). Adopting mixed race children served to establish not only a dutiful sense of patriotic belonging, but also a benevolent and generous image of the U.S.

As SooJin Pate has theorized, the notion of a generous U.S. evolved in conjunction with neocolonial power through a project she calls "American humanitarianism empire." By illuminating the U.S. military's extensive involvement in humanitarian missions such as orphan rescue during the Korean War, Pate contends that such military action, was "a way to assuage the explicit colonial practice of U.S. military occupation before, during, and after the Korean War...Through this particular form of neocolonialism, the U.S. is able to preserve its myth of exceptionalism while, at the same time, invest in empire-building activities in the Pacific" (23).

Thus, the United States' humanitarianism in South Korea laid the foundation upon which the Korean adoption industry was built as well as the building of each nation's citizenry. For South Korea, transnational adoption reinforced notions about which kinds of bodies should be excluded from the nation and thus, created a stateless population, in need of a home, within its borders. Some argue that South Korea's dependence on U.S. humanitarian relief initiatives to resolve this social crisis crippled the sustainable development of a social welfare system for children, and that this dependent mentality has expanded into other parts of Korean society as well (Choe). For the U.S., it bolstered the image of a benevolent world leader that welcomed foreigners onto its shores and into its homes, while whitewashing the atrocities committed by the U.S. military during the Korean War as well as American political interests in occupying Korea. Furthermore, Pate suggests that transnational adoption served as a method of colonial assimilation that transformed the burdensome biopolitical excess of the Korean War into productive American citizens (73-74). The families who adopted biracial, and later full-blooded, Korean children had little awareness of the geopolitical violence that underpinned the making of their happy new families.

THE AMERASIAN, THE ORPHAN, AND THE "DEAD" MOTHER

The campaign to convince Americans to rescue mixed race children from the clutches of North Korean communism or South Korean racism was so successful that by the 1960s the demand for Korean children exceeded the supply. This moment marked the shift in which the majority of adoptees became "pure" Korean, but it also marked a perversion in the manifest logic of adoption. In response to an increasing demand from prospective adoptive parents in the U.S., the transnational adoption industry made a definitive move towards looking for children to place in families rather than looking for families in which to place children. This practice continues today throughout the world and has been sharply criticized by those seeking reform of transnational adoption. E.J. Graff has said, "There are simply not enough healthy, adoptable infants to meet Western demand—and there's too much Western money in search of children...As international adoptions have flourished, so has evidence that babies in many countries are being systematically bought, coerced, or stolen away from their birth families" (60). David Smolin names as the number one adoption myth that "There are limitless and huge numbers of orphans, including healthy infants and toddlers, in need of international adoption." The orphan myth provides a disturbing example of the way in which South Korea and the U.S. created the paradigm for the larger practices and problems of transnational adoption, with the Amerasian child as the prototype of the mythic orphan.

Despite the seeming disappearance of biracial children from the Korean adoption market, the practices and ideologies that were put into place in South Korea and the U.S. during the 1950s heavily influenced the system as a whole. Just as Amerasian children were subjected to a series of national policies that rendered them stateless persons, the "full-blooded" Korean children that began to replace biracial bodies were required to go through a process of deracination from country and family in order to transform them into adoptable subjects. According to Eleana Kim:

orphan status is a prerequisite for adoption in American immigration law, which means that the child has been deemed to be adoptable by either the death or the departure of both parents, or through legal relinquishment by at least one parent. The child is thereby an exceptional migrant who is 'reunited' with 'immediate family' in the U.S. and has no other legally extant kinship connections that might render her the first link in a 'chain of migration' (*Our Adoptee* 520).

Again, in this instance, both American and South Korean legal systems took an active role in producing "orphans." On the South Korean end, an "orphan *hojuk*" is created to register the child as having no relatives and no family lineage, which prepares the child for "adoption and erasure as a Korean citizen" (E. Kim, *Our Adoptee* 521). Such legal manipulations suggest that not all children classified as orphans are parentless, and indeed, there have been many examples of adoptees who have discovered that their paperwork was falsified or their birth mothers coerced into signing relinquishment papers so that they could be designated as "orphans" and their adoptions completed (Choi; Oostrom). For example, there have been some high-profile cases of missing children who were taken into custody by adoption agency directors and then sent to American families (O). Anecdotal evidence also suggests that many adoptees have discovered glaring discrepancies between official documents and the stories they were told about the circumstances of their adoptions.

The production of Korean "orphans" was also enabled by South Korean economic policies that favored rapid industrialization and growth. During the 1960s, one common explanation for continued transnational adoption was the rise in child abandonment by Korean families.[8] However, we must be critical of the notion of "abandonment" and locate it within the economic climate. In 1962 South Korea launched its first "Five Year Economic Development Plan," whose slogan was "First, Development, Second, Welfare," Under this plan, many working class families were subject to wage suppression, resulting in widespread poverty and an exponential increase in the number of children in orphanages[9]. It was not uncommon for poor families to temporarily place their children in an orphanage in order to provide for their basic necessities. As E.J. Graff has noted, in many countries throughout the world, orphanages are understood as temporary foster care homes to provide parents with relief during times of hardship. Therefore, children in orphanages often had living parents who intended to care for them, and Western adoptive families were often unaware of this. Rather than establish a long-term social welfare program for these children and their families, the South Korean government liberalized adoption, by expanding the countries where these children would be sent. By 1965, receiving countries included the Scandinavian countries, Holland, Australia and Canada (Hübinette, "Korean Adoption History"). By transferring these children overseas, the South Korean government could unburden themselves of a needy population, thereby serving national economic security interests. By the 1970s, the economic explanation for adoption was combined with other causes, such as the rise of divorce and pregnancy among single women. During the 1970s and 1980s, Korea sent more than 100,000 children abroad—two-thirds of all Korean adoptees throughout transnational adoption history.[10]

It is important to note that a child can also be turned into an orphan while the birthmother is alive and willing to take care of her own child. Under Korean family law, unwed and divorced mothers had few parental rights. Until 1979, the father was automatically given full child custody in the event of divorce. Women were then denied parental rights over her child, including visitation, from the dissolved marriage. Korean patrilineal family registry (*Hoju-Je*), which reigned the modern family system until 2007, did not recognize women to be the head of the family registry so that a single mother's relation to her child was not legally recognized. Under the government's drive for population control, children of divorced parents and single mothers without immediate family protection were continuously and conveniently turned into "orphans" by severing all ties from their existing kin, thus rendering the biological family "dead."

THE BIRTHPLACE OF SOCIAL DEATH

Extending the notion that orphans are produced through the removal of the child from her family, community, and nation, Jodi Kim argues that: "a particularly elided yet significant condition of possibility for transracial adoption is the conjoined 'social death' of the adoptee and the birth mother" (*Empire* 169). She contextualizes the social death of birth mothers in the circumstances that make it difficult or impossible for these women to keep their children and argues that: "Profound natal alienation, or the capacity to give life but the severing of rights to claim and parent that life, radically circumscribes the quality of the lives of birth mothers such that they undergo a social death" (*Two Mothers* 857).

The ideological underpinning of this "death," however, is that "the figure of the Korean birthmother…is depicted as either a prostitute or an unwed teenage mother. Her supposed sexual deviance from a prescribed norm …exchanging money for sex, being unwed at the time of pregnancy, and/or having sex at an inappropriate age—deems her unfit to take care of her own children" (Pate 227).[11] This ideology is evident in Kim Jin Yeol's 1974 seminal study on South Korean birthmothers in which she identified the cause of "the foreign adoption problem" as "disadvantaged" women such as prostitutes and bar hostesses, as well as other working class women who do not live under their fathers' or husbands' rule. Likewise, in the biopolitical discourse on the adoption of biracial children born in Korea, there is a consistent theme that the children have no future in Korea not only because of racial discrimination, but also because their mothers' presumed association with the camptowns means that they are incapable of parenting. This implies that at the heart of societal beliefs about "unfit" motherhood lies the unregulated sexuality of the birthmother.

Though the majority of birthmothers may not have participated in sex work, they still carry the stigma of having conceived a child through allegedly promiscuous, accidental, or transgressive forms of sex.[12] The notion of excessive and immoral female sexuality, epitomized by the figure of the prostitute, extends to all birthmothers who fall outside the patriarchal family order.[13] If the camptown was the birthplace of militarized prostitution and subsequently, the first group of "war orphans" to be sent to American families, then it was also the birthplace for the ideologies that would govern transnational adoption. The "illegitimate" Amerasian child and the "unfit" sex worker mother are symbolic figures that justify the rationale for sending children to the West. When the child has no possibility for a decent life in Korea and the mother is clearly unfit because of her sexual deviance, then it is easy to naturalize transnational adoption as the best choice for birthmothers and their children.

Many of the adoptees who were violently extracted from their original kin, however, have grown up haunted by the ghosts of their social deaths, as have their birthmothers. Over the past two decades, South Korea has witnessed the return of adult adoptees in search of their birth families. Consequently, search and reunion stories began to air on television and soon grew into a pop cultural phenomenon (*A'Chim MahDang*). Through these television shows and other media, the figure of the Korean birthmother has emerged (Hosu Kim). Unlike the overarching characterization of the birthmother who should relinquish her baby—as sexually promiscuous and unfit to mother, the emergent narrative of the birthmother looking for her adult child portrays a different kind of woman. She is elderly or middle aged, an unfortunate mother who had to make a painful decision out of economic necessity or in the absence of the baby's father. Adoption was a noble choice for her child's better future. None of these birthmothers came forward revealing a background in sex work.

This emergent figure of the Korean birthmother in contemporary media representations, then, is carved out through the careful elimination of the woman's history in the camptown. For instance, when biracial adoptees appear in search and reunion narratives, the social stigma against their mother's association with American men and the child's having been born into the camptown is downplayed, but often in the background. These details are covered over by a generic story about widespread poverty as the immediate cause for adoption. Therefore, the figure of the biracial child's birthmother is transformed into a sacrificing mother who chose adoption as her motherly duty. By not revealing the larger context of the birthmother's life, we do not see the societal mistreatment and hardship she suffered. We see only a devoted mother who has waited her whole life for her child's return.

These acts of search and reunion, in a sense, have failed. For the biracial adoptee, the search fails to find the past and instead begets another thing missing. For the birthmother, made socially dead when her child was sent away, a second death is played out through the violent suppression of her history. Underneath this newly made birthmother, a camptown sex worker shimmers as her ghostly double.

THE KINSHIP OF VIOLENCE

By having located the phenomenon of Korean transnational adoption in the U.S. camptown, we have tried to illuminate the invisible figures in Korean adoption studies—the sex worker mother and her biracial child as "social problems" whose expulsion from Korea spurred a permanent adoption industry and profoundly affected the character of nations. We believe that a critical analysis of transnational adoption as a product of U.S. militarism can recast the image of the war orphan from an object of pity and humanitarian desire to a politically powerful subject at the crossroads of nations. Through the reclamation of the camptown as one's birthplace, these newly visible subjects complicate the narrative of U.S.-Korea relations as a familial alliance, illustrated by the common phrase *hyeol-maeng* (혈맹), or "alliance by blood," which implies the forging of an unbreakable bond between two equal nations.

We conclude by meditating on the ways in which the Korean War and its unending aftermath have broken apart families and created new ties across different groups of people who were born of the dark history of war and biopolitical violence. Here are some of the reverberations that ripple through the modern Korean diaspora and beyond.

Let's recall for a moment the iconic images of the orphan, alone and hungry, amidst the remnants of war-torn Korea and then the smiling mixed race children who were Harry Holt's first project in transnational adoption. Now flash forward again, from 1955 to 2010. A group of second generation Korean Americans in their 30s are sitting around a table at an informal social gathering in Minneapolis. Some of them are adoptees that have searched for their biological parents and the truth surrounding their adoption histories. The others are biracial and grew up with their Korean mothers, who were silent about the past. All of them, in one way or another, are compelled to look for their hidden family histories. A spontaneous conversation arises in which they acknowledge the fact that they are all connected through their having been repudiated by Korean society. It is a conversation that shatters the previous images of Korean orphans and adoptees, and once shattered, the image fragments are reassembled to create a new picture of kinship. One of them ironically refers to the group as "war trash," and they all laugh knowingly.

In 1966, a man arrives at the Sun Duck orphanage in Korea to retrieve his daughter, Cha Jung Hee, from whom he had been separated. The reunion takes place shortly before the girl was to be sent away for adoption. The social worker in charge of her case makes a decision that, rather than inform the American family of what had happened, she will send another child in Cha Jung Hee's place, under Cha Jung Hee's name. Kang Ok Jin, whose mother had not intended permanent relinquishment, is told by the social worker that she will go to America under the name Cha Jung Hee and that she must never tell her American family of her true identity. Kang Ok Jin is reborn as Cha Jung Hee, and then again as Deann Borshay. Her paperwork falsely states that her parents are dead, that she is a "war orphan" despite having been born after the war, and shows evidence of forged signatures. At the age of eight, she is told to forget every memory of her family, her past, and her home in Korea. Eventually she forgets, until one day, when she remembers. Her adult life becomes a journey to investigate the past and she goes on to make a stunning film, *In the Matter of Cha Jung Hee*, which documents her search for the "real" Cha Jung Hee. Although she finds a match, she also discovers that her adoption files contained photos of a third child, also called "Cha Jung Hee." The film concludes that "Cha Jung Hee" was more than an actual child. She was a "template for the perfect orphan." This practice of fabricating orphans spread to other countries along with the practice of transnational adoption.

In 2004, a young teenage girl from Cambodia is reunited with her birth family. At the age of 9, she was abducted by a child-procurer and sent to live with an American couple without the birth family's knowledge or consent. Initially, her adoptive family believes that she was an orphan but as the girl learned English and the adoptive parents investigated the matter, they realized that the child they thought needed a family already had one. They returned the girl to the family from whom she was tragically separated.

In 2006, an American couple adopts three sisters from Ethiopia through Christian World Adoption. They were told that the girls were AIDS orphans who faced a future of poverty and prostitution. As the girls learn English, they tell the adoptive parents that they had come from a middle class family that was still alive. In 2007, a woman in Guatemala reports to the police that a man locked her up and stole her baby. After a 14-month search, she finds her baby in an orphanage, just weeks before the child is to be sent to an American couple. That same year, in Nepal a child placed in temporary foster care is adopted by a couple in Spain, without the biological parents' knowledge or consent.[14] Her family is still searching for her.

In 2000, a birthmother appears on a Korean television show and tells her story: Her first son, Kenny, was fathered by an American soldier. When Kenny was seven and it was time for him to start school, she decided that it was time to let him go. One day she practiced sending him away by putting him alone on a bus. Kenny seemed fine, so she took him to a nearby orphanage. Soon, she learned that his paperwork was complete and he would be leaving. After he left, her life broke down. She hurriedly married another GI who brought her to the U.S.—once an abstract land of opportunity and freedom, now the place where her beloved secret son was living. Thirty-two years went by. So much time had passed that she stopped hoping to find her son, who was still a seven-year-old boy in her heart. But then her sister in Korea called and told her that her Kenny had come back to Korea to look for her. So she went back to Korea, for the first time since she moved to the U.S. In her mind, she returned to Kimpo airport in 1969 where she put a photo of the two of them in Kenny's pocket before saying goodbye. When it was finally time to meet her Kenny, she saw a stranger named Jeffrey Higginson. But even before their reunion someone had asked her "what if he is not your son?" "It doesn't matter," she said. "I will accept him as my own."

NOTES

[1] See Wang's website: www.fingerstothebone.com.

[2] For more on this topic, see Dorow; Sarri, Baek, and Bombyk 1998; and Yoon and Hwang 1996).

[3] Prior to the recent exchange of fire between North and South Korea, most Americans were unaware that the Korean War was never resolved and that Koreans continue to live, paradoxically, under a regime of both hyper-militarization and insecurity.

[4] For more on biracial adoptees, see Hurh; Chun; Park; Hwang and Yoon; and Pate.

[5] For more on the relationship between transnational adoption and militarism, see Duncan; Hübinette; Pate; J. Kim; E. Kim.

[6] Biracial Korean American activist Sajin Kwok has argued that transnational adoption functioned much in the same way as did abortion—it "increased the sexual availability of prostituted women…who weren't tied down with child-rearing duties."

[7] As Haeri Kim has noted, without fathers who were willing to claim them, Amerasians could not become U.S. citizens, and therefore, Kim argues that "the persistent denial of individual paternal responsibility…has produced a *stateless population* in and outside of its territories." (28)

[8] The proportion of abandoned children compared to the total number of adoptees during the 1960s reached 55%.

[9] These five-year economic development plans continued until 1996.

[10] 1985 marked a record high of 8,837 children, or approximately 1% of live births in Korea, placed in transnational adoption.

[11] The ideology that "proper" motherhood should conform to middle class heteronormative standards is the ground for South Korea's inadequate social welfare for single mothers whose children continue to be expelled from Korea via foreign adoption.

[12] For example, Yoon and Hwang (1996) identified foreign adoption as a byproduct of rapid industrialization, which displaced many young females into urban centers where they were employed as factory workers. Their independent residential arrangements might have made them prone to "improper" sexual behavior without a father figure in the household.

[13] Kim's notion of "problem women" as the culprit of "the foreign adoption problem" continues to underscore ideas about contemporary birthmothers, mostly single women in their teens and early twenties.

[14] In 2008, E.J. Graff wrote: "In many countries, it can be astonishingly easy to fabricate a history for a young child, and in the process, manufacture an orphan. The birth mothers are often poor, young, unmarried, divorced, or otherwise lacking family protection. The children may be born into a locally despised minority group that is afforded few rights. And for enough money, someone will separate these little ones from their vulnerable families, and turn them into 'paper orphans' for lucrative export" (p. 63).

WORKS CITED

"Now, Mixed Race Children in Korea Can Go to the U.S." *The Chosun-Ilbo* (Daily Newspaper). Seoul, Korea. January 29th, 1954. Print.

Cho, Grace. *Haunting the Korean Diaspora: Shame, Secrecy, and Forgotten War.* Minneapolis: MN, University of Minnesota Press. 2008. Print.

Cho, M. (Executive Producer). *A' Chim MahDang* [아침마당]. Seoul, Korea: KBS on July 5th and July 12th 2000. Television Broadcast.

Choe, Won Kyu. *Oeguk' minganwonjodanch' eui hwaldongwoa hanguksahoesaon paljone mich'in yonghyang* [Activities of foreign voluntary agencies and their influences upon social work development in Korea]. Diss. Seoul National University, Seoul, Korea 1996. Print.

Choi, Mee Suk. Personal Interview. 27 July. 2005

Dorow, Sara. *I Wish for You a Beautiful Life.* St Paul, Yeong & Yeong Book Company. 1999. Print.

Duncan, Patti. "Genealogies of Unbelonging: Amerasians and Transnational Adoptees as Legacies of U.S. Militarization in South Korea." *Militarized Currents: Toward Decolonized Future in Asia and Pacific*, ed. by Setsu Shigematsu and Keith Lujan Camacho. Minneapolis, MN: University of Minnesota Press, 2010. 277–307. Print.

Graff, E. J. "The Lie We Love". Nov/Dec 2008. *Foreign Policy* 59—66. PDF File.

Higginson, J., & Kearly, P. *Unlocking the Past.* Flat Rock, MI: A.N.Y.O. Publishing Company. 2003. Print.

Hübinette, Tobias. "Korean Adoption History." *Guide to Korea for Overseas Adopted Koreans*, ed. E. Kim. Seoul: Overseas Koreans Foundation.

2004. Print.

—. *Comforting an Orphaned Nation: Representations of International Adoption and Adopted Koreans in Korean Popular Culture*. Diss. Stockholm University, Sweden. 2005. Print.

Hwang, O., & Yoon, M. "The Study of the development of the characteristics of unwed mothers in Korea." *Dongguk Journal: Humanities & Social Sciences*, 35 (1996): 219–247. Print.

In the Matter of Cha Jung Hee, dir. by Deanne Borshay Liem. 2010. aired on September 15, 2010. PBS. Film.

Kim, Eleana J. *Adopted Territory: Transnational Korean Adoptees and The Politics of Belonging*, Durham, NC: Duke University Press, 2010. Print.

—. "The Origins of Korean Adoption: Cold War Policy and Intimate Diplomacy." US-Korea Institute at SAIS Working Paper Series. 2009: 1–26. Print.

—. "Our Adoptee, Our Alien: Transnational Adoptees as Specters of Foreignness and Family in South Korea." *Anthropological Quarterly*, 80 (2), (2007): 497–531. Print.

Kim, Ji Yeol. *Mee-hon-mo ui daehahn Yeonku* [A Study of Unwed Mothers]. Unpublished Master's Thesis, Ewha Women's University, Seoul, Korea. 1974. Print.

Kim, Jodi. *Ends of Empire: Asian American Critique and the Cold War*. St. Paul, MN: University of Minnesota Press. 2010. Print.

—. "An 'Orphan' with Two Mothers: Transnational and Transracial Adoption, the Cold War, and Contemporary Asian American Cultural Politics." *American Quarterly* 61.4 (2009): 855–880. Print.

Kim, Haeri. "Proving American Fatherhood, (Re)uniting with Asia: on the Legalization of Amerasian Immigration." Paper presented at the annual meeting of the Theory vs. Policy: Connecting Scholars and Practitioners, New Orleans Hilton Riverside Hotel, The Loews New Orleans Hotel, New Orleans, LA, Feb 17, 2010, 1–32. Print.

Kim, Hosu. "Television Mothers: Lost & Found in Search and Reunion Narratives." *Proceedings of the First International Korean Adoption Studies Research Symposium*, Seoul, Korea 125–145. Print.

Klein, Christina. *Cold War Orientalism: Asia in the Middlebrow Imagination*, 1945–1961. Los Angeles, CA: University of California. 2003. Print.

Kwok, Sajin, "Status of Korean Amerasians," unpublished manuscript. 2004. Print.

Kwon, In Sook. *Daehahn Minkook en Koondae-dah* [Korea is Military: Feminist Perspective on Peace, Militarism, Masculinity.] Seoul, Korea: Chung Nyun, 2005. Print.

Ministry for Health, Welfare and Family Affairs "The Current State of Domestic and International Adoption" (Kungaeoe ibyang hyonhwang). Seoul: Ministry for Health, Welfare and Family Affairs. 2009. Print.

Moon, Katharine. *Sex Among Allies:Military Prostitution in U.S.–Korea relations.* Columbia University Press. 1997. Print.

O, Yong-chu. *Han'guk adongbokchi kigwan'gwa sisôrûi sôl'lippaegyông'gwa paljônjôk yôinê kwanhan yôn'gu* [A study on the establishment background and developmental factors in the Korean child welfare agencies]. Diss. Soongsil University: Department of Social Work. 1994. Print.

Okazawa-Rey, Margo. "Amerasian Children of GI Town: A Legacy of U.S. Militarism in South Korea." *Asia Journal of Women's Studies* 3.1. (2003): 71-102. Print.

Oostrom, Danielle van. Personal Interview. 7 Aug. 2005.

Pate, SooJin. *Genealogies of Korean Adoption: American Empire, Militarization, and Yellow Desire.* Diss. University of Minnesota. Print.

Park, In Sun. A study on search of Korean among Young Adult Adopted Persons in the U.S.A. Diss. Ewha Women's Univeristy, Seoul, Korea. 1994. Print.

Park, Kyung Tae. *Sosucha wa Hankuk Sahoe* [Minority Groups in Korean Society], Seoul, Korea: Humanitas 2006. Print.

Sarri, R. C., Baik, Y. & Bomnyk, M. "Goal Displacement and dependency in South Korean–United States intercountry adoption." *Children and Youth Review,* 20, 87-114. 1998. Print.

Shin, E. & Kim, H. A Report on Former Kijichon Sex Workers in Kyunggi Do. Conference Proceeding, Sunlit Sisters' Center 2008 : 14–100. 2008. Print.

Smolin, David. Expert's Respond to "The Baby Business" Dec 20 The Schuster Institute for Investigative Journalism Archive, 9 Sept. 2010. Web. 20 Dec. 2010. http://www.brandeis.edu/investigate/gender/adoption/expertsrespond_Smolin.html.

Sunlit Sisters' Center. *Oral History of Former Kijichon Women.* Sunlit Sisters' Center, Korea. 2008. Print.

2.

Cheeseburger Season

GRACE M. CHO

Ten years ago my mother moved in with me for what turned out to be a seven-month stay. I had just bought a co-op apartment in Queens with my partner at the time, and the advent of my homeownership, along with the fact that I had recently turned thirty, made me feel adult enough to accept the challenge of hosting my mother. My partner generously agreed to give up his music studio so that my mother could use it as her bedroom. It was a small room tucked away in the back corner of our apartment, in a separate wing with its own bathroom, and it gave my mother the privacy she needed.

At that point in her life, she had been suffering from schizophrenia for fifteen years and agoraphobia for seven. The thought of interacting with anyone outside her immediate family caused her so much stress that she would hide in the closet or crouch behind a piece of furniture every time the doorbell rang. For most of my adult life, she refused to go outside and believed that if she moved too much, "if I even lift my finger the wrong way," she might bring harm to those around her. I think it was that same delusion that governed her behavior around eating. She denied herself the pleasure of most foods because she did not want to cook nor did she want other people to do it for her. Her diet consisted mostly of packaged ramen, rice and kimchi, and other people's leftovers. Though on special occasions, if the conditions were just right, she would allow herself to indulge in some small luxury. The last time this had happened was on Christmas, two years earlier, when she drank her first cup of coffee in five years. I woke up that Christmas morning and saw my mother standing at the kitchen window, her gaze fixed on the sky and an empty coffee mug in her hand. "I told myself that if we have white Christmas this year, I can have a cup of coffee," she said. As soon as the first flakes fell, she turned on the percolator and said, "I knew it."

During the time that my mother lived with me, I could barely coax her out of her room, and getting her to eat a proper meal was a constant battle. Her refusals to eat took on the character of a hunger strike against some force to which only she was privy. On a few occasions, however, I'd come home from work early and find her hunched over the garbage can eating a piece of bread, or I'd hear her footsteps scurrying down the hall to her room. "It's OK, Mom! It's just me!" I'd shout from the entrance. Aside from those clandestine trips to the kitchen, she spent most of her days wrapped up in a little ball with her head tucked into her chest, rocking herself on the floor of her room. Though she had been sick for years, it was the first time I really witnessed it on a daily basis. To see what had become of my mother devastated me.

When I was a child, she was the most passionate cook I knew. The experience of tasting a new food, and of learning how to cook it, captivated her so completely that nothing could break her concentration. My childhood memory is dominated by the image of my mother zipping about the kitchen in a manic fury. Though I was incapable of really knowing my mother when I was young, I felt her hunger. She wanted to eat everything, master all cuisines, and feed everyone who came within sniffing distance of her kitchen. She had grown up poor, and feeding others made her feel rich. There was a power in food that she understood for the first time when I was young. For several years she worked as a professional forager, braving the wilderness to bring home massive quantities of wild edibles. She was so fearless, so adept at foraging, that she became one of the largest suppliers of blackberries and mushrooms in the Pacific Northwest.

Despite the experience my mother had acquired with different kinds of food, her favorite meal was always a basic cheeseburger—medium rare with tomato and cheddar. Every year, when the Washington rains gave way to drier days, she would fire up the charcoal grill, throw some patties on it and declare the commencement of "cheeseburger season."

My mother's love of cheeseburgers went way back to the U.S. military occupation of Korea. As a bargirl at a U.S. naval base, she had access to luxurious American foods that most Koreans could only dream of—it was sort of a fringe benefit of serving American soldiers. Before that, she was like any other Korean, whose first taste of American food probably came from scavenging in the dumpsters outside U.S. Army mess halls. Right after the war, the American bases became a destination for hungry Koreans looking to buy bags of leftover food scraps, which were often mixed up with all kinds of inedible trash. I imagine that my mother once found a half eaten cheeseburger beneath a layer of crumpled napkins and cigarette butts, and in her half-starved state of mind, thought it was the most transcendent thing she had ever tasted. Perhaps it was the experience of getting her meals from the garbage that sparked my mother's aspirations to some day eat well.

There's a story that my father used to tell about how he fell in love with my mother because of her enthusiasm for cheeseburgers. He took her out on a date to an American restaurant at the naval base where his ship was docked. My father had been moving up the ranks of the U.S. merchant marines and was at that time, a First Mate. That gave him special access to VIP privileges.

My mother had been long out of school and had never formally studied English but she was a woman driven to learn. She memorized words one-by-one from a dictionary and paid close attention to the dialogue in American movies. She compared her speech to that of other English-speaking Koreans and felt certain that she did not have an accent. Indeed, she pronounced many English sounds correctly. The Zs that most Koreans pronounced as Js did not intimidate her. She had little trouble with long As or words ending in consonants, except for words ending in both R and L, which were especially difficult if they were followed by another consonant. Nonetheless, the fact that she believed that she spoke English without an accent illuminated her voice with the unmistakable sound of confidence.

My father was almost fifty and my mother, in her mid twenties. He looked across the table at this young beauty, and wondered if she could possibly love an old man. "Order anything on the menu," he said. "Anything at all." My father was frugal, but he believed that some things were worth the money. It was a much fancier restaurant than the other ones my mother had been to before. An irrepressible smile spread across her face, exposing her huge dimples. She was rapturous. The waiter arrived to take their order. My mother swung her feet back and forth and wiggled slightly in her seat. Her smile grew larger as she enunciated each word clearly, "I'll have a cheeseburg, please." My mother clapped her hands together and said to my father, "Oh boy! Cheeseburg is my favorite food in the whole worl!"

That was the point in the story when my father always began to get dewy-eyed and his telling would often end there. But if his emotion had not gotten too heavy, he would conclude with the words, "Your mother was the cutest thing I ever did see."

Not long after the cheeseburger date, my father initiated his engagement to my mother, which was complicated by the fact that he was already married. She suffered through the waiting—the time during which my father left Korea and went back to his American wife—and probably watched the other Korean women around her pine for the soldiers who never returned. But my father did return. There was no fairy-tale wedding for my mother, no celebration from either of their families, just the promise of America and an endless supply of cheeseburgers. And somehow that was enough.

By the time my mother moved in with me, my father was three years dead and my mother was about to turn sixty. Among Koreans, sixty is the birthday that deserves the most fanfare. At sixty, a person has achieved a milestone measured by the completion of the entire lunar zodiac. Nowadays, in the age of modern medicine, seventy has become just as celebrated as sixty.

On the days leading up to my mother's sixtieth birthday, I planned a lavish meal of her favorite foods. For the first time in months, she looked forward to the prospect of eating, though her excitement was not without conflict. One day, I approached her as she rocked herself in the little ball.

"Mom."

"Hm?" she said without looking up.

"I'm going to make *kalbi* for your birthday," I said.

She lifted her head and the dark clouds around her started to dissipate. "Be sure to put plenty of garlic in it."

"I'm also going to barbecue some chicken."

"I haven't had that for years… Why you go to so much trouble? Don't cook all that."

"Mom, it's your birthday."

"Big deal."

"It's your sixtieth birthday. There will be cheeseburgers, too."

Suddenly, she looked up and smiled. She had avoided smiling since her front tooth had fallen out a couple years earlier, but this time she couldn't help herself. She covered her mouth and kept her smile hidden behind her hand. "Cheeseburgers, huh? That sounds good."

On the day of her birthday, I set the big dining table for three and filled it with plates of *kalbi*, grilled chicken, potato salad, *kimchi*, *cong-nameul*, spinach *nameul*, cheeseburgers, sliced tomatoes and onions, baby lettuce, grilled corn on the cob, seedless watermelon, and a four layer lemon cake.

"It's time for your birthday party!" I said from the doorway of my mother's room.

"I'll just eat in here."

"No. I already set the table. Come out."

I was anticipating a struggle, but instead, my mother stood up and shuffled down the hall towards the dining room. When she came face-to-face with my partner, she stopped and said to him, "It is my birthday, after all." Then she walked up to the edge of the table, sized up the spread, clapped her hands and shouted, "*Manh-ta!* Lots of goodies!"

The three of us feasted together and my mother relished everything. It was the first time in seven years that she sat down to a meal with anyone other than her own children, and the first time she got really excited by food. In that moment, I knew that the mother who had raised me was still alive.

"Did you enjoy the meal?" I asked.

"Yeah. I been wondering if I was gonna get a birthday party this year." Her big smile returned and she said, "Oh boy! That cheeseburger is good!"

My mother's sixtieth birthday kicked off a tradition. On every subsequent birthday, I prepared a simplified version of that meal, stripped down to its essence of grilled cheeseburgers and a lemon cake. She enjoyed each birthday meal as much as she had at sixty, though I had hoped that she would live to see seventy so that I could have done the big feast again.

After my mother's death the scene of our final moments together looped inside my head for days. I fixated on the exact sequence of events, minor details of the weather, the sound of her voice. I had traveled from Brooklyn to her home in New Jersey—the apartment that was adjacent to my brother's place. As I walked from the train station, I noticed that the air was cold but smelled vaguely of budding flowers. That night I cooked *saeng-tae jjigae*, one of her favorite winter meals, knowing that the change in seasons was on the horizon. Since the year my mother lived with me, her mental health had improved enough so that she no longer curled up in the little ball or resisted eating good meals. But that night, she seemed inexplicably sad and asked me to stay a bit longer than usual, so I did. When it was time to leave, I felt a sharp pang of remorse. I had already said goodbye and had taken two steps down the stairs, but something compelled me to turn around.

"Mom," I said. "Just think that the next time I see you it will be spring. Then it will be cheeseburger season."

Those were my last words to her. Since then, I have eaten only one cheeseburger a year—on my mother's birthday. This year she would have turned seventy.

3.

The Asian Motherhood Stigma

A Historical Glance at Embedded Women's Practices in the Korean Colonial Media

MEROSE HWANG

South Korea is known as a land of female shamans. Like many colonized countries around the world, shamanism emerged in Korea under an imperial logic to racialize indigenous society. Shamans appear in the history of Korean motherhood as gendered rationality and spirituality coincided with nationalistic projects to modernize the country through the family. The misogynistic impulses of the nationalist movement were prefigured in discussions of Korean mothers as "superstitious," reinforcing the male-female social power imbalance. By employing the term, shamans, writers were able to homogenized female community leaders and characterized them as superstitious. In the late 19th and early 20th centuries, female shamans were the subject of numerous discussions and reports in newspapers and journals in Korea and abroad. The subject became a frequent scapegoat for all that was wrong with Korea, acting as a lens for a myriad of modernization topics throughout the 20th century.

Tracing the historical effects of capitalism in the late 19th and early 20th century on the Korean shaman subject provides a method for interpreting the historically recent emergence of elite motherhood and home economics. This study represents an investigation into numerous intellectual and material crossings, and the various political, economic, and cultural conditions that solicit our view of a capitalist modernity to show how the development of social regulatory discourses informed modern homemaking and ideas about class, gender, and motherhood in Korea. I consider capitalist modernity to be the global impulse of rising large-scale markets and the division of labor in which all nations are compelled, in the words of Marx and Engels, "on pain of extinction, to adopt the bourgeois mode of production; it compels them to introduce what it calls civilization into their midst, i.e., to become bourgeois themselves" ("Bourgeois" 7, "Wage Labour" 203–217). Especially focused on how social stratification was ideologically developed in early twentieth century Korean history, this chapter examines the numerous ways in which articulations of Korean women as "evil" depended intimately on a racialized reproductive subject, expressly for the exploitation of unpaid domestic labor for the larger struggle of becoming a modern nation. Shaman discourses were a conditional manifestation of modernity, expressing the economic anatomy of the classes. Highly complex social connections created by capitalism were among the most vital resources of modernity. An infrastructure for capitalist development was formed through expanded trade, diversified markets, and increased labour divisions. My analytical approach to capitalist modernity considers the transnational effects of modern industry in which social relations of human reproduction and female consumption were welcomed by global capitalist promises of progress and development.

This chapter on shamans as female pariahs in colonial Korea considers the historical process to reconceptualize Asian women for a capitalist modernity. A new arena of Korean journalists engaged in conversations about women's social behavior in a conceptual framework to regulate domestic practices, accelerate Korean development, and enhance the Japanese empire's global presence. Identifying local obstructers or inhibitors to Korea's progress was crucial to this new discursive paradigm. Journalists employed a capitalist model of accelerated growth by targeting poor women as superstitious, unmodern, and stubborn bearers of tradition. For both Japanese colonialists and Korean domestic reformers, women's destitution and sexuality became definitive elements of a stigmatized population. These writers formed Korean shamanism's particularism and indigeneity through a gendered temporality, and used the preponderance of womanly fraternization in order to explain the colony's latent (unlikely) development.

At the same time, the Japanese colonial government (1910–1945) encouraged Korean women to write for the media to showcase the Government-General's modern and progressive leadership. In the 1920s, it lifted the ban on the Korean native press, sparking dozens of printing houses to reopen. While the Japanese government permitted the native Korean presses to run again, it kept an iron fist over media content by issuing hundreds of censorship fines over the next couple of decades. Due partly to these punitive policies, writers developed strategies to self-censor while they furthered colonial campaigns to racialize and sexualize Koreans. Writers on all sides of the political spectrum united to reject traditional leadership roles played by women, and they identify shamans and womanly congregations as particularly objectionable. Indigenous journalists both appeased and resisted colonial monitors by perpetrating racist and sexist images of colonized subjects and by using these images to point out Japan's failed promises to modernize colonial Korea.

Women were not only the subjects, they were also some of the authors of this early media. A few women's journals were in print as early as 1900, but after the re-opening of the native press, women's niche writing flourished. Starting with the Japanese imperial organ, *Mainichi Shinbun* [*Daily News*], women were eventually stationed in all printing houses, and by the mid-1920s women's journals and dedicated columns reached unprecedented numbers (Y. Pak 8). Women working on "female interest" columns became the markers of modern egalitarianism. They were primarily tasked to persuade readers to produce and abide by newly imposed principles of motherhood (Y. Pak 8–11; S. Park "Making Colonial"). These writers actively discussed the configurations and boundaries of proper reproduction and care-work through the dailies and bi-monthly women's journals. As women's issues became a part of the national reform agenda in the 1920s, women's groups gravitated towards the middling politics of elite modernity and journalists increasingly embraced a new epistemology of science by rendering work in the private sphere into a public education campaign and opposed embedded, informal, communal, and kin-based knowledge systems as unmodern, uneducated, criminal practices.

The colonial media worked alongside the Japanese imperial government to constitute new political rationalities and their liberal technologies effected a new conception of economy and society. The institutionalization of public education in the early twentieth century was a marker of this modern empire. But in practice, public education was inaccessible to most girls and their families because admission to such schools required families to have, among other things, surplus human resources, cash for school fees and supplies, urban residence, and elders who would trust and support their daughters' education. Nonetheless, the media industry singularly aligned to promote girls' curriculum and public education and embraced a middle-class vision for gender equality. A new study in home economics became the central component to girls' curriculum. In the 1920s, the founder of "home economics," Ava Milam (1884-1976) travelled to China and Japan, to gradually introduce Koreans to the new field (S. Pak 77–109). The Japanese government embraced this American subject as the latest trend in girls' education and adopted it as the primary subject in girls' school (Chŏn 95–112). North American missionaries worked to piecemeal western education into girls' schools and helped to standardize and control gendered labor within and outside the home.

A small group of cosmopolitan, privileged, Korean women of letters embraced all things "new" and "modern" to represent their own progress. Their campaigns prioritized elite public over informal education and wage over non-wage labor, increasing women's double burden. For these writers, the largest platform to address these new women's issues was one that would systematically train women to accommodate and support colonial industrialization. The home economics project dovetailed with the Japanese government's increasing demand for cheap mechanized labor. As the colonial economy was pushed to expand light industries and agricultural price inflation spiked poverty rates in the countryside, young destitute women left their rural homes seeking work around industrial cities. Korean journalists feared young women flocking the cities might put the nation in peril as these newcomers permanently settled in urban areas. They also feared the mass emigration of girls might create a rural surplus of bachelors (S. Park "Colonial Industrial" 137). Writers took on the role of social reformers, believing that the key to the nation's success lay in properly educating these rural girls and they proposed that these full-time female workers attend night school for personal and national benefit. The positive principles of factory work were espoused in classrooms as a part of the girls' new urban experience. Their night schooling was intended to help foster a willing return to the countryside and necessary preparations for healthy rural motherhood (C. Kim "Kaehwagi" 57–78). In this way, women's bio-power was explicitly framed in the interest of the capitalist labor market.

It may go without saying that the print industry promoted women's education and literacy in order to boost readership, but an important facet to this industry were its methods to enhance industry-based consumption. While modern mothers were characterized as wise and prolific shoppers, evil women also figured prominently as their counterpart in the colonial media's marketing agenda. Negative reinforcements, targeting women as stumbling blocks to modern education, inhibitors to science, and transmitters of superstition proliferated in the media to steer women towards new habits of consumption. The modern superstition discourse coincided with a tumultuous and diversifying economy during a time of global agricultural depression. The print media created webs of relations in a colony that was driven by the belief that micro-level monitors like neighborhood watches, would help stabilize the economy and assuage the regional effects of the global crisis. Superstitious women were identified as agents of embedded exchange, believed to represent large informal sectors of uneven development. New political rationalities coupled with new conceptions of economy and society caused writers to view Korean women's indigenous activities negatively as challenges to economic prosperity and national progress.

In the 1930s the superstition discourse was enmeshed with concerns about the global economic depression, and a ballooning female urban labor force, along with alarming food shortages and spiking unemployment rates in Korea. In light of the economic crisis, women's magazines called on women to tighten their belts and funnel their resources for efficient and productive motherhood: to curb personal spending habits, to tightly manage their purses, and most importantly, to practice prescribed preventative healthcare. Female readers were informed about ways to provide their children with proper nutrition based on imported food products, how to use new pharmaceutical medicines, and educated on available services in government hospitals. A popular mother's journal, *Ahŭi Saenghwal [Child's Life]* introduced and described in detail the health benefits of highly processed products like toothpaste and aspirin ("Chŏnggyŏl" 20). Their study boasted their knowledge in nutritional science with conclusions such as "foods rich in cod liver oil aid in developing good teeth. Meanwhile, those households that do not mix their grains induce calcium-deficiency, causing teeth to easily rot." The magazine listed instructions and a daily regimen for mothers to oversee their children's oral hygiene, stipulating how "even small teeth must be cleaned well and brushed twice a day." A striking collage wrapped the bottom of the text with a woman in a shower cap, smiling in the shower, with a glass of milk, a basket of fruit and a toothbrush in a glass cup. All of these foreign and exotic items were valorized as rational, functional, and modern. The fact that most Korean women could not afford these products or had alternatively effective regiments was glossed over by descriptions of manufactured imports as ordinary, practical, and modern. The media dissuaded readers from experiential, inherited, and communal methods, and was highly suspect of locally-sourced, alternative healthcare medicines and practices that poor, rural mothers desired and trusted. The women's media campaign normalized rich, urban homemakers as practitioners of modern science and outsourced all aspects of childcare to major industries, placing the financial burden of this labor consumption criteria on individual households.

Political women's groups proliferated alongside the media with increasing criticisms against the colonial government in the 1920s and 30s. Printing houses that persevered through the colonial censorship system suppressed liberal editorials and redirected their energies towards safer topics like Korean essence and particularism, schizophrenically reinforcing and resisting foreign rule through such images of selves as Other. In this hybrid discourse, colonized elites advanced imperial capitalist motherhood by rendering private and communal female practices abnormal. Judging proper motherhood through a binary of science and superstition, women were asked to use their purchasing power to actively participate in and disseminate commercialized products and services. Professors wrote columns in magazines like *Urijip [Our House]* on matters such as the "Superstitious Problems in the Korean Family," praising their readers with statements like, "the people that can eliminate [superstition] are parents who are educated and who believe in reason" (32). The mother's journal, *Ahŭi Saenghwal,* took issue with "old" habits declaring, "sickness cannot be cured through superstition." A picture of a man in a lab coat, standing behind a microscope, holding up a test tube in one hand and beaker in the other, reinforced the article's message: "in this age of developed science, we cannot lean on superstitions." It reported that the "ignorant" and "uncivilized" were not the only ones to "rely on superstition" and found throughout the city, "even those among the intellectual class" place "paper charms on their doors to avoid fatality" (6). The article highlighted a newly manufactured aspirin pill as a product that could heal the common headache. Commercialized medicine was pushed into the home, forging a mother-pharmacist dyad. Rationalizing changing values in this way promised literate mothers a relationship, albeit an unequal one, with science and modernity. A writer/reader, doctor/intern relationship established the perpetual need for external, market driven instructions with the promise that, by reading and shopping, women can become savvy homemakers.

This default of superstitious motherly behavior assumed a female psyche that lagged behind the times because it was argued that women were bound to tradition. The homemaker's journal, *Urijip* illustrates this point in a 1932 article in which it begged mothers to embrace "scientific knowledge." The article presented a survey of superstitions that women believed were related to childrearing, disease, death, birth, and children's futures. It assumed that women followed superstition "out of the feeling of fear." Some "superstitious sayings" commonly heard from women disciplining their children were:

> If you whistle at night, a snake will enter the room. If two people wash their faces out of the same bowl, they will fight. If you play with grains, you will have an ugly wife. (32)

These sayings were messages to young people to spend their evenings productively, to not reuse dirty water, and to not waste food. It was admitted that "these sayings were created to stop children from doing certain things." But, the article retorted that this was nothing more than a list of "old wives' tales...a kind of irrational superstitious faith [that had] no relationship to science... If we don't realize reasons behind these prohibitive activities, then our children would do them even more." What went without mention in this article was that these sayings also had an underlying theme of shamanic ritual. Korean shamans were notorious for whistling at auspicious hours of the night, inviting ominous spirits to their gatherings, conducting water rituals and reading divinations in rice. Criticizing mothers for not "realizing reasons behind" these beliefs not only assumed that women perpetrated undesirable actions but also that they were inclined to mimic shamans, that they internalized and habituated their rituals. Social customs, traditions, and private speech were blurred together in what was perceived to be an embedded, informal, household economy. The article criticized such sayings for promoting "scientific" falsities and for being "useless." Despite the fact that these notions were "created to stop children from doing certain things," and because "this kind of irrational superstitious faith [had] no relationship to science," the outcome of this mother-speak was seen as damaging, undermining socially governed principles in diligence, hygiene, and frugality (C. Kim "Chosŏn" 12–13, 32). The dailies, like *Tonga Ilbo [East Asia Daily]*, believed "tragedy from ignorance" was the result of women's cognitive dysfunction ("Muji"). Even if these sayings were efficient and their outcomes aligned with economic austerity objectives, mothers were urged to question their very thoughts and habits.

Women's minds and bodies were treated as vessels from which irrational customs could be selectively expunged and replaced with science and mass-produced wares. The ultimate objective of this discourse was to move

Korean women away from home/community (tagged as "superstitious") births and toward western hospital (scientific) births. The media found shamans putting the country's future at risk, arguing that these women prevented pregnant women from being admitted to hospitals. A 1921 *Chosŏn Ilbo [Korea Daily]* editorial gave an anecdote of "customary" activities surrounding childbirth. A pregnant woman went into labor; she began suffering complications at which point she ordered her family to bring shamans to conduct rituals over her birth. Immediately, a group of four to five shamans gathered in the north side of the main hall and began "praying for an easy delivery." Apparently, when the shamans entered the room of the woman in labor, the family members were so mesmerized by their ritual dance that they lost sight of "nursing the patient" and forgot the critical task at hand. While this story did not claim to be based on an actual incident, it detailed what the editor believed was a typical scene of shamans involved in childbirth as retold from "common" knowledge. Readers were asked to notice when shamans "suddenly attack in this way and in these particular conditions for delivery." It clarified that women in labor command their family members to recruit shamans precisely in emergencies, when "times are urgent," and warned of women who only entrust shamans to conduct "miracle prayers" and who do not "immediately receive surgical treatment from a doctor," resulting in "cases of death." Women and families that did not receive "treatment under a doctor" were not only accused of being "superstitious," they were charged with being morally and socially irresponsible ("Misin ŭl t'ap'a").

The imperialist racialization of motherhood is perhaps most evident in the media's methods to criminalize marginalized women. Shamans were publicized as having close connections with unofficial medical specialists and even acting as unlicensed midwives ("Kiinp'yŏnmulŭl"). Beginning in the 1930s, with the start of groups like the Health Movement Society and the Korean Eugenics Association, issues of childbirth were feverishly debated alongside initiatives in selective breeding, policies in medicines, and birthing hospitals (Yoo 313). The colonial media was in the thick of criminalizing shamans for interfering with natal care. *Chosŏn Ilbo* published an article that disclosed the findings of an investigation conducted by an officer from the city of Inchŏn where he found a "wicked" shaman, by the name of Sun-pok Pak, trying to exorcise a woman who had fallen ill after childbirth. Shaman Pak told this woman that an "evil spirit needed to be driven out" of her through a "spirit releasing" ritual. To the authorities, Shaman Pak "confessed to fleeing after receiving money, rice, food, a pen, and ink" ("Inchŏn"). The media was challenged by people's preference for shamans over modern medicines. A cultural magazine editorial, *Kaemyŏng Sibo [Enlightenment Bulletin]* found that, "when a superstitious believer comes down with an illness, despite their symptoms, usually they first plead and ask the shaman and, after that process, they go to get medicine" ("Misin Pangmyŏlŭi"). The monthly magazine, *Ahŭi Saenghwal* implored:

> Whether a person is ignorant or not, why would they receive foolish words from someone who is not a doctor but who gives instruction on a curative treatment? Why do they listen to advertisements about patented medical treatments that they find in the newspaper although they haven't been properly examined? (6)

To dispel their trust, the media warned women to look out for shamans "pretending to be doctors" and "curing false illnesses." Expecting mothers were urged to "abandon listening and giving in" to them ("Kiinp'yŏnmulŭl"; "Kaegumŏkbati"). Such images of dangerous home births and licentious midwifery were meant to portray hospitals as women's "wise" and best choice. Meanwhile, these stories were evidence that women commonly chose not to admit themselves to hospitals and instead preferred options, like commissioning unlicensed midwives, herbalists, ritualists (all described as shamans in these cases), because such communal, community services were tried, trusted, accessible, and often pleasurable. Reading such stories against the grain helps us to understand the media's motive to criminalize women's unregulated practices. The enduring images of women as the bearers of tradition were not written to celebrate women; they were not even written by or for the women of the communities depicted. Rather, they were written for privileged families that had the social and material capital to overcome the sexualized and racialized stigma of impoverished motherhood.

Tracing the history of institutionalized medicine reveals the injustices to indigenous communities. Campaigns to incarcerate patients and eliminate unlicensed healthcare experts were measures to eliminate people's free will, self-determination, and management over their own bodies. The westernization of the medical field in colonial Korea included debates on the hygiene police's task to "voluntarily" or "forcibly" admit patients into hospitals. In the late nineteenth and early twentieth century, Korea faced a number of severe smallpox epidemics for which isolation hospitals were built. Those not caught by the hygiene police secretly sought out local ritual and healthcare specialists to cure their afflictions. Rituals in the treatment for smallpox became so popular that a God of Smallpox was made a regular member of women's ritual pantheon (O. Kim 38–58). As the smallpox epidemic shows, during times of widespread crisis, people actively resisted modern, state-run institutions and pursued traditional forms of healing to the extent of breaking the law and at the risk of being criminally reprimanded.

The colonial medical education and licensure system disenfranchised *ŭinyŏ* (medicine women), who the former Chosŏn Dynasty had stationed in state-sponsored clinics across the country. The Japanese colonial government issued a "medical student ordinance," limiting the educated few to pursue western medical accreditation in order to practice traditional medicines while the majority without certification were forced to take their practices underground. Starting in the mid-1920s, the colonial government adjusted its policy to also license the "traditional medicines" industry. Although this may be seen as a measure to accommodate non-western medical practices, it effectively allowed the government to co-opt and control materials that were used for producing medicines as well as the process involved in making them and to monopolize the market (C. Sin 105–139; K. Sin 227–56). A handful of exceptionally licensed women aside, women were almost entirely shut out of this new regulatory system. Due to their expensive treatments, urban-exclusive locations, male dominant practitioners, foreign sources, but mostly their lack of community engagement, these new regulatory systems were not trustworthy and female patients avoided them at all cost.

The print media urged the colonial administration and police to better monitor and restrict the movement of people for the sake of public health even while acknowledging that these new institutions were not properly equipped to accommodate the population. Ill-equipped isolation hospitals were feared as destructive institutions created by the state to incarcerate the poor and the weak (Y. Park and D. Shin 37–46; Y. Park "Anti-Cholera" 169–86; *Han'guk*). Newspapers even blamed these hospitals' poor staff and facilities for making people "panic" and resort to other means of treatment ("Kyŏnngni" 2). The press implicated the state for causing people's distrust in new medical institutions. While journalists steadily supported systematized healthcare, they also distanced themselves from the state by highlighting the government's inability to properly implement and monitor its new institutions. The media and the public both feared the negative rumors surrounding isolation hospitals; these were said to be places that people entered but never left, and as such they were considered death sentences, especially for the indigenous Korean population.

Japanese policies were meant to protect the metropole from colonial contamination. These institutions had a reputation for segregating patients according to race (only Japanese and western patients were admitted into the best hospitals). Hospitals meant for the native population were over-crowded, understaffed, underequipped, and unsterile. The police bureau was put in charge of monitoring travelers' health. In the southern coastal city closest to Japan, Pusan police were ordered to "reduce the number of Korean passengers to Japan by checking especially for alcoholics, drug addicts, or penniless floaters," believing enhanced screening of visible social misfits would help safeguard "Japan from communicable diseases" (S. Park "Making Colonial Policies" 49). "Japan wanted to manage an anti-epidemic system that aimed at centralization at the highest level, and the main axis was the police," therefore, they gave the police jurisdiction over anti-epidemic measures under the Law on the Prevention of Contagious Diseases, promulgated a few years after the annexation of Korea (Y. Park "Anti-Cholera" 173).

While the media pointed to various culprits in the spreading of diseases, they ultimately urged the public to assume their legal and social obligation to trust and participate in western/Japanese colonial medicine. Women's journals ran "health columns" and discussed hygienic practices to "prevent contagious diseases." Ahŭi Saenghwal concluded, "All diseases arise from not heeding the warnings and exclamations for sanitation and occur from neglecting good cleaning" ("Misin" 7–8). The daily, *Chosŏn Ilbo*, told a story of an outlaw mother who went to a shaman in search of a cure for her son, who was afflicted with smallpox ("Akchil" 27). The story recounted how this wayward mother left her severely sick son to attend a ritual on his behalf and how the child died during her absence. According to the paper, the mother, more than anyone else, should have been at her son's bedside, her rightful station. She should have taken her child to the isolation hospital but she was "entangled" with a shaman instead. She, like so many mothers, was portrayed as contaminated and a threat to society on multiple levels.

Another *Chosŏn Ilbo* article revealed how a family took illegal measures to attend to their daughter while she was forcibly detained in an isolation hospital ("Kyŏnngni" 2). The paper reported one family's attempt to cure their daughter who simply suffered from dysentery, hoping that this cure would release her from what they thought would otherwise be her death sentence. They hired a shaman to sneak into the hospital, conduct a secret "ritual" for their daughter, hide from the "authorities" and escape without getting caught. Outraged by their successful trespass, the paper demanded the hospital administration "express a bit more sincerity" for a matter in which the police administration held little interest. The article made clear that illicit practices such as hospital rituals endangered proper treatment of patients. Rather than questioning the hospital's poor facilities, the paper focused on its mismanagement of this situation. While their anti-shaman stories revealed women's resistance to the state's regulatory programs in public health, the media made its mission to present colonial institutions as best practices to maintain public safety. Despite people's resistance to institutionalized medicine, the media trusted that such institutions would lead the nation toward a better future.

When considering women as the writers behind these columns, it is difficult to generalize them merely as victims of a patriarchal, colonialist discourse. These women writers participated in the modern discourse that distinguished them as an elite group and their discussions served the interest of a minute urban middle class. By 1930, women comprised less than two percent of a reading population, where less than seven percent of all Koreans were able to read (Y. Kim 44; Yi 331). This small coterie of female journalists wrote as local members with insight, but without membership in shaman, superstitious, female criminal communities. They promoted distinctly "enlightened," urbane principles and practices to set them apart from the colonized masses. As seen through the print media, their methods to biologically segregate their population supported the growth of capitalist industries and such growth was seen as key to building a strong nation and empire.

The Korean print media affirmed the choices that appeared most promising to elite women under the forces of colonialism. While they expressed their motives for national reform, they subscribed to hegemonic values in a modernity that could only be had in a future without women's indigenous communities. This chapter has shown how the media helped to reconstitute the private sphere and attributed great significance to standardizing Korean motherhood, linking sexualized and racialized ideals of womanhood with the development of a citizenry devoted to a capitalist modernity. Reading between the lines of the colonial print media, it is possible to see women who catered to a spectrum of healthcare demands throughout Korea, even if it meant breaking the law. Those who did not trust the enforcement of colonial and western medicalized practices solicited local specialists through whom they met their physical and spiritual needs. During a period of intense institutional and social transformation, unlicensed female healthcare providers modified and channeled their livelihood towards sustainable occupations by amalgamating with "oriental medicines" (the Japanese colonial government created this licensure after demands to recognize these majority medical practitioners), working from designated stations in and near Buddhist and Shinto temples, and by mobilizing to secure cultural labor guilds (C. Sin 105–39; K. Sin 227–56). Women in Korea continued to resist western and colonial medical and legal regimes throughout the century, suggesting their tenacious involvement in unregulated health/spiritual care specialists and services.

WORKS CITED

"Akchil Yuhaeng Toeja: 'Mudang' i Palho Kwangsan chi Taep'yŏng won-Kun esŏ (Let's Popularize Wickedness: Rampancy of Shamans in Kwangsan-chi, Taep'yŏngwon-kun)." *Chosŏn Ilbo [Korea Daily]* (11 September 1938): 27. Print.

Chŏn, Mi-gyŏng. "1920 30 Yŏndae 'Mosŏng Tamnon'e kwanhan Yŏn'gu: 'Sinyŏsŏng' e Nat'anan Ŏmŏni Kyoyugŭl chungsimŭro (Research on the 1920s-30s "motherhood discourse": the motherhood education of new woman)." *Han'guk Kajŏng kwa Kyoyuk Hakhoeji [Association for Korean Families and Education]* 17.2 (June 2005): 95–112. Print.

"Chŏnggyŏl han Sŭpkwan ŭl Kirŭra (Cultivate Sanitary Habits)." *Ahŭi Saenghwal [Child's Life]* (6 June 1937: 20). Print.

"Inchŏn edo 'Mudang' Tte Nodongjaŭi Kohyŏl ŭl Sach'wi (A Throng of Shamans Also in Inchŏn: Swindle Laborers' Blood and Sweat)." *Chosŏn Ilbo [Korea Daily]* (12 May 1939). Print.

"Kaegumŏkbati rŭl Pyŏngt'al i Rago tto Yugi: Mudang ŭi Mal Tŭtko tto Naeda Pŏryŏ (Abandon False Illnesses Called *Kaegumokbati* and Abandon Listening and Giving to Shamans)." *Tonga Ilbo [East Asia Daily]* (29 July 1933: 2). Print.

"Kiinp'yŏnmulŭl Jŏnŏp ŭro Mudang Dobaerŭl Ŭngjing (Mudang Who Did Deceptive Work)." *Tonga Ilbo [East Asia Daily]* (1 March 1939). Print.

Kim, Chong-jin. "Kaehwagi Ihu Tokpon Kyogwasŏ e Nat'anan Nodong Tamnon ŭi Pyŏnmoyangsang" (Aspects of Labor Discourse That Appeared in Post-Enlightenment Textbook readers). *Han'guk Ŏmunhak Yŏn'gu Hakhoe [Association for Korean Literary Research]* 42 (February 2004): 57–78. Print.

Kim, Chong-man. "Chosŏn Kajŏngŭi Misin Munje (Superstitious Problems of the Chosŏn Family)." *Urijip [Our House]* 8 (Fall 1932): 12–13, 32. Print.

Kim, Ok-ju. "Chosŏn Malgi Tuch'ang ŭi Yuhaeng kwa Mingan ŭi Taeŭng" (Smallpox Epidemics and Popular Responses in the Late Chosŏn Period). *Ŭisahak [Medical Studies]* 2.1 (July 1993): 38–58. Print.

Kim, Yŏng-hŭi. "Ilche Chibae sigi Han'gukin ŭi Sinmun Chŏpch'ok Kyŏnghyang" (Trends in Newspaper Exposure of Koreans during Japanese Colonial Rule). *Han'guk Ŏnnon Hakhoe [Korean Media Studies]* 46.1 (December 2001): 39–71. Print.

"Kŏn'gang han Ch'ia nŭn Kŏn'gang ŭi Haengbok ŭl Kachŏ Onda (Healthy Teeth Bring Healthy Happiness)." *Ahŭi Saenghwal [Child's Life]* (6 June 1937): 6. Print.

"Kyŏnngni Pyŏngsa esŏ Mudang Pullŏ Kutnori: Chŏngni Kŏllin Ttal ŭl Kuisin Chakui Rago Ŏrisŏkŭn Kanghwa Ŏboi (Shamans Called to Conduct Ritual at Isolation Hospital: Foolish Kanghwa Parents Who Said Their Dysentery Affected Daughter Was Possessed by Demons)." *Chosŏn Ilbo [Korea Daily]* (8 July 1937): 2. Print.

Marx, Karl, and Friedrich Engels. "Bourgeois and Proletarians." *The Communist Manifesto*, edited with an introduction and notes by David McLellan. Oxford: Oxford University Press, 1992. Print.

—."Wage, Labour and Capital." *The Marx-Engels Reader*, second edition, edited by Robert Tucker. New York: WW Norton & Co., 1978. Print.

"Misin Pangmyŏlŭi Undongŭl Ch'oknam (The Urgency for the Movement to Exterminate Superstition)." *Kaemyŏng Sibo [Enlightenment Bulletin]* 15 (May 1935): 1. Print.

"Misin ŭl T'ap'a Hara. T'ŭkhi Puin'gye ŭi Kaksŏngŭl Ch'okham, Chilbyŏng e Ŭiyakŭl Ijŏbŏri go Mudang P'ansu ege Man Ŭiro hanŭn P'yesŭp (Get Rid of Superstition. Especially Urging to Awaken Women's Groups, Their Evil Customs That Rely Solely Only on Shamans and Fortune-Tellers and That Forget Medicine for Diseases)." Editorial. *Chosŏn Ilbo [Korea Daily]* (21 July 1921): 1. Print.

"Misin ŭro Pyŏng ŭl Koch'il su Ŏpta (Sickness Cannot Be Cured Through Superstition)." *Ahŭi Saenghwal [Child's Life]* (6 June 1937): 7–8. Print.

"Muji ka Nahŭn Ch'amgŭk; Chŏngsin Byŏngja rŭl Kamgŭm Sangbong ŭro Nant'a Ch'isa, Pyŏng Koch'in Tago Chumun Oeu Myŏ Mak Ttaeryŏ,

Mudang Wonbongŭibubu Ŭi Pŏmhaeng, Changyŏn-Kun Chosen-Ri Eso (Tragedy from Ignorance; Deadly Restrained Clubbing of Mentally Ill Person, Recited Incantation and Reckless Beating Claimed to Cure Illness, Estranged Shaman's Offense in Chosan Town, Changyŏng District)." *Tonga Ilbo [East Asia Daily]* (22 November 1934). Print.

Pak Sŏn-mi. "Kajŏnghak Iranŭn Kŭndaejŏk Chisik ŭi Hoektŭk: Ilcheha Yŏja Ilbon Yuhaksaeng ŭl chungsimŭro" (Acquisition of Modern Knowledge through So-Called Home Economics: Female Japanese Exchange students under Japanese Colonialism) *Yŏsŏnghak Nonjip [Women's Studies Journal]* 21.2 (December 2004): 77–109. Print.

Pak Yong-kyu. "Ilcheha Yŏgija ŭi Chikŏp Ŭisik kwa Ŏllon Hwaltong e kwanhan Yŏn'gu" (Research on Female Journalists' Professional Consciousness and Press Activities under Japanese Imperialism). *Han'guk Ŏllon Hakpo [Korean Journal of Journalism]* 41 (July 1997): 5–40. Print.

Park, Soon Won. "Colonial Industrial Growth and the Emergence of the Korean Working Class." In *Colonial Modernity in Korea*, edited by Gi-Wook Shin and Michael Robinson, 128-60. Cambridge, Mass.: Harvard University Press, 1999. Print.

Park, Soon Won. "Making Colonial Policies in Korea: The Factory Law Debate, Peace Preservation Law, and Land Reform Laws in the Interwar Years." *Korean Studies* 22 (1998): 41–61. Print.

Park, Yunjae. *Han'guk Kŭndae Ŭihak ŭi Kiwŏn* (The Origin of Korean Modern Medical System). Seoul: Hyean, 2005. Print.

Park, Yunjae. "Anti-Cholera Measures by the Japanese Colonial Government and the Reaction of Koreans in the Early 1920s." *The Review of Korean Studies* 8.4 (December 2005): 169–86. Print.

Park, Yunjae and Shin Dong-hwan. "Ilcheha Sarip P'ibyŏngwŏn Sŏllip Undong Yŏn'gu" (Research on the Movement to Establish a Private Isolation Hospital during the Late Colonial Period). *Ŭisahak [Medical Studies]* 7.1 (July 1998): 37–46. Print.

Sin, Chang-gŏn. "Kyŏngsŏng Cheguk Taehak e itsŏsŏ Hanyak Yŏn'gu ŭi Sŏngrip" (Institutionalization of Traditional Medical Research in Keij Imperial University). *Sahoe wa Yŏksa T'onggwŏn [Collected Works of Society and History]* 76 (December 2007): 105-39. Print.

Sin, Kyu-hwan. "Pyŏngjon kwa Chŏlch'ung ŭi Ijungju—Ilcheha Hanŭihak ŭi Sŏyang Ŭihak Insik kwa Suyong" (Coexistence and Eclecticism: the Perception and Acceptance of Western Medicine in Traditional Medicine under Japanese Colonial Rule). *Yŏksa Kyoyuk [History Education]* 101 (March 2007): 227–56. Print.

Yi, Sŭng-yun. "Ilcheha Kyŏngsŏng Pangsong ŭi Tamnon Saengsan Kwajŏng kwa Munhak ŭi Taeŭng" (Kyŏngsŏng Broadcasting Discursive Production and Literary Confrontation under Japanese imperialism). *Uri Munhakhoe [National Literature Association]* 22 (August 2007): 329–54. Print.

Yoo, Theodore Jun. *The Politics of Gender in Colonial Korea: Education, Labor, and Health, 1910-1945.* Berkeley: University of California Press, 2008. Print.

4.

Chrysanthemum

FIONA TINWEI LAM

Inside your body there are flowers.
One flower has a thousand petals
That will do for a place to sit.

Kabir, "A place to sit"

Rolls of rice paper in the corner,
jars of soft-haired brushes,
elegant cakes of watercolour,
black inkstone at the centre.

My mother held the brush vertically,
never slant, arm and fingers poised,
distilling bird or breeze into
diligent rows of single characters.

Hours rippled. Years of practice urged
the true strokes forth—stiff bamboo
now waving in white air, cautious lines
ribboning silk folds of a woman's gown.

My favourite of her paintings
was of chrysanthemums. They began
as five arcs of ink, long breaths in the emptiness
alluding to stem and blossom. Then,

from the finest brush, the outline of each petal.
Flesh flowed from the fuller one, tipped
with yellow or lavender, until every crown
bloomed amid the throng of leaves.

If only I had been paper,
a delicate, upturned face stroked
with such precise tenderness.

5.

The Purpose of This Life

DMAE ROBERTS

"I dreamed you Daddy came to me," my Taiwanese mom said nine weeks before she died from the speck that grew in her lungs.

"Do you remember anything else?" I asked her. She rarely spoke of Daddy who died two decades earlier.

She shook her head. "Just to not be afraid."

But Ma couldn't help being afraid. At 69 years old, her breast cancer returned 12 years and one mastectomy later. She told me the "9" birthdays signified bad luck in Taiwan. I laughed at her warnings when she cautioned me at 19, 29 and 39.

"Be careful this year." Her eyes narrowed with intensity. "Something bad could happen. It's a 9 birthday."

"How am I supposed to be careful for an entire year?" She hated it when I disregarded her wisdom. As I got older, I asked my Chinese girlfriends, and they couldn't figure it out. The number 9 usually signified long life and prosperity.

Yet when Ma woke up from Daddy's dream, she made me promise not to reveal her age as 69.

"If I go, you lie. I'm 70 okay?"

"Okay, okay"

"This is important."

"Let's watch a movie."

Daddy's tender message in Ma's dream to not be afraid went contrary to memories of my battling parents. I tried to think of a time when Ma and

77

Daddy, who met post-Korean War in Taiwan, didn't do battle—fighting about money, about his losing money, his not making money.

I recall happy times living near a military base on the outskirts of Tokyo. My younger brother Jack and I played with kids of all colors both Japanese and American. The military took care of us, and my parents never fought. Ma thought Daddy, then a radar specialist, would stay in the service till he retired at 35. But in August of 1964, Daddy monitored his radar screen as two American destroyers chased North Vietnamese torpedo boats into the Gulf of Tonkin, forcing them to fire. Daddy knew if he stayed in the Air Force, he would be part of a new war. So he got out and vowed to Ma he would be able to take care of us. He returned home to the U.S. to look for work while we waited a sullen six months. Ma wondered if he would leave his eight-year-old daughter and five-year-old son there in Japan. One night, Ma started crying because I tried to gulp down water to swallow the tough chicken she cooked—some of which floated down to the bottom of my drinking glass. Daddy left her with little cash to buy good food.

When Daddy journeyed back to Japan, he told Ma he had found a job selling something called *Wynn's Oil Products*, and the next moment I remember was in the foreign country of America.

I don't remember leaving Japan. It was as if I looked at one image of our Japanese house with the wire fence that housed our white Akita dog, Snow, and then I blinked to awaken at night in the back seat of a strange car bundled up with Jack in blankets trying not to freeze. There was nothing in between. No frames of transition from one image to the other. No memories of transit of the airplane ride. One moment my home was in Japan, a time burned in my heart as the happiest of my childhood. Then seconds later I wiped frost from a moving car window in the back seat, trying not to feel cold inside course wool blankets. Cut to an exterior shot of a blazing neon sign framing buildings surrounded by snow and gaudy bright lights:

Reno—The Biggest Little City In The World

And so began the carnival ride called Reno. Casinos gave Daddy coupons so we could dine on cheap lobster while marking numbers on Keno tickets at a restaurant dinner table. We sometimes won a few dollars, which made Ma shriek with delight. Gone was the safety of our Tokyo neighborhood. Instead strange men beckoned my school friends and me to come into their buildings for a reason that seemed sinister. Our world became foreign and difficult to navigate. Used to walking everywhere in Tokyo, my family was thrust into a culture where cars honked at pedestrians, especially women and children.

When Ma decided to assert her independence and go grocery shopping while Daddy was working, we got lost. Pushing a shopping cart loaded with groceries down the street, Ma made me ask strangers coming out of wedding chapels and liquor stores to help us. I tried to be brave, translating for her until we found our way home, all the while ignoring looks of hungry unshaven white men. For the first time since leaving Japan, I feared for my safety. Living in America would become repeating lessons of distrust and insecurity as we migrated three more times looking for a new home.

That night I woke up to Ma and Daddy fighting about moving away again. Ma quieted when she saw me peeking around the doorway.

Just as we settled into a life in Nevada, we made another cross-country trek to Idaho and through the Oregon high desert. America appeared to be a dry, dusty land till we reached Eugene and the lush Willamette Valley. We settled in an old two-story rental house in a tree-lined neighborhood—actual trees!

Ma made it a mission to bring kids to our doorstep.

"You be friends now?" Ma said by way of introduction to the next-door neighbors, Robbie and his older sister Sylvia.

I immediately had a crush on Robbie, who was in my fifth grade class. Jack tagged along whenever we went swimming at the pool or to the movies. A stray female German Shepherd dog showed up in our front yard one day and charmed me with her ability to sit, stay and shake hands on command. I named her Queenie, and my new neighborhood friends loved her, too. Every day after school, we'd yell "dog-pile!" and all the kids would pile on top of a tail-wagging Queenie who loved all the attention.

One afternoon I saw Robbie and Sylvia across the street and called out for them to wait for Jack and me. But they kept walking with their cousin who was visiting from out of town.

"Wait up!" I shouted, pulling Jack with me. We nearly reached them when Robbie's cousin turned around scowling.

"Flake off, you Chinese" he hissed. Robbie looked uncomfortable and pulled his cousin away.

Stunned, I imagined hitting this ugly, ugly cousin. Then I saw the look on Robbie's face. He never thought about me being Chinese before. I backed away slowly, leading Jack home. A few hours later, after their cousin had left, Robbie and Sylvia came to play as if nothing had happened. Robbie noticed my silence. Sylvia once told me Robbie only liked quiet girls. Just as Robbie thought I might be girlfriend material, we had to move again.

Ma got a job at a plywood mill outside of Junction City, a town of 2000 or so descendants of Scandinavian farmers who journeyed to Oregon to get away from the isolation they experienced in the Midwest. Several generations later, they would not welcome us, their first interracial family.

On the ride back from our first day of school, Ma waited for us at the bus stop, her hair in a fashionable bouffant. From the back of the bus I heard

"They're Chineeeeese…"

From that day on, Jack, who looked more Asian, fell victim to name-calling and pranks. I could pass for white, and I grasped for survival through silence and learned the value of not standing out. While I remained quiet at school, I came home to parents still at war.

"Why don't you find a regular job, not be salesman all the time?" Ma yelled, already tired of working at the mill.

"Lay off, woman!"

"Don't tell me lay off—"

"Kiss my ass—"

"Tell your mother to!"

I learned to hide in my bedroom and read until they calmed down. Peace came when they went outside to do their own projects around the yard: Daddy fixing the fence, Ma tending her vegetable garden. They were so opposite, not only in their backgrounds, but also in their natures and personalities. It showed distinctly in the way they butchered animals.

Daddy, the Oklahoma boy raised on 40 acres of farmland, took the brute force method, lopping off the chicken's head with a hatchet. He held its legs as it convulsed, spilling blood everywhere. I watched him through the kitchen window, my hands over my eyes, blocking out the horror.

Yet Daddy could be my strong protector when dirty work had to be done. A possum once wandered through an open door and trapped itself inside the kitchen. I'd never seen a possum before—a giant rat with a bird-like mouth that hissed and lunged at me.

I screamed. My strong Daddy came running in.

"It's a possum," he said as he walked toward it. "Stay still. Those suckers can be mean…"

With one practiced motion, Daddy grabbed the possum by the neck and dragged it out to the yard while it thrashed about in his hands. He hurled the possum away from him. I watched it waddle off into the black-berry bushes.

"Back home, your grandma used to make a good possum pie out of those," Daddy said as he wiped his hands on his overalls.

Daddy's dirty work also meant hard choices. He took Queenie to the pound a month after we moved from Eugene to Junction City. Queenie turned savage when we got out to the country, killing any small animal she could find—rats, squirrels and cats belonging to neighboring farms. Each morning we found Queenie's blood-soaked offerings on the front step. Queenie, my comfort, my friend, who slept with me at night, had become wild and uncontrollable. Daddy tried to keep her in the rickety fenced yard but she leaped over it in a single bound. I came home from school one afternoon to find her missing.

"Daddy took her away," Ma said.

Daddy's bass voice sounded gruffer than usual, "A dog like Queenie shouldn't be locked up on a leash. I paid for a week at the pound. She'll find a good home."

I asked them to let me have Queenie back.

"You not feed or water her. You too busy with school," Ma blamed me.

I took in the guilt and locked myself in my bedroom in a house I hated, stuck on acres festering with bristles and vermin. The sound of rats running on the rooftop kept me awake late at night. I cried for Queenie. If she had been allowed to live, we would have been rat-free. If I hadn't been 10 years old, I could have fought harder for her, I would have demanded Daddy go back to the pound, I could have shouted—

"Why did you move us here?"

Some months later, I tired of opening the refrigerator and finding dead chickens with heads and feet intact. One afternoon I watched my dad catch a white hen from the backyard. As he headed toward the chopping stump with hatchet in hand, I screamed at him from the kitchen window.

"Don't kill them anymore! Please Daddy, don't!"

Ma came running into the backyard and peered up at the window to see me crying.

Daddy rearranged the squawking chicken under his armpit. He took a few steps toward the chopping stump, and I rushed from the house and into the yard.

"No, Daddy!" I cried again.

"Honey, we have to eat," Daddy said with a gentleness I hadn't heard before.

Ma, the Taiwanese war survivor stepped in.

"I do this," she said to Daddy, taking the chicken into her arms. She started cooing and petting the hen, calming it down in an instant. Ma, who had lived through World War Two, understood starvation, but she also believed in reincarnation. She thanked Lady Buddha, the goddess of mercy, for steering her away from exploding bombs and planes strafing the countryside during wartime. Ma believed in kindness to farm animals, though she held no value for pets. She treated our potential food sources with respect and feared retribution in her next life for unkindness to animals.

"Bobby, get my knife and the rice pan..."

Daddy hesitated. "Chu-Yin, the girl's gotta get used to this."

Ma stared Daddy down, and he wheezed out a sigh. He set down his hatchet and stepped into the house. A moment later, he returned with a long, thin knife and a metal pan filled with rice soaking in water.

"Pour the water out," she directed me, while whispering in Taiwanese and stroking the hen. The chicken, almost hypnotized, started to close its eyes and go to sleep.

I did as she asked—under a spell myself, anticipating a strange ritual. I drained the water from the rice pan and placed it near my mother who squatted on the ground, holding the chicken close to her chest. Ma plucked a few feathers from the hen's throat while still whispering.

Then she slowly slit its throat. Blood seeped from its neck, first a trickle, then more, until it dripped in a single fine line into the pan below the chicken. Ma kept speaking quietly as the pan filled with blood. First the chicken's eyes flickered and stopped, its neck became limp, and then the full weight of its whole body lay against my mother's hands. Finally, silence.

I turned away from my mother and glanced at my father, who by this time started smoking another cigarette. I walked back into the house where I shut my bedroom door and pulled out my books: Shakespeare, science fiction, anything to take my mind off the quiet killing. Then came the familiar smell of boiled feathers and blood as Ma plucked the chicken in a vat of hot water. I listened to the sound of Ma's cleaver on the chopping board, whack-whack-whacking the chicken apart. I followed the sound to see this five-foot woman swinging her favorite knife almost half the length of her arm.

"Get the beans ready," Ma said in between chops.

She towered over me as I sat at the kitchen table, snapping green beans. Ma continued chopping while shooting sideways glances at me.

That night she cooked fried chicken for Daddy and Jack, steamed the rice blood mixture for her own dinner, and for me, she fried an egg for me to eat with the green beans and plain rice.

After dinner, while we washed dishes, I asked Ma what she whispered to the hen.

She shrugged. "I say, 'thank you for this life.' And I tell her, the next one will be better."

After we celebrated her 70th birthday (really her 69th), Ma confided to me she must have been a bad person in a prior life because she suffered so much in this one. She had a long litany of abuses: First her parents didn't want her and sold her for 20 yen. Her stepparents beat her. She starved during the war and narrowly escaped being blown up. She never learned to read and write. Daddy never gave her the rich life she wanted. I never helped her with her dream of starting a Chinese restaurant. She worked all her life to retire only to get cancer not just once, but twice.

I didn't know how to respond to her unhappiness with the landscape of her life. Not when she had two children and a husband who, though an under-achiever, had loved her and endured her tirades over the years. As her body gave out on her, and the cancer took over in her final days, I realized that despite the dozens of friends she had or my devotion to her caretaking, nothing could satisfy this woman for whom deprivation had created such an empty hole that could not be filled.

Yet I put on my best face every morning when I took care of her.

"How are you doing today, Ma?"

"Life is so comp-li-ca-ted."

That last word stretched into several words, several incarnations requiring great effort.

On her last day of life, as her lungs collapsed, I kept giving her morphine drops as the hospice nurse instructed, till she finally let go of her life, not in peace, but in great fear and pain, to die in her own bed, in her own house. Her eyes wide stayed open in a body stiff with emptiness.

One of the noble truths of Buddhist teaching is that "life is suffering." The other is to let go of the causes of suffering. Ma couldn't do that even in the last few moments, and I wonder how much I can let go.

I listed Ma's age as 70 rather than 69 on the obituary just as I had promised her, even though I didn't understand the significance of the dreaded 9 birthdays. A few weeks ago, several years after Ma's death, a Taiwanese friend explained it to me.

"It isn't the number 9. It's about completing a cycle," my friend said. "Older people like to celebrate birthdays rounded up because as they get to 59 or 69, they fear they may not make it to the good karma of the new decade. So they'd rather celebrate a year ahead and not worry."

I finally understood, and I cried.

Ma tried to seize longevity by pushing forward to the next decade before losing her hold on this one. She couldn't tell me this. We didn't know each other's language well enough. Rarely could we talk with any kind of understanding, and even after her death, I'm still trying to understand.

Buddhists believe the purpose of this life is suffering, and once you accept that, everything else is joy.

I'm ready for the joy.

6.

a wandering daughter's grammar

RITA WONG

she congregates with nomads
attentive & occasionally settling
reconjugates self with each meeting:
i am self
I is personae
i & stolen grammar
hoarded carefully in bare hands & forgotten pockets
aiya! hai been dou ah!
good fortune, i'm a tough cookie
will bend & trace those words to follow black, black hair,
the sound between my bare thighs as i walk & sidestep,
mimic & repel the roles imposed upon me

remember: timidity begets timidity
speak up, girl!

breast: used in conjunction with chicken, evoking fear. breast:
       in conjunction with lover, a welling, a swelling, of
       touch & of shyness

lip: to be used as a verb whenever possible

knuckle: layers of work ethic, prone to cracks & dryness, pun-
        ishment in a harsh climate

back: in the middle, a spot, a star, her mother said, always at
        her back, a reflexive verb, used with memory, invokes
        support, to talk at

liver: term of endearment, perhaps the inner catalyst for reliev-
        ing the outer dryness

guilt: a way of life, can be slowly unset with optimism

sisterhood: towards including mother if possible

II: Negotiating Constructions of (East Asian) Motherhood

7.

Tiger in the Hornets' Nest

The Furor over Amy Chua's *Battle Hymn of the Tiger Mother*

FIONA TINWEI LAM

A hornet's nest of condemnation was stirred up when Amy Chua released her parenting memoir, *Battle Hymn of the Tiger Mother*, in 2011. Chua, a US-born, Harvard-trained law professor at Yale who is married to a Jewish colleague, chronicles her journey to cultivate her two daughters to fulfill their potential as high achievers amongst America's elite. Chua writes about not allowing her daughters to receive grades less than an A, play anything but the piano or violin, participate in school plays, engage in social activities such as sleepovers and playdates, watch TV or play computer games, or choose their own extracurricular activities.

She describes exhausting, drawn-out power struggles where she employs threats, insults and put-downs to make her kids toe the line. She even (comically) tries out her approach on the family dogs. One time she threatens to burn her eldest daughter's stuffed animal collection if a piece is not played perfectly. Another time, she prevents her youngest daughter from having supper, going to the bathroom or getting a drink of water until a challenging piano piece is mastered. Eventually, her youngest daughter rebels at age 13, cutting off her hair, and smashing a glass at a café during a family trip to Russia, shouting that she hates her life and her mother, and that she doesn't want to be Chinese. This turning point finally results in Chua relenting—somewhat.

The Penguin version of her book contains a lengthy subtitle not contained on the British Bloomsbury hardcover: "This was *supposed* to be a story of how Chinese parents are better at raising kids than Western ones. But instead it's about a bitter clash of cultures, a fleeting taste of glory, and how I am humbled by a thirteen-year-old." However, an excerpt from the book, provocatively entitled "Why Chinese mothers are superior" that appeared in the *Wall Street Journal* is critical of "western" or permissive parenting, which in Chua's view coddles children's self-esteem to their long term detriment, in contrast to "Chinese" or authoritarian, academically-focused parenting which benefits children by gearing them for success.

The piece quickly went viral, and received over five thousand comments, with numerous blog responses appearing across the internet. The book was also discussed extensively in the media including *The Guardian, The Washington Post, The New York Times, Slate, NPR, The Globe & Mail,* and the CBC. Although her approach is not much different from that of some parents who are intensely focused on sports or other physical performance-based activity for their kids (e.g. hockey, ice-skating, tennis), some commentators expressed outrage, horror or concern, and labelled her approach abusive and damaging, pointing to the high proportion of suicides amongst Asian-American teenagers.

Despite doing some damage control and backtracking in follow-up interviews, admitting she has made parenting mistakes and would do things a "little" differently if she could turn back time, Chua has received death threats. (Her eldest daughter even come out in her defence, publishing an open letter in the *New York Post.*) Part of the negative reaction may be due to the tone of the excerpt which may have come across as arrogant, strident, or dismissive. In addition, Chua arguably reinforces existing stereotypes about the Asian "model minority" (as *Maclean*'s did in its notorious "Too Asian" a year previously). She uses the shorthand label "Chinese parenting," a misleading term that blithely ignores the diversity in parents' personalities and parenting approaches among parents of Chinese descent. Although she admits that some westernized parents of Chinese ancestry don't raise their kids her way while other ethnic and immigrant parents do, she doesn't seem to give sufficient weight to how her own strong personality and distinct socio-economic and family background make her parenting approach unique and particularly ferocious.

The author deems an extremely limited number of activities and pursuits worthwhile. It should go without saying that some Asian parents do embrace literature, theatre (which Chua dismisses as a waste of time), visual arts, and yes, even team sports. (One recalls the historic BC Mainland Cup win of a group of Chinese-Canadian young men called The Chinese Students which defeated the favoured UBC Varsity Squad in 1933, and later the Spalding Trophy in 1936).

David Brooks' response to the furor over Chua's book in *The New York Times* correctly points out that a lot of essential learning goes on outside of formal learning environments, e.g. in the cafeteria or sleepovers or at the mall, that will become necessary and indeed invaluable in both social and workplace settings later: "Chua would do better to see the classroom as a cognitive break from the truly arduous tests of childhood. Where do they learn how to manage people? Where do they learn to construct and manipulate metaphors? Where do they learn to perceive details of a scene the way a hunter reads a landscape? Where do they learn how to detect their own shortcomings? Where do they learn how to put themselves in others' minds and anticipate others' reactions?"[1]

My Hong Kong-born mother, a widowed physician and very talented musician (who played the accordion and ukulele as well as piano), would only occasionally remind us to practice, doing nothing to enforce the reminder. Under no pressure from her parents, she was self-motivated to study both medicine and music because of her interest in both areas. My parents didn't pressure me either to be a top student, doctor, scientist, accountant or pharmacist. During summer vacation, I chose to take drama and creative writing courses or did secretarial work, and during the school year, I skulked around the halls reading books and writing bad poetry, then came home to bake. A lot of my Asian classmates didn't play any instrument whatsoever. Some were very involved in sports teams. And in China itself, one effect of its one child policy has been reported to be the creation of spoilt "little emperors" in urban environments. Bottom line–only some Chinese parents are "Tiger" parents like Chua.

Nonetheless, like Chua, I wasn't allowed to go out at night and was drilled in math for a few years during elementary school. I remember my mother raging at me in the kitchen during her numerous and often futile attempts to teach me the principles of algebra years before I had to learn it in school. My ability to solve the questions diminished in inverse proportion to the volume of her berating and shouting. "If you're good at math, everyone will know you're smart," she'd say, having been a math whiz herself as a child, the implied corollary being that if I were bad at math, everyone would think I was stupid.

In the end, particularly with logarithms, physics and chemistry, I probably was and still am, as well as "lazy, cowardly, self-indulgent and pathetic" as Chua describes once calling her daughter. But given Chua's essential argument about the need to strive and practice to realize our full potential, I wonder how many of us (and how many of our children) have failed to push ourselves to strive harder in some significant area of our lives for fear of failure and lack of will or confidence, and that perhaps the denial of this fact partly underlies the tenor of the denunciations.

What also might be behind the strong reaction is the whole issue of good vs. bad mothers. Books which challenge western culture's idealization of motherhood (nurturing, encouraging, gentle, adoring, never shaming or raging) are often blasted. Think of *Conflict: The Woman and The Mother* by French feminist, Elisabeth Badinter, who created quite a stir by arguing that the romanticized notions of what is natural, inherent or ecological are eroding women's hard-won freedom, pushing them back into the domestic realm. Or the huge outcry in France at Corinne Maier's satiric bestseller, *No Kid: Forty Reasons For Not Having Children*, which humorously and subversively relates her regret at having children.

Interestingly, I recently read Jeannette Wall's 2005 memoir, *The Glass Castle*, about her and her three siblings being raised in jaw-dropping poverty by her nomadic and dysfunctional parents in different regions of the US. Whether they receive grossly negligent parenting or hyperparenting, children can and do grow up to become stable and successful adults, or the reverse. Genetics, environment, mentors, social support systems, luck— they all play a part.

Furthermore, I wonder if Chua's type of achievement and prestige based hyperparenting leads to cultivating a kind of elitism that ultimately fostered the kind of resentment toward the Chinese minority in the Philippines, and toward other similar market-dominant ethnic minorities elsewhere, who have faced violence at the hands of impoverished majorities, as is described in her fascinating book, *World On Fire: How Exporting Free Market Democracy Breeds Ethnic Hatred and Global Instability*. Much of my own approach to parenting focuses on the core values of responsibility, compassion, kindness, self-awareness and citizenship, not just individual achievement (especially challenging given my son's preference for laser tag and war games!). I want him to learn to listen, which means I have to model it myself. Given the state of the environment and the world, I want my child to understand he is part of a larger picture, that he can work with others or alone to make a difference. Like Chua, I want to prepare my child for the future—but in a different way.

A few years ago, I observed my then six-year-old son crawl under the piano to lie there, refusing to practice prior to his weekly lesson, arms firmly crossed. He had clearly mastered the art of *satyagraha*, Mahatma Gandhi's political resistance strategy, all by himself. Bemused, I pondered the options. Be authoritarian or permissive? Ignore him and go to the kitchen to make supper. Lecture him about the need for hard work, the value of music, and the cost of prepaid lessons. Drag him out from under and force him to play. Utter the typical bribes and threats that frustrated parents have uttered throughout the ages. A combination thereof?

Rather than engaging in power-lifting only to watch him slide back down underneath as had happened once before, this time I mentioned his favourite picture book from preschool, *Click Clack Moo*, about cows that go on strike when their farmer demands more milk. "I knew I should never have read you that book!" I joked, "You're just like those cows!" He chuckled, his face softening, his arms uncrossing. Laughing and taking a break was the best way out of the standoff for both of us. I found him a better music teacher (one who actually enjoyed teaching) who employed a method that would still challenge him, but where he'd have fun. Ultimately it was pleasure and creative expression through music that I wanted to instill, not its opposite, whatever the musical genre or instrument, although discipline and practice would of course be an essential component of the process.

It's a cliché to say that parenting isn't easy, and that there are contradictory theories and approaches, reflecting different stances culturally, ideologically, psychologically, and philosophically. Prior to having kids, we may have preconceptions of how we'll be different from our parents (my case) or conversely, how we will be just like them (Chua's case). But once we are parents, there are thousands of decisions to be made, and constant compromises and adjustments with the occasional about-face. When to be firm, when to be flexible, when to back down? Much as the experts might want us to believe the opposite, there is no magical, cookie-cutter, one size fits all approach because not only are each individual parent and kid different, but their environments and circumstances shift with time.

For fun, I checked out a Taoist Chinese astrology textbook to find out more about those born in the Year of the Tiger, and sure enough, Chua fulfills her destiny: "The Tiger parent is a despotic ruler at home. Children are expected to obey and show respect. Tiger parents' decisions will supersede a child's wishes... Tiger parents have high expectations for their offspring...."

Just before the year of the Tiger passed, one particular Tiger mother managed to squeeze in one last roar, although more than a few critics have roared right back.

NOTES

[1]http://www.nytimes.com/2011/01/18/opinion/18brooks.html?_r=1\
&ref=columnists

8.

Neoliberal Maternal Discourse, Tiger Mothers, and Asian American Mother-Daughter Narrative

PAMELA THOMA

If "the mommy wars" was named in American popular culture some time ago, in the late 1980s, and observers and scholars have subsequently identified the ways in which commercial media have used this purportedly deepseated conflict to produce anxiety about and to help create an industry around increasingly unattainable standards of motherhood, it shows no signs of a ceasefire.[1] The mommy wars construct is now clearly of a piece with the gender war ideology that the U.S. media typically use to frame coverage of a wide range of social issues. It is most evidently tied to our day's popular fascination with pregnancy and biological reproduction, but its intense focus on what defines the "good" mother (and thus the "bad" mother) forges ahead in a seemingly limitless expansion, drawing into its theater of influence areas that were not at first presented as relevant to mothering, such as economic threats to the American Dream. Indeed, as a popular discourse, the mommy wars is also deeply nationalist and racialized, as well as gendered and class-based. Given its title, its high profile, cross-media promotion, and its content, Amy Chua's *Battle Hymn of the Tiger Mother*, fits squarely within the mommy wars.[2]

The mommy wars is not, however, a seamless and uncontested media construct, and as the controversy that surrounded Chua's memoir illustrates, pushback against the reductive and divisive binary interpellation that pits "good" stay-at-home mothers against "bad" career mothers is substantial. For all of its problems, Chua's memoir itself pushes back in certain ways and suggests challenges to the framing of the mommy wars that the media most frequently relies upon. Notably, the Tiger Mother Chua portrays is a woman with both a career and a deep investment in her role as a mother. Chua's depiction of her experience may even be read, despite the substantial personal resources at her disposal, as a negotiation of the absurdly high demands now placed on mothers in a U.S. context that provides precious few social supports. I acknowledge the influence of the mommy wars and consider it part of a broader knowledge and public conversation about mothers, mothering, and motherhood, which I call Neoliberal Maternal Discourse (NMD). This discourse about the reproduction of contemporary U.S. society began to coalesce in the 1970s as the social philosophy of neoliberalism was unfolding. It now manifests in popular narratives of female citizenship that address the maternal in visual media forms both old and new, political rhetorics, and public controversies, as well as various print modes and genres, such as the memoir and the novel. As a deeply developed formation of print, visual, and digital media texts, NMD includes a wide range of fictional and non-fictional narratives produced by women and by men that find their way into public consciousness, whether as print texts, e-books, televisual productions, or filmic adaptations. Alongside the commercial websites and blogs that offer consumer parenting advice and the self-help narratives that are typically preoccupied with "work-life" balance, the popular genre fiction about motherhood that emerged in the late 1990s and was dubbed "mommy lit" has been particularly influential. The "new" mommy lit, as described by Heather Hewitt, is dazzling in its variety and visibility and includes "the momoir," Internet mommy lit, online blogs and zines, and the community spaces collectively called "the maternal feminist revolution." Much of NMD may also be considered life writing, a term with currency in literary studies and one that is not limited to autobiographical print texts.[3]

Now an expansive dialogue, NMD in the U.S. is fundamentally concerned with delimiting neoliberal cultural citizenship and foregrounds mainstream expressions and practices that currently define what it means to be an American, especially those that consider how best to reproduce (both biologically and socially) the normative American citizen-subject and thus the nation.[4] It frequently addresses women and immigrants, or those who most literally reproduce the citizenry, and urges them to take responsibility for and undergo private reinvention. That is, as I understand NMD, it is both part of a technology of governance that shapes citizen-subjects in particular ways to reflect the reigning social philosophy of contemporary consumer culture and neoliberal (post-welfare state) public policy, and it is a register—a kind of index—of everyday maternal practices and labor that constitute claims to belonging in U.S., with Asian American mother-daughter narrative contributing in heterogeneous ways. To be sure, although popular Asian American mother-daughter narrative is typically narrowcast within the racial field of this discursive formation and may manifest or endorse the neoliberal contours of it, Asian American narratives also disclose the racialized maternal labor that has been and is customarily denied and thus invisible in national narratives of female citizenship and belonging (Tapia 22). U.S. citizen-subjects are born and reborn, as Ruby Tapia observes, through different maternities in the racialized productions of the maternal in public discourse.[5]

I underscore in this chapter that the contested nature of the shifting terrain of cultural citizenship in the U.S. was more brightly illuminated when Asian American mother-daughter narrative was pulled fully into the limelight of popular discourse about mothering in 2011 via the spectacle that was Chua's memoir. Certainly, mother-daughter narrative was a well-established form in Asian American literature long before Chua's contribution, the mommy wars, and NMD, and elsewhere I have analyzed the relationship between the contemporary development and popularization of the category "Asian American women's literature" and the concerns that constitute NMD, with respect to specific fictional print narratives or novels.[6] Here I briefly consider additional texts that circulate in dialogue with or as intertexts for *Battle Hymn of the Tiger Mother* within the mommy wars and as part of the larger dialogue in NMD. Rather than simply one more throwaway act in a media circus that insists on divisive and militaristic metaphors, I argue that *Battle Hymn*, associated Asian American women's life writing, and the controversies surrounding these texts are closely linked to current revisions of both the American Dream and citizenship in the U.S. and are therefore a compound site of important cultural and political struggle. First, I discuss definitions of cultural citizenship for women in the U.S. today as manifest in NMD, then I contextualize Chua's tiger mother figure within NMD, and finally I analyze a selection of recent life writing by Asian American women about motherhood and parenting that is also part of Asian American mother-daughter narrative or matrilineal discourse in Asian American literature.

CITIZENSHIP, NEOLIBERAL MATERNAL DISCOURSE, AND REPRONARRATIVITY

Neoliberalism depends upon a political economic rationality that rigorously seeks to reorganize governance, society, and citizenship (Ong II) around the transactions of the marketplace, asserting that this will maximize social good (Harvey 165). Neoliberalism is thus anxious to modify the production and reproduction of the citizen-subject and is considered a deeply biopolitical form of advanced capitalism.[7] Accordingly, contemporary neoliberal citizenship for females has seen significant change since neoliberalism became hegemonic as the social philosophy of the global economy in the 1990s, involving what Angela McRobbie has termed "the new sexual contract." This contract requires female subjects "to make good use of the opportunity to work, to gain qualifications, to control fertility, and to earn enough money to participate in consumer culture" (54). To ensure women take up the increased expectations of this set of requirements, neoliberal societies, which purport to leave governance up to individual choice-making in the marketplace, enlist non-governmental forces and institutions, such as the media, in the tacit instruction of subjects for self-governance that will align with neoliberal values, feelings, and behavior. According to some scholars, neoliberalism attempts to manage subject making through the production of an affective experience of belonging in the cultural sphere, which well-schooled citizen-subjects then translate into appropriate consumption and production (labor) as defined by advanced global capitalism. In this view, cultural discourses are underwritten by changes in material relations; in the U.S., changes predictably appear in updated transformation or reinvention narratives of the American Dream.

In NMD, women are frequently represented as members of the nation only to the extent that they adhere to a model of motherhood that adopts the ethos and practices of the marketplace. The narratives and texts that comprise NMD often detail a version of contemporary Americanness for female subjects defined in the national imaginary by an ideology of transformative femininity, one that centralizes bourgeois motherhood, which is composed of consumer-based affective and material practices associated with the white, middle-class nuclear family.[8] Put another way, NMD engages a repronormative model of cultural citizenship for female subjects characterized by striving participation in motherhood and consumer culture. As overlapping and feminized domains, motherhood and consumer culture are popularly regarded in the contemporary U.S. as empowering and transformative, promising positive regeneration but also needing careful self-discipline (McRobbie 54). The new sexual contract as McRobbie has described it reminds us, in fact, that this model of motherhood depends upon labor, reproductive and productive, that enables consumption. Finally, NMD highlights mother figures who model and literally reproduce good choice-making citizen-subjects.

NMD thus provides an opportunity for understanding the material and biological imperatives of gendered cultural citizenship, or the close links among the economic, biological, and cultural dimensions of contemporary belonging in the U.S. Nikolas Rose conceptualizes biological citizenship as a neoliberal mandate for self-governance, self-care, and responsibilization in which "individuals themselves must exercise biological prudence for their own sake, that of their families, that of their own lineage, and that of the nation as a whole" (24). Moreover, the intertwined economic, biological, and cultural dimensions of neoliberal citizenship are racialized as much as they are gendered. As a contemporary cultural formation, NMD is a site of power over life that registers the differential forms of biopolitics in which the neoliberal regulation of life "reduces *certain* life to bare life. At the same time it also invests in the lives of others, as in the maintenance of lifestyles" (Sharma 139, emphasis in original).

We can draw a line, then, between the repronormative cultural citizenship for white women customarily valorized in NMD in the contemporary U.S. and the "Republican Motherhood" in the late 18th and 19th centuries when "popular literature … prescribed the 'moral mother' as provider of nurturing guidance to future citizens of the republic," which was imagined to be white and property owning or middle-class (Solinger 270). With the shift from agrarian to industrial production, the white republican mother who limited fertility and who possessed expertise in increasingly complicated infant care and domesticity became a cultural icon, all in an effort toward reproducing good citizenship in an America in turmoil over slavery and growing abolitionist movement. Today, in the move from industrial production to a post-industrial global economy, popular discourse in the U.S. again exhibits deep concern about changes in the body politic, registers the neoliberal goal to reorganize citizenship, and locates these shifts in the maternal figure. As Ann Kaplan argues, the imaginary or mythic mother erupts in popular discourse when changes in social formation, particularly economic and technological changes, produce new threats to the status quo (15).⁹ Importantly, then, NMD is a site of sustained and intense struggle.

The context of national change and Chua's anxieties about change, particularly for her children, were visible to many readers of *Battle Hymn of the Tiger Mother*, despite the heavy narrative shadow of over-generalization about culture, ethnicity, and motherhood. More than recession aware, the economic crisis is actually central to the book, with social instability and decline serving as the backdrop for "the risks [Chua] is willing to take to invest" in the future of her daughters.¹⁰ After observing that lots of people, from every cultural group and all walks of life, work hard and attempt to influence their children to do the same, Patricia Williams suggests that readers "not spend too much time wondering why Chua assigns her neurosis to her Chinese-ness, rather than her aspirational American upper middle-class-ness," or even concern themselves so much with her "obsession" with academic success; instead, Williams directs our attention to Chua's "pathological yearning for dominance, control, standing, and respect. Chua does not just want perfect scores; she is desperately afraid that she and her daughters will be drowned in the cold goop of what she endlessly refers to as 'decline.'" Such positioning in relation to social change, understood as degeneration, is now even clearer with the publication of Chua's most recent book, *The Triple Package: How Three Unlikely Traits Explain the Rise and Fall of Cultural Groups in America*, which she co-authored with Jeb Rubenfeld, her husband.

Crucially, for the demonstration of social belonging in our time, consumer practices of bourgeois motherhood publically communicate or display alignment with mainstream neoliberal values, and these practices include the consumption (as well as the production) of popular media narratives of female transformation, such as *Battle Hymn of the Tiger Mother*. In fact, in a mediatized society, where commercial media has increasing authority to define reality, belonging mandates that engagement with mainstream cultural narratives be displayed, visible, and semiotically legible to others. So, at the same time that many U.S. states have passed equal marriage laws and popular culture recognizes in certain ways that families have changed, especially for female belonging NMD seems to insist on a public "repro-narrativity" or "the notion that our lives are somehow made more meaningful by being embedded in a narrative of generational succession" (Warner 7). I suggest elsewhere that the increased demands for publicity under neoliberal cultural citizenship are not totalizing and have offered both constraints and opportunities for shaping contemporary belonging in the

U.S. for Asian American women.[11] But, and particularly with respect to childhood, I heed recent queer theorizations, such as Lee Edelman's reproductive futurism (5–6) and Jasbir Puar's homonationalism (4), which again warn us, as Michael Warner did two decades ago, that "the outlook is grim for any hope that childrearing institutions of home and state can become less oppressive" (9). In NMD, the narrative of reproduction is far less about the transformation of life than it is about the maintenance of "normal" life.

TIGER MOTHERS AND MATERNAL MODEL MINORITY FIGURES

As a contribution to NMD, Chua's *Battle Hymn of the Tiger Mother* centralizes the figure of the Asian American mother and reverberates with a variety of mainstream mommy wars texts, perhaps most resoundingly with the divergent political celebrity personas of Michelle Obama's "Mom-in-Chief" and Sarah Palin's "Mamma Grizzly."[12] While Chua claims that she intended more irony than most readers recognize, the memoir provides, to be sure, a narrative of transformative femininity for Asian American women that centralizes bourgeois motherhood and the consumer-based affective and material practices associated with the construct of the white, middle-class nuclear family. Towards the beginning of the memoir Chua confides:

> Like every Asian American woman in her late twenties, I had the idea of writing an epic novel about mother-daughter relationships spanning several generations, based loosely on my own family's story. This was before Sophia was born, when I was living in New York, trying to figure out what I was doing working at a Wall Street law firm. (30)

In this passage, not only does giving birth to Sophia create a transformation that provides clarity, but it also seems to communicate and display a sense of cultural belonging, functioning as a substitute or equivalent for the great Asian American novel which would have traced a series of transformations across generations in the model of Asian American female bildungsroman. In the plot lines of these narratives, Patricia Chu observes, mother-daughter relationships are often transformed through mothers and daughters completing similar emotional searches for inner strength, literally revisiting the motherland for cultural identification, or even suffering through feminized impoverishment to arrive at mutual middle-class comfort in the

United States; as Chu asserts, "the literary genre of the *bildungsroman* is a central site for Asian American re-visions of American subject formation," with gendered stories of authorship so strong that they may replace the well-married hero plot (11).

Moreover, although the passage from Chua's memoir may seem to suggest a kind of postfeminist retreatism or a withdrawal away from wage labor in favor of mothering and family life, the memoir actually illustrates how Chua merely reforms her professional life, molding an academic career as a professor of law at Yale University around the consumerist demands of middle-class motherhood in suburban America. Her well-paid professional labor enables, for example, the piano and violin lessons and international travel that she focuses on in the memoir. In several ways, the book is a meditation on the transformation of Chua's financial capital into cultural capital for her daughters so they too may access the well-lived or "good" life in the U.S. that Chua so spectacularly projects, textually and extratextually. Although the narrative depends upon maternal labor, Chua's framing shifts away from directly telling the story of maternal labor, both productive and reproductive, which has been the case historically, as public discourse in the U.S. has always repressed or occluded the facts around the exploitation of women's labor, particularly women of color, in reproducing the nation. Instead, the narrative in *Battle Hymn* foregrounds a tale of maternal and consumer transformation.

In certain scenes *Battle Hymn* does not uphold neoliberal values or illustrate consumer-based practices. This is evident when Chua recalls insisting that her daughters make their father a genuinely sincere birthday card rather than buy one, when she relays that her own immigrant mother pleaded with her to abandon a neo-traditionalist parenting style, and when she describes how she denied her daughters sleepovers, a ritual site for the production of normative, consumption-based femininity.[13] In the book, Chua repeatedly also rails against shopping malls and crass consumerism. Again, however, these practices and decisions reveal a hierarchy among taste cultures, since Chua devotes a fair amount of narrative time to describing her willingness to fork over plenty of cash for the right sort of distinctive commodities. Nevertheless, *Battle Hymn of the Tiger Mother* undeniably created extratextual space for wrestling with the neoliberal model of transformative femininity when it positioned the figure of the Asian American woman as a model American citizen, a *maternal model minority*, under the limelight and provoked a public controversy about maternal labor and differential neoliberal biopolitics, which has extended well beyond the initial uproar at its publication in early 2011.

The June 2012 Pew Center Report entitled "The Rise of Asian Americans" used the tiger mother figure made famous by Chua to praise Asian American women for fertility within heterosexual marriage and in concert with a neoliberal model requiring a managed combination of family, education, wage labor, and consumption. The Report includes Chinese, Filipina, Indian, Vietnamese, Korean, Japanese American, and "Other Asian" women in aggregate statistics that cameo Asian Americans as "the highest-income, best-educated and fastest-growing racial group in the United States." It also claims that Asian Americans "place more value than other Americans do on marriage, parenthood, hard work and career success" (3) with particular emphasis on Asian American women's high rates of out-marriage, citing Priscilla Chan's marriage to Facebook founder Mark Zuckerberg as a positive example.[14] The Pew Center Report constructs "the Asian American woman" as a female model minority citizen-subject for the neoliberal era, and the proliferation of this discursive construction compels interrogation of neoliberal citizenship.[15]

In short, the contributing and striving neoliberal citizen-subject "fits snuggly with the independent, self-supporting image of the model minority," and the new sexual contract of feminine citizenship has inspired another configuration of this racialized narrative of Americanization (Das Gupta 55). Related to the sexual model minority that Susan Koshy has theorized, in which the mediating figure of the Asian American woman becomes "emblematic of the perfect match between family-centrism and sex appeal," the maternal model minority is emblematic of a match between ideal motherhood and neoliberal capitalism's values, which combine for the normalizing reproduction of the nation (16–17). In another powerful rearticulation of Asian American femininity and similar to the sexual model minority that "buttress[ed] and reviv[ed] a besieged ideal of the *American* family," the maternal model minority helps manage a cultural struggle over shifting narratives of the American Dream under a neoliberal political economy that relies upon a new formula of feminized labor, consumption, and subjectivity (17, emphasis in original).

The figure of the maternal model minority is positioned in popular discourse in triangular relation to, on the one hand, the figure of the high-powered career woman, typically coded white, who has repudiated motherhood entirely or at least as her primary identification and social value.[16] On the other hand, the maternal model minority plays in contrasting relation to the figure of the "bad mother," often coded black, who both refuses to responsibly mother and refuses to labor in the marketplace. The "cultural difference" of the figure of the Asian American maternal model minority positions her between extremes within the racial field of NMD, where she balances motherhood with employment to prudently manage family and fertility. In NMD, maternal model minorities instruct all female worker-consumers to update their "skill set" for a late capitalist marketplace in which they must participate in the transformations of motherhood and consumer culture and reproduce the social order to be counted as citizens.

The racialized, gendered, and nationalist ideological claims of the mommy wars have publically operated since the late 1980s to establish thinly veiled rationales for the ongoing exploitation and devaluation of women's labor, unpaid and paid, and this has become even clearer in the past few years as rationales emerged in recessionary culture which called for women's sacrifice to, and makeover responsibility for, economic recovery. As if in response, Chua's book claims that "Chinese Mothers" are superior because they subscribe to a neo-traditionalist model of parenting that produces "successful" (diligent, aspiring, culturally sophisticated) Americans. While Chua attempts to include in her definition of the Chinese mother exceptional men and women of other ethnic groups, her primary claim is that her personal example of mothering, albeit not without missteps, is best and, by implication, authentically Chinese. Moreover, she contends that her version of motherhood—a twenty-first century version of Republican Motherhood—is what the U.S. needs to become more competitive in the global economy.

In *The Triple Package: How Three Unlikely Traits Explain the Rise and Fall of Cultural Groups in America*, Chua and Rubenfeld return to the image of the model minority, broadening discussion of the possession of successful cultural traits to several racial and ethnic groups in the U.S. and minimizing its gendered form in the maternal figure that was front and center in the first book. While *The Triple Package* attempts a sort of sociological study, it suffers from the same postracial illogic as the earlier memoir, namely ignoring the relevance of racial inequality, citing the success (defined strictly in conventionally material terms) of one sector of a marginalized racial-ethnic group as evidence that racism and white supremacy do not exist, and asserting that what it really takes to succeed in the U.S. and for the U.S. to regain its lost stature is a certain combination of cultural values or attitudes. Rather than changes in public policy that might address structural inequalities and social barriers to upward mobility, the authors contend that new (read neoliberal) values and thus success may cultivated by the individual willing to work hard; the magic number in Chua and Rubenfeld's formula is three, with superiority, insecurity, and impulse control comprising the fairy dust combination. The nationalist dimensions of the book's culturalist thesis of the book is most elaborately articulated in the concluding chapter, "America," where the authors conveniently ignore the scholarship on neoliberal political ideology as a reinvigoration of the American Dream, instead claiming that the problem with American society today is that, "[a]fter two hundred years, America lost its Triple Package, damaging our economy, our health, our relationship to future generations" (200). The purported loss of American Dream values has created complacency in all save for those driven by patterns of social marginalization to prove themselves worthy. Clearly, this postracial and acontextual argument has widespread appeal, but it disregards reigning political culture of the U.S. and erases specific immigration histories, to say the least.

Most disturbingly, the popularity of Chua's books may be linked to neoliberal or "new" eugenics, which Asha Nadkarni analyzes in relation to the reproductive nationalism and eugenic feminism that have roots in U.S. imperialism and that now often accompany sophisticated innovations in biotechnology, as well as economic development projects (203–204). This technology has produced the Human Genome Project and the capacity to identify disease at the genetic level, and it has led to hundreds of biotechnology "products," including a variety of reproduction-assisted technologies, such as genetic diagnosis or screening, the in vitro fertilization or so-called "3 parent baby" procedure that the FDA is currently considering for approval, and transnational gestational surrogacy. These are all recognizable as routes to the transnational capitalist reproduction of modern, healthy subjects. Medical discourse surrounding these innovations is problematic not only because it clearly positions them in commercial terms that indicate they will only be available to those who can afford them, but also because it tends to reduce complex social health problems and processes to biological explanations and solutions. Not unlike fertility clinics that use race and ethnicity in egg and sperm collection and marketing (Almeling 57), race-based biomedicine reinforces the biological meaning of race (Roberts 799). Finally, biomedicine largely subscribes to a neoliberal model of mitigating health risk through privatized care. In neoliberal biomedicine, it is the individual who must identify predisposition to disease or "abnormality" and adjust accordingly to create healthy and happy offspring and a successful national future, as well as participate in the development of those less fortunate in the U.S. and in the global South by bringing them into global economic relations. While Chua and Rubenfeld do not limit their comments to Asian Americans nor present a biologically deterministic argument, and their book would not likely be considered part of the area of life writing that recognizes the genome as a "book of life" which exists alongside narratives about human life in the genomic age, the authors are certainly making cultural and material claims that may be deployed in the neoliberal chapter of eugenics discourse and use the paradigm of the model minority to develop them (Jurecic 777).

RECENT ASIAN AMERICAN MEMOIRS ON MOTHERING

Chua's *Battle Hymn of the Tiger Mother* and the maternal model minority must be positioned within the contested site of NMD, but it should also be contextualized in relation to Asian American literature and particularly mother-daughter narrative or "matrilineal discourse." In Asian American literary studies, and stretching back to the beginning of the early contemporary period with Jade Snow Wong's *Fifth Chinese Daughter* (1943), popular mother-daughter narrative, and particularly the memoir, has been discounted or discredited for pandering to a mainstream audience. The debates surrounding Maxine Hong Kingston's *The Woman Warrior: Memoir of a Girl Among Ghosts* (1976) may be the most high profile example in the life writing category, but Amy Tan's best-selling novel *The Joy Luck Club* (1989) was also upbraided for participating in mainstream feminist "sugar sisterhood" and "model minority discourse."[17]

Feminist scholars in Asian American literary studies have, by contrast, theorized matrilineal discourse as counternarrative to patriarchal texts, correctives to mainstream feminist texts that do not recognize the salience of race or ethnicity, or extensions of maternal discourse that recast the Freudian family romance.[18] In addition to mothers, matrilineal discourse highlights Asian American female authorship, maternal presences or surrogate mothers, and daughters' perspectives.[19] If some critical responses to the discounting of contemporary Asian American mother-daughter narrative seem simplistically celebratory and may be read as defensive reactions, recent treatments such as Chu's are mindful of the complex negotiation of discursive constraints within which Asian American female authors must work and Asian American women are obliged to read. Asian American mother-daughter narrative often disrupts the generational succession of repronarrativity through focusing on daughters as authors, narrators, or characters. While some narratives may remain repronormative, particularly when they idealize or abject mother-daughter relationships, focusing on the daughter potentially presents opportunities to queer family narratives or even upend heteropatriarchal capitalist myths.[20] Generational succession is a compelling trope for Asian American women writers given the social history and ongoing constraints for belonging that mandate heteronormative family formation, participation in global economic wage labor, and responsible self-care for immigrant women.[21] As part of the more recent scholarly appraisal, studies such as Erin Khuê Ninh's *Ingratitude: Debt-Bound Daughters in Asian American Literature* signal a measured approach to reading mother-daughter narrative that declines the summarily dismissive impulse and an unconditionally recuperative one.

Within the forms and genres associated with contemporary Asian American mother-daughter narrative, there is a wide diversity of representation, including firm rejection of neoliberal maternality and explicit ideological pushback to its most conventional manifestations, especially the maternal model minority. Not long after Chua's first book was published, Asian Women United, the California-based collective that has produced videos and several anthologies, including *Making Waves: An Anthology of Writings By and About Asian American Women* (1989) and *Making More Waves: New Writing By Asian American Women* (1997), issued a Call For Papers for a new anthology titled *Mother of All Stories.* "Spotlighting the Varied Experiences of Asian American Pacific Islander Women," the collection will include essays, short stories, or other creative works in a print volume, and selections will appear in blog and Tumblr projects as well. The volume aims "to uncover and share stories of the many Asian women who break the confining molds of the self-sacrificing and sentimental Joy Luck Mom or the unrelenting and unaffectionate Tiger Mom" (Asian Women United). Although print media may be the most well known form of Asian American mother-daughter narrative, other screen texts, and especially blogs, play a substantive and dynamic part in life writing within the larger arena. The site Asianmommy.com features a list of thirty-four Asian American blogs, which is only a sampling of the many more that make up the 4 million mommy blogs in existence, as estimated by Cori Howard (quoted in Jones). There are also, of course, Asian American contributors to non-ethnic specific mommy blogs, some of whom, including Grace Hwang Lynch, posted critical responses to Chua's *Battle Hymn of the Tiger Mother.*

Importantly, before Chua made her spectacular entry into mother-daughter narrative and effectively named all Asian American women "Tiger

Mothers" and thus solidified them as constitutive figures of NMD, there had been serious challenges to the maternal model minority figure. One example from a daughter's perspective comes from performance artist Margaret Cho, whose stand up comedy has parodied her Korean immigrant mother's conventional notions of beauty, sexuality, and, controversially, her accent.[22] Similarly, a one-woman show that ran for seven months off Broadway and inspired the publication in 2008 of Sandra Tsing Loh's *Mother on Fire: A True Motherf%#$ Story About Parenting*, preceded Chua's memoir by several years. Loh's story is not, decidedly, an updated narrative of Republican Motherhood for the neoliberal era. In fact, this bestselling *New York Times* notable book traverses the same terrain of educational success for one's children that Chua's memoir covers, but it moves in a very different direction.[23] As one reviewer writes, "Loh's ability to write a book about a year in the life of a mom, source material for many a tepid memoir (or 'momoir,' sigh) and upgrade it into a—dare I say it?—galvanizing treatise on somber topics like public school education, class, and midlife consumerism, all the while eliciting at least one snort of laughter per page, is no less than a feat of genius" (Paul). "Tired of being an obedient participant in this, the high-water period of feminism's Conde-Nast-icization …where our Self-hood—or Self magazine-hood—boils down to …how am I feeling …and what should I buy?" Loh's narrative draws critical attention to an important affective maneuver of neoliberal maternal discourse when it functions to create a feeling of belonging among mothers based on self-making consumption (263). She additionally connects contemporary motherhood to the transformation narrative it so frequently inhabits when she writes, toward the close of her memoir, that, "Instead of cliché, affluent lives of anxiety, paranoia, narcissism and buying overpriced baby products online, modern motherhood has catapulted us atop a tsunami of optimism and oxytocin—old school, archetypal, biological!" (267).

Somewhere in between the Tiger Mother memoir and the Mother on Fire memoir is Mei-Ling Hopgood's *How Eskimos Keep Their Babies Warm And Other Adventures in Parenting (from Argentina to Tanzania and Everywhere in Between)*. Consistent with its rejection of easy categories in which to place mothers, Hopgood's 2012 book resists generic classification. Structured as a kind of travel narrative in which descriptions of different cultural and national contexts that the author has "visited" reveal specific parenting practices that seem particularly effective but depart substantially from the reigning model of the "new momism" in the U.S., this hybrid form of life writing takes as its primary purpose the refusal of the good versus bad mothering in the mommy wars of NMD. On Hopgood's website, a review from Booklist praises the author for "Eschewing the confrontational 'tiger mother' style," and showing "respect for everyone she speaks with and everything she learns." Although Hopgood is billed, like Chua, as a suburban American mom and is also an academic, the similarity pretty much ends there, not only because Hopgood was an expatriate living in Buenos Aires when she wrote her book but also because Hopgood does not claim to possess authentic Chinese cultural knowledge, nor does she position herself as an expert on a particular form of parenting.[24] In contrast to *Battle Hymn*, in *Eskimos* the author's personal views, practices, and background are embedded in insights about how she discovered that, "While no culture can claim to be the best at any one given aspect of parenting, each has its own gems of wisdom to add to the discussion" (262). With reference to studies by sociologists, anthropologists, and child-care experts, and based on interviews with researchers and lay informants alike, Hopgood concludes that, "It's unhealthy to enclose ourselves in parental parochialism, ruled by the plaintive, guilty insistence that there is a single, best way to raise children" (262). Instead, the book encourages parents to experiment with parenting methods.

In *How Eskimos Keep Their Babies Warm And Other Adventures in Parenting*, two of the eleven chapters focus specifically on East Asian parenting practices, and both subtly challenge stereotypes of the rigid self-discipline or "impulse control" that Chua so blithely associates with Asian cultures and considers so important. In the chapter on how Chinese are successful at "elimination communication" or early potty training, Americans are represented as too rule bound and invested in developmental models that claim children can only be trained after a certain age (88). Hopgood learned from Ivy Wang, a woman from northeastern China who lives in Beijing and writes for a parenting blog in California, that "the key ... is being relaxed about nudity, body waste, and accidents" (90). In the rural method Wang espouses, young children are allowed to eliminate whenever and wherever they need to, wearing a diaper (*kaidangku*) that has a split down the back, but when they do eliminate, parents make a sound that the child soon recognizes as a signal and responds to accordingly. In the chapter on how Japanese "let their children fight," Hopgood again troubles the popular misperceptions that are Chua's stock in trade. In this section of *Eskimos*, the author relies upon a comparative study by Joseph Tobin of kindergartens in Kunming, China; Kyoto, Japan; and Honolulu, Hawaii, which concluded that Japanese teachers "scrupulously avoided confronting

or censuring" disruptive students, preferring to let children learn to take responsibility for social interactions and work out conflicts among themselves
(177). In addition to undermining stereotypes of Asian cultures as authoritarian, the chapter also underscores that Asian cultures are not all the same
or interchangeable. The organizational structure of Hopgood's book also
steers the reader away from making easy or deterministic conclusions about
the links between parenting style and culture, since each chapter considers a
cultural practice in a specific location but then ends by providing a shorter
corroborating discussion of another context. The chapter on how Tibetans
cherish pregnancy ends, for instance, with a brief outline of the long history
of social policy that makes Sweden "a prenatal paradise" (171–2).

In her final chapter, Hopgood tackles head on the question of "How
Asians Learn to Excel in School." She is careful here not to overgeneral-
ize or treat all Asians as a single, monolithic group, and she traces popular perceptions in the U.S. to high profile media attention to successes, as
in the spelling bee prowess of South Asian America students, for example. Hopgood also broadens what is often understood to be an Asian parenting obsession with academic success to widespread anxieties in the U.S.
about national decline, citing a recent poll in which parents reported their
biggest worry was that their child "won't get the education and opportunities she needs to reach her potential" (251), as well as the very real material
conditions of economic insecurity parents are experiencing. While Hopgood does not deny aggregate performance patterns on standardized testing, she clearly recognizes them as aggregate, attributes them to cultural context, and explicitly rejects genetic explanations for aptitude or achievement.
She ends the chapter by highlighting a cross-cultural comparative study of
fifteen year olds in thirty-four "wealthy" countries on 2009 standardized
tests in reading, math, and science, as reported by the Organisation for Economic Co-operation and Development; if East Asian countries are well represented, Western countries such as Canada, Estonia, the Netherlands, and
New Zealand are also among those that rank highest. Finally, Hopgood attributes her own interests in academic success to her adoptive, American
(white) parents who were both teachers, rather than to her Taiwanese birth
and Chinese cultural heritage.

In this chapter I have used the controversy surrounding Amy Chua
and ideas in both of her books to emphasize that Asian American mother-
daughter narrative, whether in autobiographical or fictional modes, participates in a broader conversation about mothering that is closely linked to
revisions of both the American Dream and citizenship or belonging in the

U.S. While not all are accessible or legible to a mainstream audience, Asian American mother-daughter narrative is deeply heterogeneous, rather than homogenous, and functions as a space within NMD where subjects wrestle with neoliberalism's increased demands for consumption and labor from women, specifically the mandate to responsibly manage fertility and family via consumer practices for the good of the nation. As part of NMD, the mother-daughter narrative of Asian American women writers has been important both in affirming the cultural citizenship of Asian American women and in articulating its racialized and material limits, contributing insight into contemporary reformulations of citizenship that insist on recycling national myths of Americanness defined by consumer-based transformation narratives.

NOTES

[1] See Pozner on the creation of the "Mommy Wars" in the late 1980s by media and publishing industries (104–106). Douglas and Michaels also look to the media as the origin for the current commercial preoccupation with motherhood but describe it as the "new momism," or a highly romanticized view of motherhood with impossible standards that vilifies those who can't meet them while seeming to celebrate those who try (4–26). The new momism emerged in public discourse in the midst of the women's movement of the 1970s, exploded in the media in 1980s to "redomesticate the women of America through motherhood," and triumphed in the marketplace by the late 1990s, when "conspicuous consumption ... conquered childhood, motherhood, and the nursery" (Douglas and Michaels 9, 300). See also Hays on "intensive mothering."
[2] In January 2011, just before Chua's book was released, she published the essay "Why Chinese Mothers Are Superior" in the *Wall Street Journal*, which was composed of "controversial sections" from *Battle Hymn of the Tiger Mother* and obviously intended to create a media spectacle about mothering in the United States that starred Asian American women, all in a bid to sell the book. And sell it did, quickly rising to the #7 position on Amazon.com. Publicity for the book was also produced through appearances of Chua on high visibility venues such as the *Today Show*.
[3] According to the website for the Oxford Centre for Life-Writing, "Life-writing involves, and goes beyond, biography. It encompasses everything from the complete life to the day-in-the-life, from the fictional to the fac-

tional. It embraces the lives of objects and institutions as well as the lives of individuals, families and groups. Life-writing includes autobiography, memoirs, letters, diaries, journals (written and documentary), anthropological data, oral testimony, and eye-witness accounts. It is not only a literary or historical specialism, but is relevant across the arts and sciences, and can involve philosophers, psychologists, sociologists, ethnographers and anthropologists."

[4] For discussions of cultural citizenship, see Rosaldo, Stevenson, and Miller. For discussion of Asian American cultural citizenship, see Lim and Thoma.

[5] I paraphrase the description of Tapia's argument on the back cover of her book.

[6] See chapter two, "Asian American Mother-Daughter Narrative and the Neoliberal American Dream of Transformative Femininity" of my book *Asian American Women's Popular Literature: Feminizing Genres and Neoliberal Belonging* (38–78).

[7] For discussion of biopolitics and neoliberal subjectivity, see Rose.

[8] The white, middle-class nuclear family remains tethered to the male breadwinner and female homemaker model, even if it little resembles most families in the contemporary U.S. See the "Race and Racism" entry in the *Encyclopedia of Motherhood* (O'Reilly) for discussion of the model of the white, middle-class family (1047–1053).

[9] See Kaplan's second chapter, "The Historical Sphere" in *Motherhood and Representation*, 17-26, and "Sex, Work, and Mother/Fatherhood" 180-219.

[10] The quotation is from the book jacket. Chua's logic is the logic of "reproductive futurism," as Edelman has theorized (2–4).

[11] See the introduction to *Asian American Women's Popular Literature*.

[12] For discussion of Michelle Obama and Republican Motherhood, see Guerrero.

[13] I thank an anonymous reader of *Asian American Women's Popular Literature* for emphasizing this important point.

[14] The Report provoked a good deal of protest, including a critical statement from the Association for Asian American Studies.

[15] As Clare Jean Kim influentially theorizes the dynamic figure of the model minority, the persistence and continuation of racial triangulation takes place in specific historical formations; the contemporary model minority manifestation first emerged in the mid-1960s with immigration policy and economic changes (118-120). While Asian Americans are positioned as models relative to African Americans in a black/white binary of racial dynamics that reroutes African American claims to equal rights and full citizenship,

the model also rests on the presumption that Asian Americans are "culturally distinctive" or immutably foreign in relation to white Americans. In this sense, the model minority thesis rests on a double or even contradictory discourse.

[16] Here I borrow and modify Kim's theorization of the "racial triangulation of Asian Americans" (106–108).

[17] See Wong for a harsh assessment of "Asian American matrilineal discourse" as racial accommodation (177) and Palumbo-Liu for discussion of mother-daughter writing as a form of "model minority discourse" that posits the "healing" of racial wounds as a route to assimilation.

[18] See Sugiyami for discussion of recent maternal discourse.

[19] "Matrilineal discourse" is Grice's term; she identifies narrative codes of "the fiction of matrilineal discourse" and provides a summary of Asian American women writers' interventions in the form (35-51). For a discussion of the more general "maternal discourse" in women's writing, see Hirsch, who locates it in postmodernist plots that revise or reject the Freudian family romance (15-16).

[20] See my discussion of revisions to the fictional mother-daughter narrative in *Asian American Women's Popular Literature: Feminizing Genres and Neoliberal Belonging* (38-78). See also Ninh's *Ingratitude: The Debt Bound Daughter in Asian American Literature* offers insightful analysis.

[21] See discussion of "derivative citizenship" in Parreñas and Tam.

[22] The representation of her mother is clearly a persona Cho performs as part of her comedy. For discussion of Cho's performance art, see Lee. For linguistic discussion of "Mock Asian," see Chun's "Ideologies of Legitimate Mockery: Margaret Cho's Revoicings of Mock Asian."

[23] For a review of Loh's one-woman show, see Martinez. For a review of her book in relation to Chua, see Howe's "Move Over Tiger Mother."

[24] See Hopgood's first memoir *Lucky Girl* for discussion of her upbringing in the U.S. and her experience meeting her birth family. Hopgood is surrounded by all sorts of parenting advice and judgments and is clearly influenced by attachment parenting that is currently popular. As Hays has argued, intensive mothering in the U.S. requires experts to whom mothers defer and pay dearly for guidance, but Hopgood is more cosmopolitan and resistant to commodified parenting.

WORKS CITED

Akass, Kim. "Motherhood and Myth-Making: Despatches from the Front-line of the US Mommy Wars." *Feminist Media Studies.* 12.1 (2012): 137–141. Print.

Almeling, Rene. *Sex Cells: The Medical Market for Eggs and Sperm.* Berkeley: University of California Press, 2011. Print.

Asian Women United. *The Mother of All Stories.* Oakland: Asian Women United, Forthcoming.

Asian Women United of California. *Making Waves: An Anthology of Writings By and About Asian American Women.* Boston: Beacon Press, 1989. Print.

—. *Making More Waves: New Writing By Asian American Women.* Boston: Beacon Press, 1997. Print.

Chua, Amy. *Battle Hymn of the Tiger Mother.* New York: Penguin, 2011. Print.

—. "Why Chinese Mothers Are Superior." *Wall Street Journal.* Dow Jones and Company, 8 Jan. 2011. Web. 9 Jan. 2011.

Chua, Amy and Jeb Rubenfeld. *The Triple Package: How Three Unlikely Traits Explain the Rise and Fall of Cultural Groups in America.* New York: Penguin, 2014. Print.

Chu, Patricia P. *Assimilating Asians: Gendered Strategies of Authorship in Asian America.* Durham, NC: Duke University Press, 2000. Print.

Chun, Elaine W. "Ideologies of Legitimate Mockery: Margaret Cho's Revoicings of Mock Asian." *Beyond Yellow English: Toward a Linguistic Anthropology of Asian Pacific America.* Eds. Angela Reyes and Adrienne Lo. Oxford: Oxford University Press, 2008. 261–287. Print.

Crittenden, Ann. *The Price of Motherhood.* New York: Picador, 2001. Print.

Das Gupta, Manisha. *Unruly Immigrants: Rights, Activism, and Transnational South Asian Politics in the United States.* Durham, NC: Duke University Press, 2006. Print.

Douglas, Susan J. and Meredith W. Michaels. *The Mommy Myth: The Idealization of Motherhood and How It Has Undermined Women.* New York: The Free Press, 2004. Print.

Edelman, Lee. *No Future: Queer Theory and the Death Drive.* Durham, NC: Duke University Press, 2004. Print.

Grice, Helena. *Negotiating Identities: An Introduction to Asian American Women's Writing*. Manchester: Manchester University Press, 2002. Print.

Guerrero, Lisa. "(M)Other-in-Chief: Michelle Obama and the Ideal of Republican Motherhood." *New Femininities: Postfeminism, Neoliberalism, and Subjectivity*. Eds. Rosalind Gill and Christina Scharff. New York: Palgrave McMillan, 2011. 68–82. Print.

Hays, Sharon. *The Cultural Contradictions of Mothering*. New Haven: Yale University Press, 1998. Print.

Hewitt, Heather. "You Are Not Alone: The Personal, the Political, and the 'New' Mommy Lit." *Chick Lit: The New Woman's Fiction*. Eds. Mallory Young and Suzanne Ferriss. New York: Routledge, 2006. 119–39. Print.

Hirsch, Marianne. *The Mother/Daughter Plot: Narrative, Psychoanalysis, Feminism*. Bloomington: Indiana University Press, 1989. Print.

Ho, Wendy. *In Her Mother's House: The Politics of Asian American Mother-Daughter Writing*. Walnut Creek, CA: AltaMira Press, 1999. Print.

Hopgood, Mei-Ling. *How Eskimos Keep Their Babies Warm And Other Adventures in Parenting (from Argentina to Tanzania and Everywhere in Between)*. Chapel Hill, NC: Algonquin Books, 2012. Print.

—. *Lucky Girl*. Chapel Hill, NC: Algonquin Books, 2009. Print.

—. *Mei-ling Hopgood*. Web. 19 February 2014.

Howe, Ben Ryder. "Move Over Tiger Mom: This Mother's on Fire." 24 April 2011. *National Public Radio*. Web. 6 June 2014.

Jones, Beth-Anne. "Cori Howard of the Momoir Project." *4Mothers1blog*. 13 July 2012. Web. 15 Oct. 2012.

Jurecic, Ann. "The Art of Medicine: Life Writing in the Genomic Age." *The Lancet*. Vol. 383. 1 March 2014. Web. 3 March 2014.

Kaplan, E. Ann. *Motherhood and Representation: The Mother in Popular Culture and Melodrama*. New York: Routledge, 1992. Print.

Kim, Clare Jean. "The Racial Triangulation of Asian Americans." *Politics & Society* 27.1 (1999): 105–38. Print.

Kingston, Maxine Hong. *The Woman Warrior:Memoirs of a Girlhood Among Ghosts*. New York: Vintage, 1975. Print.

Koshy, Susan. *Sexual Naturalization: Asian Americans and Miscegenation*. Stanford: Stanford University Press, 2004. Print.

Lee, Rachel C. "Where's My Parade?": Margaret Cho and the Asian American Body in Space." *TDR/The Drama Review* 48.2 (2004):108–132. Print.

Lim, Shirley Jennifer. *A Feeling of Belonging: Asian American Women's Public Culture, 1930–1960.* New York: New York University Press, 2006. Print.

Liu, Betty Ming. "Parents Like Amy Chua Are the Reason Why Asian Americans Like Me Are in Therapy." *Betty Ming Liu.* 8 Jan. 2011. Web. 21 Jan. 2011.

Loh, Sandra Tsing. *Mother on Fire: A True Motherf%#$ Story About Parenting.* New York: Three Rivers Press, 2008. Print.

—. "Sympathy for the Tiger Moms." *The Atlantic.* 24 February 2011. Web. 6 June 2014.

—. *The Madwoman in the Volvo: My Year of Raging Hormones.* New York: Norton, 2014. Print.

Lynch, Grace Hwang. "*Battle Hymn of the Tiger Mother*—Book Review." *Open Salon.* 13 Jan. 2011. Web. 27 Apr. 2011.

Martinez, Al. "A Heart Worn Upon Her Sleeve." *Los Angeles Times.* 22 August 2005. Web. 17 May 2014.

McRobbie, Angela. *The Aftermath of Feminism: Gender, Culture, and Social Change.* London: Sage, 2009. Print.

Miller, Toby. *Cultural Citizenship: Cosmopolitanism, Consumerism, and Television in a Neoliberal Age.* Philadelphia: Temple University Press, 2007. Print.

Nadkarni, Asha. *Eugenic Feminism: Reproductive Nationalism in the United States and India.* Minneapolis: University of Minnesota Press, 2014. Print.

Ninh, Erin Khuê. *Ingratitude: Debt-Bound Daughters in Asian American Literature.* NewYork: New York University Press, 2011. Print.

O'Reilly, Andrea, ed. *Encyclopedia of Motherhood.* Thousand Oaks, CA: Sage Publications, 2010. Print.

Ong, Aihwa. *Neoliberalism as Exception: Mutations in Citizenship and Sovereignty.* Durham, NC: Duke University Press, 2006. Print.

Oxford Centre for Life Writing. "What is Life Writing?" 28 May 2014. Web. 3 June 2014.

Palumbo-Liu, David. *Asian/American: Historical Crossings of a Racial*

Frontier. Stanford: Stanford University Press, 1999. Print.

Parreñas, Rhacel Salazar, and Winnie Tam. "The Derivative Status of Asian American Women." *The Force of Domesticity: Filipina Migrants and Globalization.* New York: New York University Press, 2008. 110–133. Print.

Paul, Pamela. "The Art of Momoir." *The New York Times.* 24 August 2008. Web. 20 May 2014.

Pozner, Jennifer. *Reality Bites Back: The Troubling Truth About Guilty Pleasure TV.* Berkeley: Seal Press, 2010. Print.

Puar, Jasbir. *Terrorist Assemblages: Homonationalism in Queer Times.* Durham, NC: Duke University Press, 2007. Print.

Roberts, Dorothy. "Race, Gender, and Genetic Technologies: A New Reproductive Dystopia?" *Signs* 43.4 (Summer 2009): 783–804. Print.

Rosaldo, Renato. "Cultural Citizenship, Inequality, and Multiculturalism." *Latino Cultural Citizenship: Claiming Identity, Space, Rights.* Eds. William V. Flores and Rena Benmajor. Boston: Beacon Press, 1997. 27–38. Print.

Rose, Nikolas. *The Politics of Life Itself: Biomedicine, Power, and Subjectivity in the Twenty-First Century.* Princeton: Princeton University Press, 2007. Print.

Sharma, Sarah. "Baring Life and Lifestyle in the Non-Place." *Cultural Studies* 23.1 (2009): 129-148. Print.

Solinger, Rickie. "Racializing the Nation: From Declaration of Independence to the Emancipation Proclamation, 1776-1865." *The Reproductive Rights Reader: Law, Medicine, and the Construction of Motherhood.* Ed. Nancy Ehrenreich. New York: New York University Press, 261-274. Print.

Sone, Monica. *Nisei Daughter.* 1953. Seattle: University of Washington Press, 1979. Print.

Stevenson, Nick. *Cultural Citizenship: Cosmopolitan Questions.* Berkshire: Open University Press/McGraw-Hill, 2003. Print.

Sugiyama, Naoko. "Postmodern Motherhood and Ethnicity: Maternal Discourse in Late Twentieth-Century American Literature." *Japanese Journal of American Studies* 11 (2000): 71–90. Print.

Tapia, Ruby C. *American Pietas: Visions of Race, Death, and the Maternal.* Minneapolis: University of Minnesota Press, 2011. Print.

Thoma, Pamela. *Asian American Women's Popular Literature: Feminiz-*

ing Genres and Neoliberal Belonging. Philadelphia: Temple University Press, 2014. Print.

Warner, Michael. "Introduction: Fear of a Queer Planet." *Social Text* 29 (1991): 3–17. Print.

Williams, Patricia. "The Tiger Mama Syndrome." *The Nation.* 3 February 2011. Web. 3 May 2014.

Wong, Jade Snow. *Fifth Chinese Daughter.* New York: Harper and Row, 1945. Print.

Wong, Sau-ling Cynthia." 'Sugar Sisterhood': Situating the Amy Tan Phenomenon." *The Ethnic Canon: Histories, Institutions, and Interventions.* Ed. David Palumbo-Liu. Minneapolis: University of Minnesota Press, 1995. 174–210. Print.

Young, Morris. *Minor Re/Visions: Asian American Literacy Narratives as a Rhetoric of Citizenship.* Carbondale: Southern Illinois University Press, 2004. Print.

9.

Korean American Mothering and Model Minority Children

JUNE H. SUN AND HYOJOUNG KIM

MODEL MINORITY EXPECTATIONS AND KOREAN
AMERICANS

Coined by William Petersen in 1966, the term "model minority" was first used to describe marginalized Japanese Americans who had achieved material success in the United States in spite of discrimination and internment camps. This term was supposed to be a response to the Civil Rights Movement of the 1960s. While Petersen and other researchers used the term to describe "model minorities" as the antithesis of "problem minorities" (e.g., African Americans) during the Civil Rights movement (an article on Chinese Americans as the model minority followed in the same year), the meaning of the term evolved to describe people, expectations, and a sense of burden, while continuing to pit racial groups against one another, suggesting "good" and "bad" racial minorities. Furthermore, as Marie Lo suggests in this volume, the myth of the model minority continues to be relevant today, reflecting western anxieties about Asian capital and economic competition.

Those stereotyped as "model minorities" are known for their success in society. Success, in this context, refers to economic or material success resulting from high academic achievement, labor market participation in highly paying job sectors such as law, medicine, and business, and high performance in the job market. Doris Nhan states that Asians have come to be known as model minorities due to accomplishing these various components of "success" in the American society. However, the concept of being a model minority is a double-edged sword. While being perceived as a model minority might indicate success in terms of academic and career achievement, the term is also a harmful stereotype since not all Asians are (economically or materially) successful and the concept of the model minority is more myth than social fact. It reinforces negative perceptions of other communities of people of color. And, as Nhan suggests, the model minority stereotype is not helpful to Asian Americans and many Asian students find the label burdensome. The Asian students in Nhan's study feel that failing to live up to the stereotype means that they failed to meet expectations. As a result, performance expectations may cause performance anxiety. A different group of Asian students in Richard Bernstein's research also felt that the model minority expectation worked against them. The students were burdened by the label and its expectations to the point of not being able to ask for help when they fell behind in class. Likewise, the university chancellor who partook in Bernstein's research confirmed that the stereotype works against Asian students who need help and creates difficulties and disadvantages for them.

Indeed, the myth of the model minority affects students at the social, interpersonal, familial, and individual levels. Consistent with this perspective, Korean American high school students in the U.S. conveyed that their parents went as far as telling them who to socialize with in order to become more assimilated and successful at school. These findings in Stacey J. Lee's research indicates that parents, too, are affected by model minority pressures. Deep involvement and investment in their children's academic and professional success demonstrates, as well as perpetuates, these pressures.

Lee furthermore asserted that the notion of perpetuating the model minority myth and stereotype was so pervasive that parents would not only have a say regarding friendships but also create a culture around the stereotype where parents are expected to raise model minority children within the immigrant community. Eunyoung Kim's study on the model minority stereotype and career choice among second generation Korean American students found that the stereotype was based on a cultural model of the meaning of success. Coming from a culture in which Confucian ideals of hard work and educational accomplishment are highly valued, the American model minority expectations paralleled the native Korean model and definition of success. With the hardships resulting from immigration added into the equation, the model minority myth and stereotype became tantamount to the American dream. Unfortunately, the myth and stereotype became a burden and placed unwelcome pressure within families, especially on second-generation students. The Korean American cultural model of success defines the meaning of success within Korean American families. Kim's qualitative study found that the model defined success in the United States as making a lot of money or gaining social prestige by entering a reputable profession—in this case, being a medical doctor, attorney, or other professional. The cultural model is based on "doing the Korean thing" as defined by the subjects in the study. The "Korean thing" in Kim's study is based on the success of Korean Americans who have become model minorities in society. Hence, the Korean American cultural model in Kim's study is a collective description of the model minority expectations within an ethnic group.

Since the family is the primary unit of support and socialization, the fires of the model minority myth and expectations were kindled within families. Karen Pyke's study on Korean American and Vietnamese American students found that conversations between Korean and Vietnamese students and their parents revolved around academic success. While the Vietnamese students also valued education and had similar complaints about their "strict parents" as the Korean students, as discussed by Bic Ngo and Stacey J. Lee, Vietnamese students have qualitative differences in parental education, income level, and immigration status (usually refugee status) when compared to many Korean American immigrant parents with higher income and education levels. The study indicated that Korean parents work long hours and carry on short conversations that have to do with grades and career choices without discussing much of anything else. While the students desired to have conversations that resemble the "typical American family" as portrayed in the media, the parents were only able to focus on highlighting the importance of succeeding in making a life and name in the United States.

This chapter presents the data from a study focused on parenting, more specifically, mothering techniques of Korean American immigrants with their college-aged children in relation to model minority expectations and how they translate into parenting or mothering practices regarding grades, curfews, and friends. Stacey Lee found that Korean American immigrant mothers believe that assimilation (which translates into academic success by acquiring fluency in the English language) happens through socialization with the "right" friends. Therefore, the mother's model minority expectations might affect their preferences when it comes to their children's friends and acquaintances. After all, society has long believed that friends are a reflection of the self, as demonstrated by Cicero's quote, "A friend is, as it were, a second self." Hence, a model minority student would be expected to have the right friends—either fellow high achieving Asian American students like themselves or high achieving white friends, showing how parenting success and failures (or even parental control) extends into friends and social circles. The model minority expectations of a mother may be expressed in her parenting style in the way the mother conveys her message about grades, curfew, and friends.

SUBJECTS AND DATA

The data for this study was collected by Sun in 2008. Subjects were recruited from universities in southern California: University of California, Los Angeles (UCLA), University of Southern California (USC), California State University, Long Beach (CSULB), and California State University, Northridge (CSUN). Ethics clearance was obtained from the primary institution, California State University, Los Angeles, and host institutions: UCLA, USC, CSULB, and CSUN. Prospective subjects were identified by visual Asian traits. The principal investigator approached students with an Asian visage and inquired about their Korean heritage. Participation in the survey was solicited upon confirmation that the subjects were of Korean descent. Subjects were expected to complete a 10-page survey pertaining to parenting, model minority issues, ethnic identification, and sexual socialization. A total of three hundred surveys were distributed with one hundred surveys for white Americans and two hundred surveys for Korean Americans. Two hundred and seventy nine surveys were completed and returned (with eighty white American surveys and one hundred ninety nine Korean American surveys). In this chapter, we report on the Korean American subsample of 199 surveys and highlight mothering practices in relation to model minority expectations.

METHODS

The data was analyzed using ordered logistic regression on STATA since the dependent variable is an ordinal variable. J. Scott Long and Jeremy Freese suggest that ordered logistic regression is best for analysis when the dependent variable is an ordinal variable. According to the authors, this version of logit analysis examines the relationship between two pairs of outcome groups and can only be used for data that meets the proportional odds assumption. Long and Freese cite McKelvey and Zavonia's 1975 and Winship and Mare's 1984 studies on the importance of using ordered logistic regression when analyzing an ordinal dependent variable; the ordinal dependent variable creates a non-linear model which violates the requirements for linear regression modeling, resulting in incorrect conclusions (183).

Dependent Variable—Model Minority Mother

The dependent variable in this study was the "Model Minority Mother" variable, which asked the respondent if the respondent's mother told the respondent she or he needed to "do better than others" in order to overcome racism. In other words, the respondent was asked if their mother emphasized the importance of reinforcing the myth of the model minority in order to avoid or overcome disadvantages due to being a racial minority. The dependent variable had five answer choices in the Likert scale format ranging from 1 = Never to 5 = Always.

Key Independent Variables

The key independent variables consist of various "mothering" perception variables related to grades, curfews, and dating. The mothering variable is based on Macoby and Martin's parenting typology. Macoby and Martin found four major categories for parenting: authoritarian, authoritative, democratic, and uninvolved parenting. Authoritarian parents had expectations and made demands without allowing their children to voice their opinion. Authoritative parents allowed their children to voice their opinion without enabling them to act on their choice; the children were required to do as they were told by their parents. Democratic parents allowed their children to make decisions only after listening to the parents' insight and input. Uninvolved parents did not bother discussing issues with their children and the children were left alone to make decisions on their own.

In this study, the respondents were asked if their mothers "told me what to do, without listening to my opinion" (authoritarian mothering), "listened to my opinions but she ultimately decided what I do" (authoritative mothering), "expressed her opinion but ultimately allowed me to decide what I had to do" (democratic mothering), and/or "did not discuss the issue and did not appear to care about my opinions" (uninvolved mothering).

Mothering—Grades: An immigrant mother may be expected to tell her child to "do better than others" in order to overcome any possible discrimination due to being a racial minority and survive and succeed in their "new" or "non-native" country. These mothers can be expected to have stricter expectations about grades. Since education and job opportunities are connected, mothers who emphasize the need to behave as model minorities are expected to be perceived as being more authoritative or authoritarian about grades and academic performance.

Mothering—Curfew: A mother who expects her child to adhere to the model minority stereotype will be more likely to enforce curfew than mothers who do not have such expectations. Since staying out late can be seen as a conflict of interest with doing well in school and getting a well-paying, high status job, mothers who expect their children to perpetuate the model minority myth and meet expectations will want their children to come home on time. Mothers with higher expectations of model minority behavior are expected to be stricter with curfew or not want their children to go out at all.

Mothering—Friends: In the same spirit as the mother with model minority expectations related to her child's significant others, the same mother might be concerned about who her child socializes or associates with. Since people are prone to peer pressure, the mother with model minority expectations would be concerned about her child's peer group and friends. The mother might have a preference for her child befriending white Americans so the child can immerse himself or herself within the dominant–white–social network or have a preference for having her children socialize with other high achieving white or Asian Americans as was found in Eunyoung Lee's study. Lee found that Korean immigrant mothers wanted their children to socialize with white students in order to expedite the assimilation process and felt that associating with other Asians, especially Koreans, would hinder their children from learning proper English, which was viewed as the gateway to academic success. These same mothers feared that their children would speak their native language if they socialized with other Korean students at school, which would prevent them from developing a sense of belonging in the mainstream white culture and decrease their desires and chances of success within it.

Control Variables

Gender: The gender of the child may affect the relationship and respon-
siveness towards his or her mother. Nancy Chodorow's 1978 work on gender and mothering suggests that females may feel closer to their mother
due to being the same gender while males may feel the tendency to respect their mothers more. Although gender may affect the mother-child
relationship differently, including emotional and mental proximity, gender is expected to have a significant effect in terms of model minority parenting. Chodorow's study suggests that daughters tend to internalize their
mother's identity while sons tend to grow more distant from their mothers' identity as they grow older and associate themselves with their fathers.
Expanding on Chodorow's thesis, Miriam M. Johnson asserts that males
may develop a sense of misogyny in that they need to differentiate and separate themselves from their mothers while daughters, although they feel the
need to become separate as well, do not need to develop a separate gendered
identity—they remain and continue being female. In a similar vein, J. Jill
Suitor and Karl Pillemer found that mothers may favor their adult daughters over sons for issues related to closeness and care. Their findings suggest
that there are gendered differences in mother-child ties.

Age: The age of the child may affect the mother's tendency to emphasize the importance of being a model minority. Due to differences in socioeconomic levels and the challenges of surviving in a new country as immigrants, Koreans who immigrated in more recent decades (late 80s to the
present) may not have experienced the same types of racial struggles and
hardships as their counterparts who immigrated earlier. However, if the
college-aged children are offspring of immigrant parents who immigrated
in the early 60s to mid-80s, the parents might have expressed their concern
about performing as model minorities in the American society. The early
60s to mid-80s cohort of immigrants left South Korea when it was still in its
stages of development and had not reached the industrial and capitalist success of what it is today; this group of immigrants did not feel up to par with
American standards of living even if many immigrated with advanced degrees. Those who were previously middle-class usually experienced downward social mobility due to lack of English proficiency and had to apply
for American professional licenses in communities with very small numbers of people of color. Due to this struggle, the immigrant parents may
have placed greater emphasis on mastering English and academic success.

The cohort effect as studied by Norman Ryder, suggests that people can create continuity and coherence through infusion. However, social changes come about from changes in resources, education, socialization, and other social factors. When this concept is applied to immigrants coming from South Korea, a country that underwent major technological and cultural changes starting from the late 1960s, it can be expected that Korean immigrants in the United States will vary qualitatively by their immigration cohort. Paul Schultz's literature review of immigration cohort affirms the qualitative differences between cohorts. While the later cohorts may have more resources due to changes in the country of origin, Schultz emphasizes that the assimilation rate upon arrival can decrease due to availability of other co-ethnic immigrants. Alejandro Portes and Robert D. Manning found that the assimilation of immigrants may be hindered due to the creation of immigrant enclaves, which may encourage segmented labor market participation within the immigrant community or away from mainstream American society.

2nd Generation: Similar to age, the immigrant generation is expected to have a significant effect on whether or not the child is expected to perform as a model minority. Although the expectations are dependent on the mother's opinions and experiences, respondents who classify themselves as 2nd generation are expected to hear more about the need to act as a model minority than their 1st and 1.5 generation counterparts who immigrated later as older children with their parents since the parents of these 2nd generation immigrants came of age as 1st and 1.5generation immigrants who struggled with the difficulties of assimilation themselves. This question was a respondent self-identification question. Respondents who were not born in the United States but came here at a very young age and consider themselves to be more "American" than "Korean" might have chosen to identify themselves as being "2nd generation."

Religion (Protestant): Other than Buddhism, South Korea is home to two major Western religions, Protestantism and Catholicism. Catholicism has its roots in French missionaries introducing the religion to the country while Protestantism was introduced by American missionaries who established institutions such as schools, hospitals, and churches with the support of the Korean monarchy. Catholicism, on the other hand, was not accepted and Korean Catholics suffered from religious persecution. Protestant Koreans were aided by missionaries to pursue their education by studying abroad in the United States. Hence, people who identify themselves as Protestant may be more accepting and hold American values of individualism, freedom, and material success as their ideal standard. The Koreans who adopted Protestantism as their religion were more accepting of American customs and traditions when compared to their Buddhist and Catholic peers. Having been introduced to American institutions such as hospitals and schools, the Korean Protestants were socialized into American practices and material goods. Korean students who studied abroad in the United States not only acquired education and degrees but also acted as conduits for introducing and perpetuating the American culture and its practices along with material goods. While the notion of maintaining one's identity may be an issue for immigrants with concerns relating to the possibility of interracial marriage for their children, Pyong Gap Min found that Protestant Korean parents preferred their children to marry a fellow Protestant with ethnicity or race having less importance.

In addition to the notion of Korean Protestants having a more "Americanized" value system when compared to people from other religious backgrounds, Max Weber's findings on Protestantism and capitalism can also explain the effects of religious affiliation on model minority expectations. Weber's suggestion of Protestants having an uncertainty about their afterlife status when compared to Catholics who were able to enter heaven by prayer and repentance on Earth left the Protestants to adopt a spirit of industrialism which led to more Protestants adopting capitalistic and industrious tendencies than their Catholic peers. As a result, Protestants were seen as being more industrious and equate their success and material achievements with faithfulness. The Protestant students in this study are expected to be more influenced by the concept of being a model minority than those who identify with other religious beliefs.

Religiosity: The religiosity of the child may be linked to the mother's model minority expectations. As reported by Elaine Ecklund and Jerry Park (3), participating in a religion may function in two ways to either support or dispel the concept of being a model minority. Firstly, citing Rudiger G. Busto's study on Asian American Evangelical College Fellowships, Ecklund and Park emphasize that religious participation helps "reinforce" the model minority image in Asian Americans. On the other hand, the researchers cite Ecklund's previous study on how religious participation can be used to challenge the notion of being "economic" model minorities. While the issue of religious affiliation and religiosity may affect the model minority expectation in different ways, a mother who expects her child to behave as a model minority might expect her child to attend religious services with greater frequency, which suggests that the child is a "good, religious" child.

FINDINGS

Univariate Analysis

The univariate analysis (Table 1) shows that the dependent variable, mother's model minority expectations is quite evenly distributed across response categories with mothers reminding their children of their minority status. 19.08% of the respondents indicated that their mothers never reminded them of having to act as model minorities while 22.54% of the respondents said their mothers rarely reminded them. 23.70% stated that their mothers reminded them occasionally while 19.08% and 15.61% reminded them often and always, respectively.

The students' ranking of their mothers' parenting style based on the Macoby and Martin typology indicate that most mothers were somewhat involved (ranging from authoritarian to democratic) when it came to grades or academic performance with only 10.99% of respondents stating that their mothers were uninvolved when it came to topics related to school and grades. The curfew question received similar responses with 15.79% of the mothers being described as uninvolved. When it came to mothers stating their preference for who their children should associate with, 19.37% mothers remained uninvolved and did not voice their opinions about their children's friends.

The respondents in the survey had a mean age of 20.45 years with 46.11% identifying themselves as being first generation immigrants or not having been born in the United States. 53.77% of the respondents are males and 61.34% of the total respondents identified themselves as being Protestant. Overall, 15.54% of the respondent indicated never attending any sort of religious service while 39.90% indicated attending religious service more than once a week.

Bivariate Analysis

The bivariate analyses (Tables 2–4) show that mother's model minority expectation is not correlated with different types of mothering except for uninvolved mothering when it comes to issues related to friends. Uninvolved mothers were less likely to have model minority expectations in regards to friendships at the 0.05 significance level. In other words, the more uninvolved the mother related to friend issues, the lesser the model minority expectations.

Variable	Survey Questions Used	Response Categories	Frequency (%)	Mean	S.D.
Model Minority Mother	As you were growing up, how often did your mother say you should do better than others so as to overcome disadvantages as racial minorities in the U.S.?	1 = Never 2 = Rarely 3 = Occasionally 4 = Often 5 = Always	33 (19.08) 39 (22.54) 41 (23.70) 33 (19.08) 27 (15.61)	2.90	1.34
Mothering (Grades)	Please indicate what the discussion(s) was/were like by answering with the responses below.	1 = Authoritarian 2 = Authoritative 3 = Democratic 4 = Uninvolved	58 (30.37) 48 (25.13) 64 (33.51) 21 (10.99)	2.25	1.01
Mothering (Curfew)	Please indicate what the discussion(s) was/were like by answering with the responses below.	1 = Authoritarian 2 = Authoritative 3 = Democratic 4 = Uninvolved	49 (25.79) 45 (23.68) 66 (34.74) 30 (15.79)	2.25	1.01
Mothering (Friends)	Please indicate what the discussion(s) was/were like by answering with the responses below.	1 = Authoritarian 2 = Authoritative 3 = Democratic 4 = Uninvolved	23 (12.04) 36 (18.85) 95 (49.74) 37 (19.37)	2.25	1.01
Female	What is your gender?	0 = Male 1 = Female	107 (53.77) 92 (46.23)		
Age	How old are you?			20.45	2.21
2nd Generation	What is your immigration generation? (recoded)	0 = Not 2nd Generation 1 = 2nd Generation	77 (46.11) 90 (53.89)	0.54	0.50
Protestant	What is your religious affiliation? (recoded)	0 = Not Protestant 1 = Protestant	75 (38.66) 119 (61.34)	0.61	0.49
Religiosity	In the past twelve months, how often did you attend religious services?	1 = Never 2 = Less than once a month 3 = 1–3 times a month 4 = About once a week 5 = More than once a week	30 (15.54) 26 (13.47) 23 (11.92) 37 (19.17) 77 (39.90)	2.25	1.01

Authoritarian = Mother basically told me what to do, without listening to my opinion at all.
Authoritative = Mother listened to my opinions but she ultimately decided what I had to do.
Democratic = Mother expressed her opinions but ultimately allowed me to decide what to do.
Uninvolved = Mother did not discuss the issue and did not appear to care about my opinions.

Table 1: Survey Questions and Descriptive Statistics

Multivariate Analysis

Ordered logistic regression analysis was used to analyze the dataset for this project. Three different regression models were created to explore the topic on hand. We looked at model minority expectations by mothers and mothering behavior pertaining to three different types of situations or issues: grades (academic performance), curfew, and friends.

Mother's Model Minority Expectation and Grades—Table 5 A total of 146 cases were used for this portion of the study. Missing cases were deleted with listwise deletion. We found that the model minority expectations of the mother had no significant effect on mothering related to grades. However, model minority expectations had a significant negative effect on the 2nd generation immigrant variable at the 0.05 significance level suggesting that mother's model minority expectations is more prevalent amongst 1st and 1.5 generation immigrant children.

Mother's Model Minority Expectation and Curfew—Table 6 A total of 145 cases were used for this portion of the study. Missing cases were deleted with listwise deletion. We found that the model minority expectations of the mother had no significant effect on mothering related to enforcing curfew. However, model minority expectations had a significant negative effect on the 2nd generation immigrant variable at the 0.10 significance level suggesting a weak but significant relationship between mother's model minority expectations and 1st and 1.5 generation immigrant children.

Mother's Model Minority Expectation and Friends—Table 7 A total of 146 cases were used for this portion of the study. Missing cases were deleted with listwise deletion. We found that the model minority expectations of the mother had a weak but significant effect on mothering related to concerns over friends of respondents. Both mothers who were perceived as being authoritarian mothers and democratic mothers were shown to have a positive relationship with model minority expectations at the 0.10 significance level. The findings suggest that respondents who perceived their mothers as being more authoritarian and democratic than authoritative or uninvolved expected their children to adhere to the model minority stereotypes.

DISCUSSION

The findings of this study show that type of mothering does not have a significant relationship to model minority expectations. However, in two of the three models, we found that nativity (birthplace) affected model minority expectations. One possible explanation for the finding is that first generation parents and their first or 1.5 generation children (respondents who immigrated as older children) are subject to more hardships than 2nd generation children and their first generation parents. Although the generational classification depends on nativity, the parents' decade of immigration affects the socioeconomic status of the entire family. If the respondent's parents arrived in the United States with very little resources from South Korea and experienced downward social mobility, then it is likely that they will remind their children to work hard for material success—and act as "model minorities"—to avoid the same fate. However, if the family immigrated with resources, the student and the parents may not have experienced socioeconomic hardship. On the other hand, if the respondents are second-generation immigrants, they may be children of 1st and 1.5 generation immigrant parents. Given the age and the demographics of the Korean American population, it is highly likely that these second-generation immigrant respondents may have parents who were educated in the United States with 1.5 generation immigrant status. These 1.5 generation immigrants are familiar with the American culture and tend to be bicultural. In addition, the 1.5 generation immigrants have more social capital when compared to more recent first generation immigrants who must find their own niche and acquire resources. As a result, the children in different immigrant status strata will have qualitative differences in terms of resources and model minority expectations where the children with greater levels of social capital and economic stability are able to meet the model minority stereotype with greater ease than first generation immigrants who need to acquire proficiency in the English language and assimilate into mainstream society prior to attempting to become model minorities.

In this study, the expectation to "succeed" is indicated by model minority expectations. While the cohort effect for immigration has salience, the overall demographic information for the students tells a different story. More than half of the students have fathers with college, graduate, or professional degrees and combined parental income in the middle to upper-middle class level. Such demographic background could also be a factor in the parents' desire to have their children maintain and continue their success in the American society since the fathers have worked so hard to meet expectations associated with the model minority, especially material forms of success.

Due to the model minority stereotype, students reported feeling conflicted between assimilating into the American culture and following through on model minority expectations or reducing their level of assimilation and not performing as well in school as was observed by Felicia Lee. Lee also interviewed a high school guidance counselor who had the impression that students who behaved as model minorities were from families who had middle class status in their home country while Asian students who struggled and did not meet the model minority expectations were from families with lower income and education levels. Such findings suggest that the myth of the model minority may appeal more to Asian Americans from middle- and upper-class backgrounds and may also be a story of how the myth is a manifestation of middle- and upper-class desires and expectations.

CONCLUSION

The idea that minority status is a stigma that needs to be overcome continues to be pervasive in immigrant communities. Felicia Lee's interview with Asian American high school students in New York and Richard Bernstein's article reveal that the model minority myth and stereotype has created a burdensome stigma, which prevents Asian students from going to their teachers for help. Researchers and journalists (including Bernstein, Felicia Lee, Stacey Lee, and Nhan) have found that the model minority stereotype can be damaging to Asian American children. Our study found that immigrant children who did not consider themselves to be 2nd generation felt the burden of their minority status more than their 2nd generation counterparts. Although Asian Americans may use the model minority stereotype to their advantage, it can be deleterious and burdensome when the student or employee is unable to meet the expectations of the stereotype. For example, in 2011, the popular television show, *Glee*, had an episode called "The Asian F." The show depicted an Asian American student getting an "A-" on a chemistry exam and being severely reprimanded for bringing home anything less than an "A". While the episode poked fun at Asian American parents' expectations of their children, it also showed a student's (and the student's parents') internalization of the myth. Such representations through media portrayals reinforce and perpetuate a damaging stereotype that stigmatizes Asian Americans students.

Future studies on this topic are needed to understand the effects on Asian American students who internalize the model minority stereotype. Although Yoon Sun Choi and Benjamin B. Lahey's study on Asian American model minorities found that overall, Asian American students engaged in less problematic behavior (such as criminal behavior and drug use) than other minority groups, the rates of problematic behavior are actually similar to those of white students. Nhan reports that 25% of Asian Americans have undergraduate college degrees compared to 22% of the entire American population, suggesting that Asian Americans may accomplish more than their minority counterparts. However, the rates of delinquent behavior, whether aggressive or non-aggressive, when compared to other racial groups are still present. Researchers are urged to investigate whether Asian American student, as a trend, are assimilating and becoming more Americanized, or whether they are remaining Ronald Takaki's "perpetual foreign-

ers" who are subject to the myth of the model minority and other stereotypes. Scholarly pursuits that endeavor to understand this experience from
Canadian and other perspectives will also contribute richly to the literature
since assimilation patterns vary by countries.

With the term "Asians" representing a wide range of ethnicities, socioeconomic status, and ethnic community resources in the United States,
researchers may consider investigating the differences between Asian ethnic groups and their rates of accomplishment with regard to the instru-
mentality of model minority stereotypes. Bic Ngo and Stacey J. Lee (2007)
conducted a study on various Southeast Asians students of Vietnamese,
Laos, Cambodian, and Hmong descent, and found that these students were
expected to be high achieving because of the model minority stereotype.
However, Ngo and Lee found that some of the students, rather than trying
to excel in school, engaged in delinquent activities. Out of the four groups
in the study, Vietnamese American students were the highest achieving followed by Lao Americans, Cambodian Americans, and lastly Hmong Americans. The researchers attributed parental education levels prior to immigration for Vietnamese success. For the Hmongs, Ngo and Lee discussed the
cultural notions of education and gendered expectations supporting or hin-
dering education. Hmongs saw education as being instrumental to survival
and success in the American society but at the same time, expected females
to be less educated to be compliant wives for males, suggesting that expectations associated with the myth of the model minority rely on intersecting
ideas about gender, race, and class.

Ngo and Lee found that Southeast Asian American students who became distanced from their cultural identity or their culture of origin were
more prone to engage in delinquent activity. Felicia Lee's article also emphasizes the importance of socioeconomic status of immigrants prior to
their arrival in the United States. Although the model minority myth and
stereotypes may apply to Chinese Americans as a whole, Lee emphasizes
that socioeconomic status creates different groups of Asian Americans—
ones where the model minority stereotype may hold and others where the
stereotype does not hold but affects them negatively. The Chinese American students in Lee's article are children of immigrants who left their rural
villages with very little resources in the first place. These students end up
with less access to resources than middle class, educated immigrants. The
same can be said about other Asian groups who leave their countries with
very little resources. For example, Southeast Asian Vietnamese and Cambodian refugees bring very little resources and capital to the United States. As

a result, Southeast Asian immigrant children may have a harder time living up to the model minority myth and feel even more burdened by associated expectations.

With such differences in socioeconomic status and rates of accomplishments among different Asian groups, the myth of the model minority may mask the suffering of Asian Americans who need help. In addition to being a stereotype, myth, and burden, the notion of the model minority is also a hindrance and disservice that prevents the rest of America from realizing that there are significant differences among Asians, just as there are in other racial groups. Superficially, the model minority myth and standards of success and benefits may seem like the "pull" factor but all it does is create divisive attitudes towards Asians, causing them to be "model perpetual foreigners." Once Asians leave their home countries to immigrate to the United States, they come to pursue the American dream and to create a new home. Stereotypes and expectations such as the model minority myth create an incomplete sense of assimilation and acceptance where only Asian American model minorities are recognized as upstanding citizens and Americans due to their success and not their failure, which leaves out a whole contingent of Asian Americans who strive to call America, their new home. It is quite common for the American media to identify the racial or ethnic background of criminals of color while successful minorities are identified as Americans. Hence, further research is needed to determine the process and expectations instituted by the model minority stereotype to determine its effects and degree of burden in general—and specifically for East Asian communities.

WORKS CITED

Bernstein, Richard. "Asian Students Harmed By Precursors' Success." *New York Times*. New York Times, 10 July 1988. Web. 13 April 2013.

Choi, Yoonsun and Benjamin B. Lahey. "Testing the Model Minority Stereotype: Youth Behavior Across Racial and Ethnic Groups." *Social Science Review*. 80.3. (2006): 419–452. JSTOR. Web. 9 January 2013.

Chodorow, Nancy. *The Reproduction of Mothering*. Berkeley and Los Angeles: University of California Press, 1978. Print.

Ecklund, Elaine Howard and Jerry Z. Park. "Asian American Community Participation and Religion: Civic Model Minorities?" *Journal of Asian American Studies*, Volume 8.1 (February 2005): 1–21. JSTOR. Web. 5

April 2013.

J, Debbie. *Amy Chua: Life of a Tiger Mother*. San Francisco, CA: Hyperink. 2012. Print.

Johnson, Miriam M. "Women's Mothering and Male Misogyny." *Maternal Theory: Essential Readings*. (Ed. Andrea O'Reilly). Toronto, Canada: Demeter Press, 2007. Print.

Kim, Eun-Young. "Career Choice among Second Generation Korean-Americans: Reflections of A Cultural Model of Success." *Anthropology and Education Quarterly*. 24.3(1993): 224–248. JSTOR. Web. 9 January 2013.

Lee. Felicia R. "'Model Minority' Label Taxes Asian Youths." *New York Times*. New York Times. 20 March 1990. Web. 13 April 2013.

Lee, Stacey J. "Behind the Model-Minority Stereotype: Voices of High- and Low- Achieving Asian American Students." *Anthropology and Education Quarterly*. 25.4(1994): 413–429. JSTOR. Web. 9 January 2013.

Long, J. Scott and Jeremy Freese. *Regression Models for Categorically Dependent Variables Using STATA*. College Station, TX: STATA Press. 2006. Print.

Maccoby, Eleanor E., & Martin, John A. "Socialization in the context of the family: Parent—child interaction." *Handbook of Child Psychology: Vol. 4. Socialization, Personality, and Social Development*, edited by P. H. Mussen (Ed.) and E. M. Hetherington (Vol. Ed.). 1–101. New York, NY: Wiley. 1983. Print.

Min, Pyong Gap. *Preserving Ethnicity through Religion in America: Korean Protestants and Indian Hindus across Generations*. New York: NYU Press. 2010. Print.

Ngo, Bic and Stacey J. Lee. "Complicating the Image of Model Minority Success: A Review of Southeast Asian American Education." *Review of Educational Research*. 77.4 (December 2007): 415–453. JSTOR. Web. 9 January 2013.

Nhan, Doris. "Asians often Burdened as Model Minority." *National Journal*. 11 May 2012. Web. 5 January 2013.

Park, Julie. "On Tiger Moms." *The Point*. 5. (Spring 2012). Web. 4 May 2013.

Portes, Alejandro and Robert D. Manning. 2008. "The Immigrant Enclave: Theory and Empirical Examples." Pp. 646-657. *Social Stratification*. 3rd Edition. (Ed.: David B. Grusky). Westview Press: Boulder, Colorado. Print.

Pyke, Karen. "'The Normal American Family' as an interpretive Structure of Family Life among Grown Children of Korean and Vietnamese Immigrants." *Journal of Marriage and the Family.* 62.1(2000): 240–255. JSTOR. Web. 9 January 2013.

Ryder, Norman. "The Cohort as a Concept in the Study of Social Change." *American Sociological Review.* 30.6 (December 1965): 843-861. JSTOR. 30 March 2013.

Schultz, T. Paul. "Immigrant Quality and Assimilation: A Review of the US Literature." *Journal of Population Economics.* 11.2 (May 1998): 239-252. JSTOR. Web. 4 April 2013.

Suitor, J. Jill and Karl Pillemer. "Choosing Daughters: Exploring Why Mothers Favor Adult Daughters over Sons." *Sociological Perspectives.* 49.2 (Summer 2006): 139–161. JSTOR. Web. 30 March 2013.

Takaki, Ronald. *Strangers from a Different Shore.* New York, NY: Little Brown and Company. 1998. Print.

Weber, Max. *The Protestant Ethic and the Spirit of Capitalism.* (2nd Ed.) New York, NY: Routledge. 2001. Print.

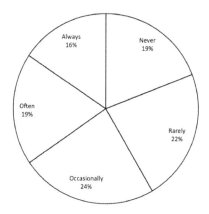

Figure 1: Model Minority Expectations

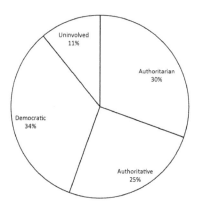

Figure 2: Mothering (Grades)

	1	2	3	4	5	6	7	8	9
1. Authoritarian Mother									
2. Authoritative Mother									
3. Democratic Mother									
4. Uninvolved Mother									
5. Model Minority Expectation	0.11	0.12	−0.09	0.02					
6. Female	0.12	−0.09	−0.07	−0.15	0.00				
7. Age	−0.05	−0.06	0.01	−0.03	−0.06	−0.00			
8. 2nd Generation	0.18	0.08	−0.20	−0.03	**−0.17**	0.10	0.00		
9. Protestant	−0.24	0.02	0.17	0.05	0.06	0.11	−0.05	−0.10	
10. Religiosity	−0.15	0.03	0.13	−0.03	0.06	**0.19**	−0.00	−0.05	**0.48**

Statistical significance at 0.05 level is indicated in bold.

Table 2: Pearson's Correlation Coefficients—Mothering (Grades)

	1	2	3	4	5	6	7	8	9
1. Authoritarian Mother									
2. Authoritative Mother									
3. Democratic Mother									
4. Uninvolved Mother									
5. Model Minority Expectation	0.05	−0.06	0.04	−0.05					
6. Female	0.12	−0.09	−0.07	**−0.15**	0.00				
7. Age	−0.05	−0.06	0.01	−0.03	−0.06	−0.00			
8. 2nd Generation	**0.18**	0.08	**−0.20**	−0.03	**−0.17**	0.10	0.00		
9. Protestant	**−0.24**	0.02	**0.17**	0.05	0.06	0.11	−0.05	−0.10	
10. Religiosity	**−0.15**	0.03	**0.13**	−0.03	0.06	**0.19**	−0.00	−0.05	**0.48**

Statistical significance at 0.05 level is indicated in bold.

Table 3: Pearson's Correlation Coefficients—Mothering (Curfew)

	1	2	3	4	5	6	7	8	9
1. Authoritarian Mother									
2. Authoritative Mother									
3. Democratic Mother									
4. Uninvolved Mother									
5. Model Minority Expectation	0.06	−0.03	0.12	−0.17					
6. Female	0.00	−0.00	**0.16**	**−0.20**	0.00				
7. Age	0.04	0.02	0.06	−0.13	−0.06	−0.00			
8. 2nd Generation	0.02	−0.10	−0.03	−0.12	**−0.17**	0.10	0.00		
9. Protestant	−0.14	0.08	0.08	−0.06	0.06	0.11	−0.05	−0.10	
10. Religiosity	−0.12	0.03	**0.16**	−0.14	0.06	**0.19**	−0.00	−0.05	**0.48**

Statistical significance at 0.05 level is indicated in bold.

Table 4: Pearson's Correlation Coefficients—Mothering (Friends)

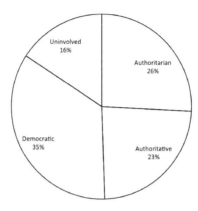

Figure 3: Mothering (Curfew)

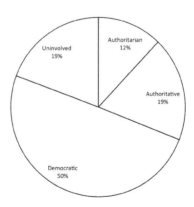

Figure 4: Mothering (Friends)

Independent Variables	Ordered Logistic Analysis	
Intercept 1	−2.96	(1.84)
Intercept 2	−1.78	(1.83)
Intercept 3	−0.79	(1.83)
Intercept 4	−0.24	(1.83)
Authoritarian Mother	−0.21	(0.60)
Authoritative Mother	−0.71	(0.62)
Democratic Mother	−0.71	(0.59)
Female	0.04	(0.30)
Age	−0.03	(0.08)
2nd Generation	−0.62	(0.31)*
Protestant	−0.04	(0.37)
Religiosity	0.04	(0.12)
Number of Observations	146	
LR test (Chi-square)	7.33	
Pseudo R-square	0.02	

*$p<0.05$; Robust Standard Error are reported in parentheses.

Table 5: Regression Analysis—Mothering (Grade)

Independent Variables	Ordered Logistic Analysis	
Intercept 1	−2.77	(1.72)
Intercept 2	−1.59	(1.71)
Intercept 3	−0.64	(1.71)
Intercept 4	0.39	(1.71)
Authoritarian Mother	0.19	(0.55)
Authoritative Mother	−0.22	(0.53)
Democratic Mother	−0.06	(0.49)
Female	−0.02	(0.31)
Age	−0.05	(0.08)
2nd Generation	−0.57	(0.31)*
Protestant	0.10	(0.38)
Religiosity	0.01	(0.12)
Number of Observations	145	
LR test (Chi-square)	5.03	
Pseudo R-square	0.01	

*$p<0.10$; Robust Standard Error are reported in parentheses.

Table 6: Regression Analysis—Mothering (Curfew)

Independent Variables	Ordered Logistic Analysis	
Intercept 1	−2.42	(1.67)
Intercept 2	−1.22	(1.66)
Intercept 3	−0.22	(1.67)
Intercept 4	0.83	(1.67)
Authoritarian Mother	1.30	(0.71)*
Authoritative Mother	0.36	(0.49)
Democratic Mother	0.80	(0.43)*
Female	−0.17	(0.31)
Age	−0.05	(0.08)
2nd Generation	−0.49	(0.31)
Protestant	0.05	(0.37)
Religiosity	−0.02	(0.12)
Number of Observations	146	
LR test (Chi-square)	9.53	
Pseudo R-square	0.02	

*$p<0.10$; Robust Standard Error are reported in parentheses.

Table 7: Regression Analysis—Mothering (Friends)

10.

Bad Mothers and "Abominable Lovers"

Goodness and Gayness in Korea

TIMOTHY GITZEN

Tears stream down Taesub's face as he speaks, fear and shame only two of the countless emotions he probably feels in these moments. As the camera shifts to the other side of the table his stepmother sits across from him. Tears fall from her eyes as she listens and implores: "Is it me? Because I didn't provide you with what you needed? And made you become isolated and lonely?" she asks through the tears. "This isn't something you did, but because of this I was isolated and lonely," he responds. His stepmother later asks, "I always think, 'What am I lacking?' I know this is something you are born with. Whatever happens, you're our child. Even if heaven and earth collapse, that won't change."

Taesub claims that he is *dongsŏngaeja* (homosexual) and his mother feels powerless to help him, not from himself but from a society, a world that she feels will forever demonize and terrorize him. Case in point: this episode of the South Korean television drama *Life is Beautiful* spurred mothers throughout the country in September 2010 to demand that SBS, the television broadcasting company responsible for the show, take responsibility if their sons "become gay and die from AIDS after watching *Life is Beautiful*" (VITALSIGN). Within the drama itself, Taesub's boyfriend's mother—a character that stands as antithesis to Taesub's stepmother—calls her son a "monster," to which he replies, "But you gave birth to me."

The melodramatic tensions within *Life is Beautiful* are no doubt played out in the lives of gay sons and their mothers throughout Korea. The

jockeying between homosexuality as a choice or as an uncontrollable phenomenon of birth may not be new, but the simultaneous love and devotion that Taesub's mother has for her son and the near disdain that seemingly other mothers have for homosexuality is a far less familiar topic of
discussion. My own ethnographic experience illustrates that these contrasting feelings for the same person—the gay son—can be felt by the "good"
mother. Goodness is both a discursive formation and a material or affective
reality—the circulation of certain discourses and experiences garner affective value and are thus deemed "good." We, in turn, orient towards those
discourses and experiences in the hopes of being or achieving goodness,
even if that being or achievement is merely a "promise" (Ahmed, *Promise
of Happiness*). As I illustrate in this chapter, a mother's goodness is entangled with her child's goodness and so mothers expect certain things from
their children in order to foster both the goodness of the children and the
mother. In what follows, I discuss what it means to be a good child, particularly a good son, and how gay sons and their mothers confront that goodness, but at the heart of the discourses of goodness is the heteronormative
expectation for sons to marry and procreate.

I conducted ethnographic research while a graduate student at Yonsei
University in South Korea between 2007 and 2010 and then again during
the summer of 2011. The focus of that ethnography, from which the data
for this chapter is taken, involved self-identified gay male college students
at Yonsei University's gay social club Come Together and their relationship with their families as they navigate through their sexualities. Just as
Taesub weeps out of fear and shame, so too did my informants (all given
pseudonyms) when they shared with their mothers that they prefer men
over women. My informants and Taesub all felt ashamed, a feeling they
had been experiencing since they first realized they were "different." In this
chapter, I elucidate the connections between gay sons and their mothers in
Korea as a method for unstitching the seams of "goodness" and "gayness"
in order to explore the politics of identity that are entangled with discourses
of goodness and experiences of gayness. In other words, I contend that gay
sons and their mothers are reassembling meanings of "goodness" by incor-
porating the expectations of these mothers and the sexualities of these sons.

ASSEMBLED DIVIDUALITIES

Donghae was twenty-four when he told his mother that he is gay. The two
of them were sitting in his mother's car when he suddenly had the urge to

tell her. She was confused because she didn't quite know what that meant, to be gay. Donghae is exceptional for coming out, given how rare it is in Korea. Elsewhere I discuss the politics of coming out in South Korea and contend that it is a family thing as the reveal stays within the family, an act of secret telling and secret making that is only shared within the family and never with anyone outside of the family (Gitzen). Among my informants, only three had "come out," and in each case they did so only to their mothers, Donghae included. I asked Donaghae in the summer of 2011, nearly a year and a half after he came out, why he told his mother. He said, "I love my parents and this is being more honest." Yet the love that Donghae confesses to be the motivation for his sexual reveal to his mother is not free from the mounting expectations that his mother has of him.

Can Donghae be both gay and a good son? And can his mother be considered "good," given her (sexually) non-normative son? At the center of both these questions are the expectations that emerge between relations of kin to the nation, kin to other kin, and kin to other bodies of discourse—both mothers and sons are expected to perform in certain ways, and those expectations are intimately connected to one another. How, then, are we to conceptualize the goodness of the mother and the goodness/gayness of the son? In order to interrogate this seeming dichotomy we should first shed light on the concept of the self in Korea. The self in Korea is understood not as individually defined but as dividually assembled. Here I am using Marilyn Strathern's concept of the dividual, where selves "contain a generalized sociality within ... persons are frequently constructed as the plural and composite site of the relationships that produced them" (13). The self thus becomes a "social microcosm." In essence, the dividual is thought of as a node within a network of social relations, where gender, status, sexuality, and the family are all aspects of the malleable and continuously constructed self. Strathern's intent is to respond to the notion of "roles" and the seeming plurality to roles; the dividual is thus an attempt to theorize a multiplicity (to borrow from Deleuze) of the person. Hoon Song describes this as "infinity" in Melanesia where the self simultaneously diverges and converges: "it can be approached from the 'inside' by counting [to infinity...and] it can be contemplated from the 'outside' as if counting had already been completed" (135). In other words, rather than perceive of the self in terms of plurality, Song (135) contends that Strathern would have favored the notion of infinity, a concept taken from Jadran Mimica's study of the Iqwaye counting system in Melanesia, because rather than think of the "openness" of plurality, infinity is "closed" as counting both begins and ends with 1.

As such, if we take Song's comparison further then the infinite self, or infinite social world, both "diverges and converges at once" as it simultaneously opens and closes.

Yet simply providing a conceptualization of an infinite self in Korea does not illustrate the seeming contraction between goodness and gayness. Instead, we must also consider the expectations, or acts, of the self in relation to the connections those expectations have to other bodies (of humans, discourses, ideologies, and so on). In this regard, the dividual is very much like Deleuze and Guattari's assemblage, where parts are not simply added to the assemblage but are used in specific ways, albeit strategically based on the situation or context, to transform and reassemble into different patterns: "The assemblage, as a series of dispersed but mutually implicated and messy networks, draws together enunciation and dissolution, causality and effect, organic and nonorganic forces" (Puar 211). Parts may fall off or be added, as relationships are continuously created and severed, but rather than layered on top for one to peel off and uncover some essential self, the parts of the dividual assemblage are always in motion, always dialogical and recursive with the other parts in order to shape those parts, as a way to illustrate that there is no authentic or true self. In other words, the multiplicity of the self, a concept Deleuze borrows from Bergson, "aims at dethroning the classical metaphysical notions of essence and type" (Viveiros de Castro 223). Rather than imagine the intersectionality of identity, the multiplicity of identity (an assemblage) attends to "interwoven forces that merge and dissipate time, space, and body against linearity, coherency, and permanency" (Puar 212). As such, discourses of goodness for the mother do not come before nor are a resultant of discourses of goodness for the son. Rather, the entanglements of these discourses are co-constitutive insofar as goodness of the mother is intimately tied to goodness of the son.

Let me explain. Mothers in Korea are often considered to be defined by their children: "when a child receives high marks, goes to a prestigious university, and finds a lucrative job…this success results from good mothering" (You and McGraw 591; see also Abelmann). In addition, success is tied to production, a measure of wealth, status, and particular ideologies as to who is considered a "good" Korean citizen, as I will discuss in the next section. Success is of course relative, but for many Korean families one's success compares to others in the immediate and extended family (Abelmann). Good mothers are thus defined by the good that their children produce, namely good education, good occupations, and good families of their own. The institution of motherhood is such that to be considered rightly a woman, and properly feminine (see J. Song "Room of One's Own"), one must marry and have children. Although the preference for sons is not as prevalent in Korea as it used to be (Chung et al.), son preference was standard when Donghae was born in 1986 (Das Gupta et al.). Therefore, the expectations of the mother are predominately two-fold: produce children and nurture them to be successful. Failure to do both throws into question a mother's goodness, a badge mothers fight to earn and sustain as it provides them with leverage within the family and authority in Korean society (see Gitzen; Abelmann; You and McGraw). Expectations and goodness, in this light, are thought of in terms of production: producing kin, producing success, producing goodness. Kinship is thus envisioned as a form of production, not entirely separate from Marxist modes of production.

GOODNESS/GAYNESS

If mothers are intimately tied to the success of their children, especially their sons, then what do mothers expect of their children? There is no single answer, and even if the institution of motherhood is quite hegemonic, Korean studies scholars have shown the diversity of womanhood, femininity and motherhood in Korea (see Song "Room of One's Own"). Yet Donghae explains these expectations quite well when he said that he was expected—not implicating his mother or father—to study hard, be a good Christian, enter a good university, serve in the military, obtain a successful job, marry, and have children. These last two, though, are what serve as barriers to Donghae's "goodness," just as they serve as barriers for his mother's "goodness." Donghae laments that he studied hard, graduated from an excellent university—Yonsei University, where we met, is ranked as one of the best schools in Korea—attended church every Sunday (even sang in the choir), and finished his military service, and yet by Korean standards he is still not a "good" son as he will neither marry nor have children.

These expectations for heterosexual marriage and procreation are not simply rules to live by, but culturally contextualized conscriptions of personhood. The transmission of one's blood to his or her offspring defines what it means to be a Korean "person" (Shin; Kim). In 2000, Gi-Wook Shin (2) conducted a survey in South Korea where 93 percent of his respondents reported that "Our nation has a single bloodline." Blood, a metaphor for both culture and the nation, makes a person and is entangled with citizenship, but producing grandchildren for one's parents defines what it means to be a son, daughter, mother and father. Blood is always inherent in the biopolitics of future reproduction, and so the discourse of personhood is predicated not on current instantiations of goodness but future incarnations of goodness. "Good" mothers therefore only socially and discursively exist if their sons are "good"—in profession, pairings, and progeny. And similarly, sons (and of course daughters) only socially and discursively exist if they fulfill these expectations, the three "p"s of personhood.

Thrown open, goodness is an object, as Sara Ahmed would term it. She contends that goodness garners affective value as it circulates across time and space, akin to the Marxist commodity. Can we then construct an understanding of goodness in conversation with non-normativity, the self-identification of "gay," that Donghae and my informants claim? My goal here is not to discuss what it means to be gay in Korea, or even provide a linguistic or historical genealogy of gay in Korea, except to say that my use of the word gay follows Donghae's and all of my informants' use of the word, both in English and with its Korean counterpart, *iban*. On the surface, the claim of a non-normative identity is in stark opposition to the makings of a social person in Korea as Donghae will not marry a woman and will not produce grandchildren for his parents. Simultaneously, his mother's goodness will be questioned as Donghae will not be able to—or chooses not to, as some in Korea may perceive—marry and have children. This yields guilt for Donghae, an only child, much in the same way as it yields guilt for Taesub being the eldest child of his family.

And yet neither is so immersed in guilt that they entertain the possibility of "playing" straight, but neither mother makes such demands of her son. Their mothers know full and well the social ramifications for having gay sons, but that does not deter either from their steadfast devotion to their sons, enhancing simultaneously the guilt both sons feel and their love for their mothers. The tension between guilt and love of the sons unveils further entanglement to their assembled dividualities by illustrating the connection between filiation and alliance. Eduardo Viveiros de Castro's essay on the use of Deleuze in anthropological conceptions of kinship proves useful, for he suggests that "post-prohibition kinship is, therefore, conceived in terms of a reciprocal presupposition between alliance and filiation that is actually (politico-economically) ruled by the former and virtually (mythically) by the latter" (233). As such, where filiation is concerned with production—the production of kin through the reproduction of substance (as in blood)—alliance is a form of becoming, "an assemblage of becomings" (223). For Deleuze and Guattari, a shift in focus took place between the two volumes of *Capitalism and Schizophrenia* from a "human economy of desire" where alliance limits filiation, to a focus of the "cosmic economy of affects (of desire as an unhuman force)" where it is filiation that limits alliance (238).

Taken together, the goodness/gayness duality may in fact be speaking to the differences between filiation and alliance. On the one hand, goodness is thought of as a molar form of production, where "social production is desiring production in a coded state… the task of the *socius* is the marking of bodies (memory creation)" (Viveiros de Castro 232). If we recall, goodness of the mother is predicated on her son's goodness, but the constitution of the son's goodness depends on producing offspring. Changmin, another self-identified gay college student, admitted that he feels guilty for not being able to produce grandchildren for his parents as the only proper way to produce grandchildren is through heterosexual reproduction. In this sense, filiation is not between parent and child but between parent and grandchild—the child is the vehicle of filiation and goodness. Even if marriage (an alliance) is part of one's goodness, I contend that heterosexual marriage is yet another vehicle to filiation; a childless couple in Korea garners much less goodness than a couple with children. On the other hand, gayness is molecular, if only because in Korea it is not thought of as a possibility, a movement, or a community of people (at least not by public discourse). Gayness as an alliance would account for works like Kath Weston's *Families We Choose* where she illustrates the differences between "chosen families" for gays and lesbians and the given family of one's birth, but it also allows for the possibility of movement in the form of becoming.

It is not necessarily Viveiros de Castro's contention that alliance trumps filiation, for if anything it is made to seem, at least within the "cosmic economy of affects," that alliance is limited by filiation. Goodness no doubt limits gayness, both discursively and experientially, for even if Donghae's mother accepts his son's sexuality (or at least ignores it), the expectations that surmount and continue to gather will forever limit Donghae's movement within his own sexuality. Taesub's mother weeps because she knows that Taesub will forever lead a more difficult life because he is gay, regardless of how good he is—he is simply not good *enough*. Yet we must not also assume that gayness as an alliance is simply the relationship between self-identified gay individuals, for even Weston argues that for some gays and lesbians, the given/ birth family is still integral to the conception of the chosen family—for some, one does not necessitate the destruction of the other, but neither do they harmoniously coexist.

By way of example, when Donghae had his first inclinations that he was "gay" and not just different in high school, he began searching online for others like him. He came across a classmate of his that was in the school's Christian club of which Donghae was also a member. "I was frustrated that he could be Christian and gay," Donghae admitted, a hint of rage in his voice nearly ten years after the incident. "You are frustrated with yourself, too, huh?" I asked after a few moments of silence. He nodded. "I was lying, but so was he!" He rationalized, at the time, that he was "better than that guy (*nom*)" because he "didn't tell anyone." Though he never spoke to the classmate—as it would make the entire situation, and his identity, too "real"—and quit going on the website, he studied harder and tried to be a better son, Christian and student as a way to compensate for his queer "lacking" (see Ahmed *Promise of Happiness*). Donghae believed, and feared, that when one is gay one cannot be other things, as if Judith Butler's "totalizing I" (566-568) is a conscious totalization. For Donghae growing up, there was no way to conceptualize his identity as both gay and Christian (or even gay and a son) because discursively his non-normative sexuality stood in opposition to what it meant to be a son and a person. Yet once he came out, and once he acknowledged that honesty is a form of love that he shares with his mother, he was able to construct both a social and an intimate understanding of personhood through the affective attachments he shared with his mother and others in his dividual network, myself included. In other words, his mother's acceptance, or even her non-instigation, of his sexuality proved to be the encouragement he needed to allow the tensions and entanglements to persist without necessitating a clean resolution.

Lauren Berlant notes that "incompatible needs and fantasies induce ambivalence" but that "there is no cure for ambivalence" (685). The unfitting pieces of Donghae's sexuality and his mother's quest for goodness will never be harmonious, because there is no erasure to ambivalence. And so we arrive back at the goodness/gayness distinction, for my claim is not singularly that goodness is always a form of filiation and gayness is always an alliance because neither Deleuze nor Viveiros de Castro would be so definite in ascribing categories. Rather, my foray into the distinctions and connections between filiation and alliance is to illustrate a shift in focus that allows for the possibility of movement between goodness and gayness. Perhaps, instead, we should speak of the goodness/gayness duality as an alliance and the relationship between the mother and the son as an alliance. For on the surface, or discursively, goodness does seem to align with filiation and the biopolitical mechanisms of blood and production, but if we only conceive of gayness as a form of alliance then we neglect the fact that alliances as becomings are *forces*, "bypassing filiation as substance" (Viveiros de Castro 240). Yet I would instead contend that alliances do not necessarily bypass substances as much as they make substances virtual. Claiming tension and ambivalence between discourse and experience is not new for anthropologists, but the very notion of a 'becoming' introduces the temporal element into the ambivalent. Filiation is characterized by production: a past-to-present-to-future r*eproduction* of substance, but alliance does not take this causal relationship as given and instead envisions a new relationship with a different connection.

To create an alliance between goodness and gayness, much in the way Donghae and Taesub do with their mothers, is to allow for affective attachments that connect mother and son by making the mundane exceptional. Becomings are about perspective, and so from one perspective the everyday-ness of the interactions between mothers and their gay sons are but acts of filiation as reproduction structures goodness. Yet from another perspective of the same everyday-ness, we see the exceptional take form as gayness is not what structures interaction but gayness and goodness are the interaction, an interaction that simultaneously shapes gayness and goodness. In other words, the simultaneity of goodness/gayness is only possible as an alliance, as a becoming, for it is not about the performance of a role but about the perspective of multiplicity (or dividuality) and the ways in which the relationships that form the multiplicity are made and unmade.

BECOMING MOTHER, BECOMING SON

My intention throughout this chapter is certainly not to imply that straight sons and daughters always fully enact and embody "goodness"; no project of the self succeeds in having a clean resolution. The assembled dividual is not solely housed within one conception of sexuality, nor one body of discourse, and so the category of the non-normative, the gay other, is revelatory of this failure and simultaneously solidifies the discursive cohesiveness of "goodness" in instantiating an "outside" that proves heteronormative solidarity. In other words, the failure of a straight son is never as severe as a gay son's failure given that the straight son can eventually "choose" to offer progeny as penance to "goodness." Even if the discourse of gayness is not prevalent in mainstream Korean thought, it can still serve as a radical "otherness" that protects the lesser trespasses and ideological "goodness" of the normative (Sedgwick).

As such, Donghae is attempting to construct his good son-ness, or fil-ial piety, by using whatever tools he has available to him, but ironically all he has is his bad son-ness, or unhappiness-causing, non-normative sexuality (see Ahmed *Promise of Happiness*). His mother is, in a sense, doing some-thing similar. On the backs of non-normativity, mothers and sons build a system of normativity. But more importantly, they simply recreate an idea of loyalty, dedication, and familial love, as if to say, "I like boys, yes, but I'm still a good son," or "my son is gay, I know, but he is still my filial son."

The multiplicity of the person, the person as a dividual assemblage of becomings, allows for seeming contradictions and actions. Perhaps the ob-vious question is simply, 'Why would a mother reject and exile her son for being gay?' But in borrowing both the dividual and the assemblage from Strathern and Deleuze, I must instead ask, "Why would we assume the mother to have such a relationship with the son where we would therefore assume a different action?" In other words, why does the mother react to her gay son in the way that she does despite the mounting pressure for her to produce a good son? And why is it that some mothers act in this way—accepting or making the son's non-normative sexuality a non-issue—while others reject the son's sexuality and chooses instead to ignore it and assume falsity? Strathern is apt to address these types of questions, Viveiros de Cas-tro (225) contends, for separation-as-relation illustrates that "relations make a difference between people" to the extent that assuming collectivity and sharedness limits the possibility and, Strathern would argue, the reality that relations are predicated on difference and disjuncture.

Returning, then, to Taesub's mother's question at the start of this chap-ter regarding whether she was the cause of his loneliness and sexuality, she implicitly asks if she is at fault for being a bad mother. She is reverting to a causal temporality; her bad-motherness somehow caused Taesub's bad-sonness (in the form of his gayness). The mother is the cause of the son's non-normative sexuality. This reads like a page from psychoanalysis, no doubt, but this is the Deleuzian intervention, for when conceiving of the relationship between mother and son as an alliance, the causal temporality of filiation—the substance—becomes virtual and mythical and therefore is only rhetorically actualized. Viveiros de Castro (240) astutely suggests that "it is alliance that has a double incidence, not only to regulate 'sexuality as a process of filiation,' but also as 'a power of alliance, inspiring illicit unions or abominable lovers.'" This "double incidence" provides a strong case for goodness/gayness as a form of alliance, but actualized within my ethnogra-phy and the lives of these mothers and sons, the seemingly "bad mothers" play the role of the "illicit unions or abominable lovers," calling forth an ethical dimension. If substance becomes virtual, and we 'lose' the past, then we are left with mothers and sons (re)creating a new past, a new relationship not bounded by the causal past. The guilt Changmin speaks of for not being able to produce grandchildren, a very Christian guilt of future repayment, is thus a product of substance made virtual by alliance as becoming. The very notion of becoming suggests that we may be capable of much more than we initially presume, that by living by the rules of the "human economy of desire" we see only as far as what we produce. But to think beyond that, to think of the alliance between mother and son as becoming something else is to think of affective connections that may go without saying, or come without knowing.

Alliance is therefore predicated on intimacy between those it connects, those it relates, be it the intimacy between mothers and sons or between goodness and gayness. The intimacy shared between gay sons and their mothers may be predicated on normative emotions of happiness, as Ahmed (*Promise of Happiness*) might suggest. Happiness is a normative direction we orient towards (and are oriented towards) and in our movement towards that utopic goal of happiness we experience what we believe to be happiness. Intimacy is a technology of the state, as Foucault might argue, for as Berlant notes, "intimacy involves relations that largely proceed by way of what goes without saying" (686). But intimacy is also a queering technology of the dividual assemblage and its constant, in-motion reassembling of affective parts, such as happiness, that hold immense value. In other words, Donghae and his mother are steadfast in their subscription to national projects of personhood and productivity, but they are also navigating through and around these discourses in ways that allow for Donghae's non-normativity without destroying the importance of social personage.

I have attempted to chart ambivalence throughout this chapter as a way to illustrate that good mothers and gay sons are not necessarily exceptions to the rules of either goodness or gayness, but that they in fact are working both within and outside these rules and desires to allow for their inclusion. For Taesub, Donghae, my informants and their mothers it may seem as if they are making the best out of a terrible situation but in fact they are re-examining what it means to be "best" and "terrible," "good" and "bad," and even "mother" and "child." But their ambivalence precludes an end to their examination as it does with every assembled dividual; it will forever continue through the tears they shed and the smiles they exchange.

ACKNOWLEDGEMENTS

I would first like to thank the editors of this collection, Patti Duncan and Gina Wong, for their comments and efforts. I would also like to thank Hoon Song, Stuart McClean, Carla Jones, and David Valentine for reading drafts of this chapter and providing amazing feedback. Finally, special thanks are due to Jennifer Patico who read countless drafts of this chapter with her now-famous patience and brilliance.

WORKS CITED

Abelmann, Nancy. *The Melodrama of Mobility: Women, Talk, and Class in Contemporary South Korea.* Honolulu: University of Hawai'i Press, 2003. Print.

Ahmed, Sara. *The Cultural Politics of Emotion.* New York: Routledge, 2004. Print.

—. *The Promise of Happiness.* Durham: Duke University Press, 2010. Print.

Berlant, Lauren. "A Properly Political Concept of Love: Three Approaches in Ten Pages." *Cultural Anthropology* 26.4 (2011): 683–691. Print.

Butler, Judith. "Imitation and Gender Insubordination." *Social Theory: The Multicultural and Classic Readings.* 4th ed. Ed. Charles Lemert. Boulder: Westview Press, 2010. 562–573. Print.

Chung, Woojin, and Monica Das Gupta. "The Decline of Son Preference in South Korea: The Roles of Development and Public Policy." *Population and Development Review* 33.4 (2007): 757–783. Print.

Das Gupta, Monica et al. "Why Is Son Preference so Persistent in East and South Asia? A Cross-Country Study of China, India and the Republic of Korea." *The Journal of Development Studies* 40.2 (2003): 153–187. Print.

Deleuze, Gilles, and Felix Guattari. *A Thousand Plateaus: Capitalism and Schizophrenia.* Minneapolis: University of Minnesota Press, 1987. Print.

Foucault, Michel. *The History of Sexuality: An Introduction, Volume 1.* New York: Vintage Books, 1990. Print.

Gitzen, Timothy. "The Promise of Gayness: Queers and Kin in South Korea." MA thesis Georgia State University, 2012. Print.

Kim, Eleana J. *Adopted Territory: Transnational Korean Adoptees and the Politics of Belonging.* Durham: Duke University Press, 2010. Print.

Mimica, Jadran. *Imitations of Infinity: The Mythopoeia of the Iqwaye Counting System and Number.* London: Berg, 1988. Print.

Puar, Jasbir K. *Terrorist Assemblages: Homonationalism in Queer Times.* Durham: Duke University Press, 2007. Print.

Sedgwick, Eve Kosofsky. *Epistemology of the Closet.* Berkeley: University of California Press, 1990. Print.

Shin, Gi-Wook. *Ethnic Nationalism in Korea: Genealogy, Politics, and Legacy.* Stanford: Stanford University Press, 2006. Print.

Song, Hoon. "Two Is Infinite, Gender Is Post-Social in Papua New Guinea." *Angelaki: Journal of the Theoretical Humanities* 17.2 (2012): 123–144. Print.

Song, Jesook. "'A Room of One's Own': The Meaning of Spatial Autonomy for Unmarried Women in Neoliberal South Korea." *Gender, Place and Culture* 17.2 (2010): 131–149. Print.

—. *South Koreans in the Debt Crisis: The Creation of a Neoliberal Welfare Society.* Durham: Duke University Press, 2009. Print.

Strathern, Marilyn. *The Gender of the Gift.* Cambridge: Cambridge University Press, 1988. Print.

VITALSIGN. "Union of mothers create anti-gay ad because of drama 'Life is Beautiful.'" *allkpop.* 1 Oct. 2010. Web. 2 Feb. 2014.

Viveiros de Castro, Eduardo. "Intensive Filiation and Demonic Alliance." *Deleuzian Intersections: Science, Technology, Anthropology.* Ed. Casper Brun Jensen & Kjetil Rodje. New York: Berghahn Books, 2010. 219–254. Print.

Weston, Kath. *Families We Choose: Lesbians, Gays, Kinship.* New York: Columbia University Press, 1991. Print.

You, Hyun-Kyung, and Lori A. McGraw. "The Intersection of Motherhood and Disability: Being a 'Good' Korean Mother to an 'Imperfect' Child." *Human Development* 42.4 (2007): 579–598. Print.

11.

Ideology, Gender, and Entrepreneurship

Implications for Perceptions and Experiences of Mothers in Taipei, Taiwan

TALIA ESNARD

Increasingly, entrepreneurial activities play a critical role in the changing nature of Taiwan's economic and social landscape. As Anderson and Lee citing Busenitz and Ghung-Ming Lau note, "the emergence of new and small businesses is now widely recognized as having a significant impact on economic development... [a reality that is] particularly evident in the People's Republic of China (PROC) [of which Taiwan is part] since the implementation of economic reforms in 1978" (775). However, when we take into consideration the recent liberal reforms and the political movement away from the historical statist experiences of Asian countries, self-employment as a viable economic option for women remains a relatively new and encouraging phenomenon. At the macro level, Sanyang and Huang signal that this translates into a forty percent (40%) representation of women across various sectors who have in some way or the other "contributed immensely to the success of small and medium enterprises to build the economy (884)." Most recently, based on a 2011 international survey, PROC President Ma Ying-Jeou revealed that such trends have led to significant growth of female entrepreneurs in Taiwan with a ratio of men to women involved in business startup activity as just under 2:1 (10.2% males and 5.6% females) in comparison to Korea's 3:1 or Japan's 5:1.

Such emerging economic trends however have not removed concerns for entrenched form of gender based structural inequalities that continue to shape among others, the heavy concentration of women entrepreneurs in low-capital and low-skilled trades within Taiwanese society (Scott). In such contexts, the traditional social and cultural fabric of Asian societies continue to serve as major deterrents to female entrepreneurship (Shieh, Lo and Su; Renzulli, Aldrich and Moody; Poutziouris, Wang and Chan). More specifically, researchers asserted that Taiwan remains a "patriarchal East Asian society" (Devasahayam and Yeoh 14) within which the position of female entrepreneurs, and by extension women, are inextricably linked to normalized paternalism, and related hierarchical structures of the family (Shieh, Lo and Su; Poutziouris, Wang and Chan). Given the relevance of such misogynistic ideologies on ethnic and economic practices, Scott (Sweet and Sour 219) argued that "when [we look] at Taiwan from the perspective of its female entrepreneurs, cracks appear on the edifice of patriarchy."

However, even with such socio-cultural constrains, other scholars also underscore broader socio-economic and by extension ideological shifts that also characterize the nature and degree of female entrepreneurship in contemporary Asian societies (Zhang and Pan; Chua). While these socio-economic developments do not undermine growing concerns for the gendering of entrepreneurship in Taiwan, they do raise some pertinent questions that relate to practice and experience within such complexities. Specifically, the burning question of how this convening of ideological orientations, including paternalism and neo-liberalism, impinge on the entrepreneurial and maternal practices of women who attempt to navigate the two, remains unaddressed. Thus, while existing scholarship continues to advance theoretical interrogations of gender and entrepreneurship in western societies, such a focus renders the dynamics of female entrepreneurship particularly in the case of those who are also mothers as unproblematic.

It is within such contexts that Yunxiang Yan urges researchers to rethink the corporate model of the Chinese family (which stresses its inherent economic functions) and shift towards deeper understandings of the gender relations that underlie family dynamics. Given the abovementioned conflicts, this chapter explores and interrogates, through an analysis of in-depth narratives, the ways in which these economic, religious and culturally embedded ideologies affect the perceptions, experiences and practices of mothers as entrepreneurs in Taiwan. The main contention of this chapter therefore is that the involvement of these Taiwanese women in entrepreneurial activities has not only placed them in direct path of the clash between the cultural, economic and religious ideologies but also complicates (with some variation) the possibilities and constraints of their engagement as well as the ways in which they respond within these divergent domains.

What follows therefore is an introduction of the guiding theoretical premises and constructs for my study. The inherent emphasis herein is on the theoretical utility of feminist social constructivism and its implications for understanding the complexity and fluidity of the experiences and practices of selected female entrepreneurs in Taipei, Taiwan. In the subsequent section, I address the central nature of interlocking ideologies on the social and economic experiences of women in Taiwan through an examination of related literature. With this backdrop of literature, I discuss the phenomenological methods of inquiry for this study, and finally the emerging themes in the narratives of mothers as entrepreneurs in Taipei, Taiwan.

FEMINIST-SOCIAL CONSTRUCTIVISM

Postmodern feminist efforts at interrogating and decentering gender offer oppositional yet insightful epistemological alternatives for understanding women's lived experiences. In her seminal work, *Gender Trouble*, Judith Butler locates such understandings within situated discursive contexts by which women through their interaction with each other *perform* gender. *Performativity* as a powerful vocabulary thus marks out the "discursive practice[s] that brings into being or enacts that which it names and so marks the constitutive or productive power of discourse" (Butler 134). This, for Butler emerged out of "personal/cultural history of received meanings subject to a set of imitative practices which refer laterally to other imitations and which, jointly, construct the illusion of primary and interior gendered self or parody the mechanism of that construction" (138). Thus, performances of gender materialize as imitations of culturally defined modes of thinking and practice that, as I demonstrate, can be connected in this case, to the ideological intricacies of Taiwanese society.

In order to achieve this, I embrace the explanatory powers of the gendered subjectivities construct as dynamic, shifting, *performative*, with ongoing understanding of gendered selves (Butler; Mascia-Lees). This notion of *subjectivities* as an extension of Butler's early writings moves away from essentialist understandings of gender and allows for scholarly work that calls attention to the multifaceted nature of subjectivity which "takes into account the many axes of identification through which a person comes to know herself" (Mascia-Lees 243) as expressed through discourse and social action.

Thus, by focusing on this notion of gendered subjectivities as situated, enacted and rationalized within dialectical contexts (Evetts; Esnard), this chapter draws greater attention to the ongoing, and competing yet interwoven nature of *"social landscapes"* and *"mindscapes"* and the ways in which mothers as entrepreneurs respond to and negotiate these subjectivities and conflicts. Using this theoretical lexis, I hope to advance our understandings of the cultural expressions and practices constituted by the fusing of a complex set of ideologies which creates dialectical points of convergence and divergence that shape the experiences of these mothers as entrepreneurs in Taiwan.

IDEOLOGY, GENDER AND ENTREPRENEURSHIP IN TAIWAN

Gender remains integral to the institutional normative and ideological frameworks (both in its cultural and structural contexts) that persistently define and limit women's economic and social activities (Evetts; Taylor; Baughn, Ahl and Marlow). In particular, powerful ideologies or "conceptual system by which a group makes sense of and thinks about the world" (Glenn 9) continue to shape gender relations as a set of "socially constructed relationships and practices organized around perceived differences between the sexes" (Glenn 3) and performed within institutions of the family and the economy. For Sangha and Gonsalves, these are fuelled by "historical emphasis on the sanctimoniousness of family life within South Asian culture [and which] plays an enduring role in South Asian mothering practices" (2). Despite such concerns, few studies interrogate the ways in which gender based ideologies create complex, often dialectical realities and processes that influence the lived experiences of mothers as entrepreneurs within Asian contexts. Such questioning is not only necessary but also timely.

STATISM, LIBERALISM AND FEMALE ENTREPRENEURSHIP

Despite neoliberal market reforms through state mechanisms in the post 1950 Chinese era, discernible cracking of traditional ideology and altered social relations, gender discrimination for women persevere (Entwisle et al.). In Asian countries like China, where family relations, gender roles, and self-employment differ from that of western societies, Zhang and Pan insisted that gender disparities in the labour market need to be understood against

the "historical experiences of labour market reforms [including collectiviza-
tion and (de)collectivization] and family relations under state socialism"
(1211). Although Zhang and Pan acknowledge the mediating effects of gender roles and unrelenting patriarchal ideals, the authors call attention to the
initial complex interactions between effects of state owned enterprises, re-
distributive sector and market reforms (including state sector layoffs) which
accounted for women's early push towards self-employment. Thus, while
initial state policies linked to ideals of market reforms moved towards fos-
tering greater economic liberalization at one end, at another, women's entry
into such regulatory regimes where patriarchal ideals supplanted equalitar-
ian ones under socialism subjected them to lingering gender discourses.

In accounting for its restricted impact, Gail Hershatter put forward the
view that the entry of women into the labour force was from the onset complicated by the contradictory assumptions upon which they were founded.
In this regard, Hershatter (1021 citing Elisabeth Croll) posits that "Mao's
statement that 'anything a man can do a woman can do also' clashed with
the widely shared belief that women were suited for lighter and less-skilled
tasks." In short, Hershatter's (1023 citing Andores) expansion of feminist
scholarship in this area, led to her argument that the "Maoist party-state had
subscribed to a reductionist theory of women's liberation, focusing almost
exclusively on bringing women into social production" based on assumptions that economic development would lead to women's equality, rather
than using the criterion of women's equality as a means to evaluate development policies. More pointedly, the author advances the line of reasoning
that this approach "neglected the complex connections between women's
economic role and cultural practices, contenting itself with a conservative
approach to family relations and other social relations in which women
were enmeshed" (1023). The net effects of such contradictory processes were
initial resistance to authority in the formative years following the cultural
revolution, rejection of management practices at the organizational level
and in the more contemporary period the proclivity for the younger generation to "locate their self-identity in discourses of femininity and motherhood, relegating worker identity as peripheral" (Hershatter 1025, citing
Rofel). Such historical complexities raise even more pointed questions not
only on the contemporary status of female entrepreneurs who work within
these dynamics but also the impact of such processes on their experiences
and coping strategies.

TALIA ESNARD

CONFUCIANISM, MYSTICISM AND ENTREPRENEURSHIP

Although largely eradicated with the democratization of Taiwan, Confucianism as "a social ethic, a political ideology, a scholarly tradition and a way of life" (Tu 3), remains a legacy of colonialism and *sinicization* or *Chinalization* (Taylor; Scott-Tanners of Taiwan). As a historical artifact, the transfer of patriarchal and Confucian ideals under the influence of China established clear "relational boundaries between men and women to divide physical space and social function" (Brige 26). Its main characteristic is that it locates "structural emphasis on the role and statuses of men and women as integral parts of the overall social order" (Lebra 210). With this weight on social action nestled within Confucian ideology, normalization of traditional respect for social hierarchy and hierarchical relations, benevolence or humaneness (*ren*), filial piety or obedience-*xiao* (obligations to parents and to one another), connections/relationships (*Guanxi*), attention to status (*mianzi*-giving face), loyalty (*zhong*), righteousness, and trustworthiness become a collective process that nurtures inner characterization and moral maturation (Wang et al.). It is important to note that these fundamental virtues of social and economic life also border on some of the teachings of Chinese mysticism, polytheistic (Pang) and ethnic practices (Scott-Tanners of Taiwan), from Daoism in the early years to the Buddho-Taoist synthesis in the later years. Thus, while at the surface, Daoism for instance stands in sharp "contrast to this vision of a completely organized and well-oiled social system, the proponents of this cosmic 'way' anticipated a return to naturalness and spontaneity of organic so-being" (Kohn 15) with a strong belief in immortality and its attainability, an accentuation of sacrifice (*si*), purification (*shai*) and thanksgiving or offering (*jiao*) which also overlaps with some aspects of Confucian teachings. Although complicated in the later years with the influences of Dao-Confucian and Buddho-Daoist synthesis (Kohn), such intermingling of religious and cultural ideologies provided multifaceted paths to understanding the meanings and experiences of Asian life (Tu).

As (Wang Yu-ting 1), Chairman of the National Youth Commission charged with the mandate to promote female entrepreneurship in Taiwan noted, "for women it's more difficult to become entrepreneurs" given the lack of support from husbands who would rather they stay at home, among other reasons, and the inadvertent effect of such dynamics on their entrepreneurial activities (Wang, *The China Post*). This cultural context of female entrepreneurship in Taiwan for Wang shapes the scalability (with more small and medium size enterprises), and typicality (service-oriented) of their enterprises with noted aversion to risk. In case of the latter, assessment from the United Nations describe this situation as one in which they assess that risk in terms of the impact of the business on their family. In sharing her personal experiences at the 21st Confederation of Asian-Pacific Chambers of Commerce and Industry (CACCI) Conference in Taipei, Wang, the then Director General of International Affairs, Global Federation of Chinese businesswomen disclosed that:

> [b]efore the age of thirty-five, the idea of setting up my own business had never occurred to me. Since [I was] a kid, I had been taught that the ideal of life was like a housewife's one. To play domestic roles properly, bringing up children and serving my husband are the ideas occupying my mind and directing my life style. It is a cultural matter, and there was, and still is, plenty Taiwanese women like me then. After opening up my own business, the pressure then immediately came from my family. My husband, a university professor, was very much stuck by the traditional notion of good family. That means a rather simple life. I was expected to fix dinner for the whole family members and to have family get together every Sunday. That was just impossible for a business woman who was at the initial stage of establishing her own business. (Wang 1)

In telling her story, Wang directed concern and attention to the role of Chinese culture as it specifically relates to norms and values that Taiwanese women inherit and the structural nature of the entrepreneurial space therein. It is in such circumstance that Porter and Nagarajan argued that women experience patriarchy inside and outside of their homes, in setting up their business and successfully running their business. With some variation in their lived experiences based on such institutional dynamics, Lu thus contends that while there is an increase towards egalitarianism in Taiwan, women's attitudes and behaviour (unlike men) remain linked to the ideological fabric of that society. In qualifying this, Wei-hsin Yu posits that "the extent to which cultural norms affect women's economic opportunities ultimately depends on whether the institutional arrangements in schools and labour markets tend to amplify or lessen the influences of these norms and preferences" (196). The empirical relevance of this therefore is the need for some scrutiny of the socio-demographic background and historical peculiarities of female entrepreneurs and the implications for understanding the experiences of female entrepreneurs in Asian societies.

METHODOLOGY

In order to gain a greater understanding of the modes of maternal thinking and practices of mothers as entrepreneurs, this study utilized a phenomenological method of inquiry (van Manen) and embraced the "constructivist and interpretative view of human consciousness" (Willis 14). As a form of interpretative phenomenology, it focused on the narratives and the "underlying meaning of the experience and emphasize[s] the intentionality of consciousness where experiences contain both the outward appearance and inward consciousness based on memory, image, and meaning" (Creswell 52) and where the notion that "consciousness is always directed at an object" (Creswell 59) or phenomenon, and its reality. This use of an interpretative phenomenological research design allowed for initial explorations of related themes surrounding the development of expressed meanings and experiences of selected mothers who are also entrepreneurs in Taiwan.

Given the focus of the study, I engaged in the combined use of purposive and snowballing sampling strategies to understand experience through the use of in-depth interviews, the ideological contexts that guide Taiwanese women's perceptions, experiences, challenges of mothering, and entrepreneurship for three female entrepreneurs in Taipei, Taiwan. These female entrepreneurs were selected based on their ability to speak English, their engagement in a new or existing venture, their proximity, availability, and on their status as mothers. Interviews were conducted in English, transcribed, manually coded, analyzed on an ongoing, open-ended, inductive basis (Reissman) where analytic memos (Maxwell) were written throughout the data collection stage as a way of establishing patterns in the data to formulate textual and structural descriptions (Creswell) that captured the essence of the what and how of their experiences. The main limitations of the study are that (i) the execution of interviews in English restricted the ability of interviewees to expand on their accounts of inherent conflicts and coping strategies related to mothering and entrepreneurship; (ii) interviews were only conducted with mothers who were female entrepreneurs in urban Taiwan, that is Taipei; and (iii) the use of a small sample of participants did not allow for generalizations beyond the narratives of those interviewed.

FINDINGS

The objective of this study was to explore the salience of ideological frameworks as discursive contexts on the perceptions and experiences of mothers *as* entrepreneurs in Taiwan. Here, the three main themes that emerged in the data were: (i) situated gender *as* troubling, (iii) entrepreneurship *as* trouble and, (iii) mothering *as Mianzi* (showing face).

Situated gender as troubling

A central theme within the narratives was the constant confrontation with gendered dilemmas within subjects' multiple roles as a female entrepreneur, wife and mother and its disconcerting effects. More specifically, the stories tell of the continued hold of patriarchal ideals in all spheres of social interaction and its resultant emotional distress and anxiety. As a case in point, Gia, a 42-year-old excursion planner with high school education and two teenage girls, from Southern Taiwan, frequently battles subtle and direct cultural dilemmas in her everyday attempt to balance her emerging entrepreneurial role with that of the social expectations of her role as wife and mother. While she argued that this is stronger in rural Taiwan, she traced this quandary to persistent patriarchal ideals in Taiwanese society. In that regard, she stated that "traditionally, people thought that women can't handle difficult things and need to care for family instead. The interesting thing is that this still happens today." In providing a critical instance within which she was affected by such gendered thinking, Gia shared that:

> I once told my husband that I wanted to expand my business and I was so disappointed when he asked me whether the idea makes any sense when we take into consideration what I have to do for him and the children. He also suggested that I would not be able to handle the three. So I did it to prove to him that I can. Men laugh if you fail, if you open a small business that's ok but if you want to go big, it becomes a joke. Men can fail while in business but women aren't given the chance to. Women still have to play the supportive role in Taiwan, they can't start businesses carefree.

Here, Gia's open expression of discord with marginalizing expectations of women even in their role as entrepreneurs sheds light on the weight of patriarchal systems of social hierarchy and relations on her economic activity as well as her direct attempts to defy such masculine spaces. In recalling another worrying experience, Gia described the case of "one colleague who for 15 years worked with satisfied clients and after fifteen years she still receives a touch on the back and mention of being a good girl." In both instances recalled, the stories point to persistent issues of power relations in the family and the workplace as constrained by ideological imperatives.

In recognizing the plurality of her subjectivity and those of other women around her, Lisa, a 35-year-old fashion designer with two young children who is planning to do a Masters in Business Administration (MBA) in the United Kingdom, drew on the intersectionality and salience of gender and ethnic practices and the collective obscuring effects of that interaction. With a heightened sensitivity towards gender issues gained from her undergraduate education, Lisa engaged in a more critical reflection on the status of Taiwanese women. In the case of the former, she located her gender identity within the "patriarchal culture and the saying that women are narrow minded and hard to teach" and traced an understanding of her own invisibility to the absence of women in the writings of Confucius and the more powerful expectation of submission and adherence to his teachings. Thus, she reasoned that although this element of passivity differs for women in comparison to their male counterparts, it transcends throughout the society as in her words, "Confucius has taught us great things: to be nice, respectful, have manners...I respect him as a philosopher but I think that he makes Taiwanese people too passive. So it is always Huānying [meaning welcome] for everything." However, she also linked this reserved nature of what she sees as Taiwanese behaviour to her ethnic beliefs, particularly those related to non-action and freedom of mind. Here, she disclosed that the:

> ...leader of Daoism is also very important as he is more spiritual and talks more about the universe while Confucius talks about the physical world and interactions with people. So if you compile understandings of Confucianism and Daoism then you can learn a lot about Taiwanese people.

Yi'F reminds us that practices of Daoism "interacted and often coalesced with the activities and doctrines of Confucianism and Buddhism" (173). Though independently distinct in their focus (Confucianism-social behaviour; Buddhism-afterlife and Taoism-spiritual and physical healing), the three ethnic practices form an amalgam of teachings that converges with folk tradition to shape a colourful moulding process that influences self-cultivation, transformation and social identity (Moore-Oldstone). One of the major implications of this is the need for future research that explores and further unveils the interplay between gender, ethnicity and ideology as experienced in Asian contexts.

Entrepreneurship as *trouble*

Scott argued that ideals of liberalization and empowerment of women through entrepreneurship stand in direct opposition to many aspects of Confucianism and Daoism including the expectations of being a virtuous wife and a good mother. Within this environment, the findings show that, at one end, all the respondents attempt to take hold of the many opportunities available in the economy. Lisa for instance stated that "Taiwan is expanding with many small to medium size business and there are lots of opportunities for women to play a part but with certain limitations." Specifically, at another end, she also acknowledged that "we have more women in business but they still face discrimination." Here, the dynamic and integrative nature of patriarchal and liberal ideologies also created many points of contention or clashes in their everyday lives as mothers and wives who are also entrepreneurs. These also produce noted contradictions between ideals of family, career and entrepreneurship (Shieh, Lo and Su). Thus, Lisa's story pointed to the partial tolerance of her entrepreneurial activity by her husband and her own internalisation of what her husband articulates as her cultural priorities. She stated that:

> …he is generally tolerant of the idea as long as it does not affect my role as a mother and a wife. Now both of my kids have left home so I have a little bit more freedom but no matter what circumstances that may emerge my family come first. During the time when the kids are around, it is very busy and I have to rush things. I can only function when they have gone to school. When they are at home, they are the priority.

Similarly, Cher, a 29-year-old financial consultant, marketer, MBA graduate with one toddler and a teenager shared that:

> In Taiwan, a woman is supposed to be perfect and simple; that is, being a mom and a housewife. I am not that perfect wife because for many years I have tried to balance my business with my roles as a mother and my husband still believes that I have

deprived my children of important values and experiences because of that.

Here, Cher's attempt to balance romanticized notions of a good mother and righteous wife with that of her entrepreneurial activities remains a thorn in the flesh, a violation of cultural normative and a source of major dissension within the home. Similarly, perceptions of entrepreneurship as trouble are also evident in the concerns of Gia's husband. Thus, Gia reports that "I want to expand my business but my husband thinks that it will not be good for my family," a statement that for Gia is tied to the traditional expectations for women in Asian societies. She revealed that "since his retirement, things have gotten worse between us and his presence [at] home upsets everything." More specifically, she pointed to constant power struggles in the home between herself and her spouse. Thus, she disclosed that:

> when my husband was the one working I managed to get some time for myself and my business. Now that he is retired he tries to run the house and denies me of my space to do what I need to do for my business. Now he tells me how much time to spend in it, how to run it, and tells me that he has worked for so many years to give me a nice life but by saying that he does not recognise what I have been doing. That really bothers me.

In telling her story, Gia locates her anxiety with the need for her husband to reassert and transfer his authority from the workplace to the home. Within this transitory period of retirement and reintegration into and reconfiguration of household relations, Gia expressed that she constantly struggles to maintain some measure of independence both within the home and in her business. In her home she shared that "it is a troubling time in our marriage. I feel that he needs to go out, be with his friends and that I will do what I have to do. Traditionally couples find a way to live with each other so we will find a new life somehow I suppose." It is important to note that while Gia recognises her sources of contention, she remains powerless in her ability to escape such conflicts and to address the wider social web within which it is framed. For Gia, part of this powerlessness emerges out of her own deeply internalized sense of religiosity and passivity that were entrenched in early socialization as a child growing up in rural Taiwan.

However, despite her passive expressions of resistance, she remains troubled by her husband's perception of her entrepreneurial activities as a threat to the family milieu. Thus, she divulged that "beneath the table I complain a lot to my children and I also remind them of how important I have been in their lives and how important I am now...but it is an emotional challenge here at this point." This power struggle and invisibility for Gia extends into her business as she communicated that "even when I go out in public and meet other business persons, it is so funny that they give my husband the business cards, not me. I am not [seen as] the business person." This narrative brings to the forefront the wider perceived inadequacy of her internal power struggles in so far as society reproduces these patriarchal ideals within public places. Within this climate, Scott reminds us that women are indeed aware of the gendered and ideological nature of power relations that generally work to the advantage of men and to the disadvantage of women both within the home and places of business. As a way of coping with the underlying contradictions and conflicts associated with navigating the two roles, the findings confirmed that these women (albeit with some variation) actively participate in and resist this perceived power game.

Mothering as *Mianzi (giving face)*

Mianzi or attention to status dictates that many peoples of Asian cultures present an image of self that is consistent with the expected social attributes within their society. It speaks to the "sense of worth that comes from knowing one's status and reflects concern with the congruency between one's performance or appearance and one's real worth" (Huang 71). In the case of this study, the findings revealed that despite their engagement in entrepreneurial ventures, the internalization of the cultural boundaries that regulate social behaviour inadvertently shape attention to their status as mothers and the performance of the roles, expectations and unquestionable commitment to their children. This sort of cultural obedience or show of their culturally assigned roles (also related to Confucian values of filial piety, and Guanxi) is evident in the ways that these women taught their children to be submissive, moral, and respectful of hierarchical relations in and outside of the home.

Thus, at one end, Lisa's maternal practices remain consistent with filial obedience or the emphasis given to children's obligations to parents and to one another even after death with the teaching of Confucianism and ethnic practices. She divulged that "I teach my kids that they need to respect their parents and their culture. They need to honour and take care of their parents in life and death." Cher makes a similar connection. She expressed that "my children are blessings from the Gods and they too must also take care of me." As part of her ethnic practices, Lisa explained that her "children learn the sacred life. I carry them to the mountain to do homework while enjoying the fresh air and the sacredness of the mountains. I make them make wishes to the God and yes they do come true for all of us." Similarly, Gia suggested that there is a need for religious sacredness in the way she raises her children. She noted that my "kids are not allowed to watch the television. We don't have one in the home. We don't expose them to all the things on television. They are not ready for that so I take them to the park, teach them to play a sport, make them get in touch with animals and their natural environment." This affinity for the natural and the spiritual for Yi'F can be explained by the religious emphasis on the moral fabric of Daoism which promotes thriftiness, purity, and control of desire, simplicity, and wordless beauty.

However, in looking more closely at their responses, the narratives also imply that these women not only harbour opposition to the deep seated cultural and ideological fabric of their society but also resist and to some extent reshape the ways in which these affect their expected roles as mothers and entrepreneurs. More specifically, Lisa spelled out her grievance with the reality that "while the role of women is changing from that of staying home to having many women involved in their own venture, women are still not seen as important as men and therefore have to follow their culture." As a response to this, Lisa communicated that while she teaches her children to respect their culture and hopes that one of them will stay in the business; she also instils in them during their private time (unknown to the father) the need for them to identify their own ambitions, to seek their own independence and embrace moments of parental separation. Similarly, Cher revealed that she "teaches her children to do whatever they want" and explore opportunities for career development outside of Asia. She explicated that this is in direct opposition to her husband's unchanging traditional position that their daughter should stay in Taiwan to find a husband to care for her. Thus, Cher narrated that "my husband tells my kids that they need to get a husband and I say let them take their time, they are young and he asks who is going to take care of them. This is a reminder of the cultural boundaries and a reason why [I should] not cross them."

Despite her initial jovial response to the discussion, Cher remained haunted by the oppositional stance (by her husband and the wider society based on the lack of social support) with regards to raising her kids, a reality she juxtaposed that is directly affected by his attachment to traditional ways of life and her exposure to a more open one. This is consistent with Sara Ruddick's argument that the burdens of acceptability in the socializing of children or in shaping an acceptable child and the powerlessness associated with that process produce a deep sense of inauthenticity where mothers respond to dominant values that can sometimes differ significantly from their own. In this case, the findings show that in their attempt to be mothers as entrepreneurs under conditions of persistent patriarchy, they often engage in contradictory displays of conformity and resistance. For Ruddick this conformity to the demands of acceptability typifies not only an adherence to societal notions of a good mother but also a betrayal of their own interest in the development of their children.

Mothering practices appear to be mediated by social hierarchy in the marriage. In addition, all three female entrepreneurs alluded to the persistent power and authority of the mother-in-law in the contemporary family. Narratives also suggest that the level and extent of involvement in their lives by the mother-in-law also affects their maternal thoughts and practices. With heavy involvement so too is the conflict. Lisa for instance uttered that:

> [My] mother-in-law and I get along …she is here for two months. She lives in the USA and once she is here she takes over and spends a lot of time with the children and the house is no longer mine…I am no longer the mother, she is. She takes over the caring for my husband, her son and our kids. His mother is close to him…you should understand that in Chinese family the daughter-in-law has to honour and respect the relationship between her husband and his mother. As long as she is here, the relationship she has with her son takes precedence over the one that I have with her son.

Scott's work (Sweet and Sour) hints that this circumstance remains central to the authority of the mother-in-law and the effects of such social process on the maternal practices of women in Taiwan. In this case, Lisa saw herself as a total stranger in their marital household with the presence of her mother-in-law who comes with greater social authority. Given this, Lisa described her approach to mothering while in the presence of her mother-in-law as a "tricky thing" as she has to be "very smart" in how she does things in and outside of the household or else she (Lisa) "gets hurt."

However, she admitted that the involvement of her mother-in-law also frees her from the burden of the family and gives her the ability to redirect the time and energy into her business in the process of getting things done; a freedom and level of contentment that she keeps to herself. Thus, she stated, "I give her space and time and I go out and get things done...I work on projects and proceed with some business. I get some time for myself while they bond in the meantime and I just work around all of that." She thus rationalized that the free and flexible time is atypical and the presence of her mother-in-law presents the basis for restructuring the lines of authority, respect for social hierarchy and the obligations to social relations that are expected and to which she responds favourably. However, while this mode of acceptance or conformity can be perceived as an effort to minimize inherent conflicts between the two spaces of work and home, it is also important to be cognizant of the manner in which this remains incongruent with the anguish that she encounters in the process and the ways that they collectively deny her of selfhood. Thus, the masking of her own contentions with these historical lines of power and authority in the home despite notable social changes in Taiwan remains her way of coping with or giving face to these expectations and inherently reducing possible family conflict.

CONCLUSION

Many writings and scholarship on working women in Taiwan have focused on relative improvements in the social status of women pushing achievements in: (i) independence, autonomy and decision making (Hu), (ii) social gratification and self-esteem (Shieh, Lo and Su), and (iii) self-empowerment (Scott) among others. However, little research underscores the extent to which cultural, economic, and religious ideologies as nuances of Asian culture continue to serve as constraints to female entrepreneurship as well as sources of dialectical counters that collectively affect the practices of mothering and entrepreneurship in Taiwan. As such, this chapter adds to this literature by showing that women who attempt to integrate mothering and entrepreneurship in Taiwan remain locked within, troubled by, and resistant to traditional ideals and practices of patriarchy, passivity, and morality, and the related intricacies of fusing ideologies.

In such cases, I argue that Shieh, Lo, and Su's stance that "Taiwan has a long way to go to loosen the fixed male-dominated ideologies and reach an equal and harmonious relationship between the sexes in society" (233) still holds. In short, "even in Taiwan, the society where we observe greater progress in closing the gender gap in employment opportunities, the story regarding the trajectory to gender equality is still far from finished" (Yu 200). In the interim, greater theorising and problematizing of discursive contexts and their relationship to maternal and entrepreneurial practices may provide a starting point for unearthing ideological and structural intricacies (including those related to ethnicity, gender, and religiosity). Such work is critical for thinking through the relationship between gender and labor in societies like Taiwan where traditionalism and modernism coexist to create and sustain contradictory and troubling lived realities for women who attempt to circumvent conflicts related to being mothers and entrepreneurs.

WORKS CITED

Ahl, Helene and Sue Marlow. *Exploring the Intersectionality of Feminism, Gender and Entrepreneurship to Escape the Dead End.* EGOS Symposium, Gothenburg, Sweden, 2011. Print.

Anderson, Alistair and Edward Uiu-Chung Lee. "From tradition to modern: Attitudes and applications of Guanxi in Chinese Entrepreneurship." *Journal of Small Business and Enterprise Development* 15.4 (2008): 775–787. Print.

Baughn, C. Christopher, Chua Leng-Bee, Kent Neupert. "The Normative Context for Women's Participation in Entrepreneurship: A Multicounty Study." *Entrepreneurship Theory and Practice,* 687–708. 2006. Print.

Brige, Bettine. *Women, Property and Confucian Reaction in Sung and Yuan China,* 960-1368, UK: Cambridge University Press, 2002. Print.

Busenitz, Lowell.W. and C. M. Ghung-Ming Lau. "Growth Intentions of entrepreneurs in a transition economy: the People's Republic of China." *Entrepreneurship theory and practice* 26.1(2001): 5–20. Print.

Butler, Judith. *Gender Trouble: Feminism and the Subversion of Identity.* New York: Routledge, 1990. Print.

Chua, Amy. "The Rise of China's Billionaire Tiger Women, Women in the World Series." *Newsweek.* 10 March 2012. Print.

Creswell, John. *Qualitative Inquiry and Research Design: Choosing Among Five Approaches,* 2nd Ed. CA: Sage Publications, Inc., 2007. Print.

Croll, Elizabeth *Women and Rural Development in China: Production and Reproduction.* Geneva: International Labour Office, 1985. Print.

Devasahayam, Theresa and Brenda Yeoh. *Working and Mothering in Asia: images, ideologies and identities*. Singapore: National University of Singapore Press, 2007. Print.

Entwisle, Babara, Gail E. Henderson, Susan E. Short, Jill Bouma and Zhai Fengying. "Gender and Family Business in Rural China." *American Sociological Review* 60 (1995): 36–57. Print.

Esnard, Talia "The Personal Plan is just as important as the Business Plan", *Journal of the Motherhood Initiative for Research and Community Involvement*, 3.1 (2012): 163–181. Print.

Evetts, Julia "Analyzing Change in Women's Careers: Culture, Structure and Action Dimensions." *Gender, Work and Organization* 7.1(2000): 57–67. Print.

Glenn, Nakano Evelyn. "Social Constructions of Mothering: A Thematic Overview." *Mothering: Ideology, Experience, and Agency*. Ed. Nakano Evelyn Glenn, Grace Chang, and Linda Ronnie Forcey. Great Britain, Routledge, 1994. 1–29. Print.

Hershatter, Gail. "Status of the Field: Women in China's Long Twentieth Century." *The Journal of Asian Studies* 63. 4 (2004): 991–1065. Print.

Hu, Tai-Li. "The Impact of Rural Industrialization on Women's Status in Taiwan." *The Role of Women in the National Development Process in Taiwan*. Ed. N. Chiang. Taipei: Center for Population Studies, Women's research Program, National Taiwan University, 1985. 339–55. Print.

Huang Shuanfan. "Two Studies of Prototype Semantics: *Xiao* 'Filial Piety' and Mei Mianzi 'Loss of Face'," *Journal of Chinese Linguistics* 15 (1987): 55–89. Print.

Kohn, Livia. *Early Chinese Mysticism: Philosophy and Soteriology in the Taoist Tradition*. Princeton, NJ: Princeton University Press, 1992. Print.

Lebra, Sugiyama Takie "Confucian Gender Role and Personal Fulfilment for Japanese Women." *Confucianism and the Family*. Ed. W. H. Slote and G. A. DeVos. Albany, State University of New York Press, 1998. 209–227. Print.

Lu, Yu-hsia. "Changes in Gender Role Attitudes in Taiwan 1991-2001." *Taiwanese Journal of Sociology* 48(2011): 51–94. Print.

Ma, Ying-jeou, Ma. Spotlights the importance of Female Entrepreneurship, *Taiwan Today*, 29 May 2012. Taiwan Today Archives. Web. 17 August 2012.

Mascia-Lees, Frances. *Gender and Difference: Globalizing World, 21st Cen-*

tury Anthropology. Illinois: Waveland Press Inc., 2010. Print.

Maxwell, Joseph A. *Qualitative Research Design: An Interactive Approach.* Thousand Oaks, CA: Sage, 1996. Print.

Moore-Oldstone, Jennifer. *Taoism: origins, Beliefs, Practices, Holy Texts and Sacred Places.* NY: Oxford University Press, 2003. Print.

Pang, Chien Kuo "The State and Economic Transformation: The Taiwan Case." *Developing Economies of the Third World, Outstanding Studies of Economic Development in Latin America and the Pacific-Rim.* Ed. S. Bruchey. New York: Garland Publishing Inc., 1992. Print.

Porter, G. Elaine and K. V. Nagaran. "Successful Women Entrepreneurs as Pioneers results from a Study Conducted in Karaikudi, Tamil Nadu, India." *Journal of Small Business and Entrepreneurship* 18. 1(2005): 39–52. Print.

Poutziouris, Panikkos, Yang Wang and Sally Chan. "Chinese entrepreneurship: the development of small family firms in China." *Journal of Small Business and Enterprise Development* 9. 4(2002): 383–99. Print.

Reissman, Catherine Kohler. *Narrative Analysis.* Newsbury Park, CA: Sage, 1993. Print.

Renzulli, Linda, Howard Aldrich and James Moody. "Family Matters: Gender, Networks and Entrepreneurial Outcomes." *Social Forces* 79.2 (2000): 523–46. Print.

Rofel, Lisa. "Hegemony and Productivity: Workers in Post-Mao China." *Marxism and the Chinese Experience.* Ed. Arif Dirlik and Maurice Meisner. Armonk, NY: M. E. Sharpe. 1989. Print.

Ruddick, Sara. "Thinking Mothers/Conceiving Birth." *Representations of Motherhood.* Ed. D. Bassin, M. Honey and M. Mahrer Kaplan. New Haven: Yale Press. 1994. 29–44. Print.

Sangha, K. Jasjit and Tahira Gonsalves (Eds.) *South Asian Mothering: Negotiating Culture, Family and Selfhood.* Bradford, ON: Demeter Press. 2013. Print.

Sanyang, Saikou, E. S. and Wen Chi Huang. "Small and Medium Enterprise for Women Entrepreneurs in Taiwan." *World Journal of Agricultural Sciences* 4(s) (2008): 884–90. Print.

Scott, Simon. *Tanners of Taiwan: Life Strategies and National Culture.* Westview Case Studies in Anthropology. Cambridge, MA: Westview Press, 2005. Print.

Scott, Simon. *Sweet and Sour: Life-Worlds of Taipei Women En-*

trepreneurs. Toronto: Rowman and Littlefield Publishers, Inc. 2003. Print.

Shieh, Vincent, Angela Lo and Emily Su. "Families of Employed Mothers in Taiwan." *Families of Employed Mothers: An International Perspective*. Ed. Judith Frankel. New York, Garland Publishing, Inc., 1997. 213–35. Print.

Taylor, Rodney, L. *Religions of the World: Confucianism*. Philadelphia: Chelsea House Publishers, 2004. Print.

Tu, Wei-Ming. "Confucius and Confucianism." *Confucianism and the Family*. Ed. Walter H Slote and George A DeVos. Albany, NY: State University of New York Press, 2004. Print.

United Nations. *Entrepreneurship and e-business Development for Women*. Thailand: United Nations, 2006. Print.

Van Manen, Max. *Researching Lived Experience: Human Science for an Action Sensitive Research*. Albany, NY: State University of New York Press, 1990. Print.

Wang, Erika. "Government promotes female entrepreneurship", *China Post*, 11 December, 2008. China Post Archives. Web 13 August 2012.

Wang, Shelly. *Women's Status in Taiwan: Helping Women and Women Entrepreneurs to help Themselves*. Paper presented at the 21st Confederation of Asian-Pacific Chambers of Commerce and Industry (CACCI) Conference in Taipei, Taiwan, 1 November 2007. http://www.cacci.org.tw/Speeches/21st\%20Conf/ShelleyWang-Paper.pdf.

Wang, Jia, Greg G. Wang, Wendy E. A. Rouna and Jay W. Rojewski. "Confucian Values and the Implications for International HRD." *Human Resource Development International* 8.3(2005): 311–326. Print.

Willis, Peter "The 'things themselves' in Phenomenology". *Indo-Pacific Journal of Phenomenology* 1(2001):1–16. Print.

Yan, Yunxiang. *Private life under socialism: love, intimacy, and family change in a Chinese Village, 1949-1999*. Stanford, CA: Stanford University Press. 2003. Print.

Yi'F, Wang. *Daoism in China: An introduction*. Translated. Zeng Chuanhui and Adam Chanzit, CT, Floating World Editions Inc., 2006. Print.

Yu, Wei-hsin. *Gendered Trajectories: Women, work and Social Change in Japan and Taiwan, Studies in Social Inequalities*. Stanford, CA: Stanford University Press, 2009. Print.

Zhang, Forrest Qian and Zi Pan. "Women's entry into Self-Employment in

Urban China: The Role of Family in Creating Gendered Mobility Patterns." *World Development* 40.6(2011): 1201–1212. Print.

The author would like to acknowledge the support of the Taiwanese Embassy (R.O.C.) in the granting of a 2012 Taiwan Fellowship for this research.

12.

Mothering Across Borders

South Korean Birthmothers' Perspectives

RUPA BAGGA-RAOULX

The transnational, transracial adoption of children is a phenomenon that has increased enormously over the last twenty years, but adoptions from South Korea to North America go back to the 1950s, after the Korean War, and represent by far the largest number of the movement of children to completely different environments from the place of their birth (Hübinette; E. Kim *Adopted Territory*). The experiences of Korean adoptees have been studied a good deal over the last decade, by a wide range of researchers from many disciplines including historians, sociologists, psychologists, and specialists in Asian Studies and childhood education. The authors are often themselves adopters, adoptees, social workers in the adoption field, or Korean Americans. Adult adoptees have also produced a number of personal accounts of their own experiences, both positive and negative, and the perspective of adoptive mothers has been well represented, going back to Bertha Holt's influential *The Seed from the East*, which provided a graphic account of early adoptions to the United States and the Christian motivation behind them.

My own perspective is that of an outsider to the "adoption circle," as I am originally from India and am neither adopted nor an adoptive parent. My interest in this phenomenon was sparked by getting to know adult Korean adoptees during my graduate studies in Korea and the United States. As I went on to complete a doctorate in Women's Studies, I became particularly intrigued by the relatively neglected perspective of the Korean birthmothers.

As a result of fieldwork in Seoul in 2007 that allowed me to meet with adoption workers, returning adoptees in search of their birthmothers, and the young mothers currently housed in maternity homes, I became increasingly aware of the complexity of the intersections of gender, class, race, and age in any attempt to understand why so many Korean women have relinquished their children in the past, and continue to do so. The reasons have changed over the decades, as have the motivations of those women in North America and elsewhere eager to adopt their babies. Global power relations enter into the equation, as well as the transformation of missionary endeavors into an institutionalized private-public child-care system that has allowed South Korea to rely on foreign sources to fund its social services. The continuing prevalence of extreme poverty, class distinctions, and overt gender discrimination in South Korea (E. Kim *Adopted Territory*), in spite of economic development and legal changes achieved through the efforts of women's organizations (Jones; H. M. Kim; S. W. Lee "Adoption of Feminism"), has meant that adoptions abroad have continued in spite of the shame they represent for the South Korean government and recurring efforts to curtail them.

Korea's little noticed continuing export of apparently unwanted children contrasts with that of China (recently curtailed), which replaced Korea as the main source of adoptable children in the last twenty years. Efforts there to control the size of the population by the "single-child" policy are often deemed excessive in the West, but they serve to justify the availability of "superfluous" children (Dorow "China R Us?"; *Transnational Adoption*). Korea, in contrast, is now concerned because the population is aging and the birthrate is exceptionally low. A closer look at accounts provided by South Korean birthmothers reveals some of the ways in which cultural, political, economic, and ethical issues play out in individual lives. Such personal stories contribute important insights into the ramifications of transnational, transracial adoption and suggest lines of inquiry relevant to the broader field of feminist and anti-racist debates over more recent waves of adoptions to the West from Latin America, Asia, and Africa.[1]

INTERSECTIONS OF GENDER, CLASS AND RACE

The personal narratives to be discussed here have been collected in three volumes, all presented as "letters" from Korean birthmothers.[2] They bear the titles *I Wish for You a Beautiful Life: Letters from the Korean Birth Mothers of Ae Ran Won* (Dorow); *To My Beloved Baby* (Holt Children's

Services); and *Dreaming a World: Korean Birthmothers Tell their Stories* (Han), a sequel to *I Wish for You a Beautiful Life*. All published through adoption agencies and based on texts collected in Christian maternity homes, these volumes indicate the extent to which the adoption process is both gendered and feminized. Both birth and adoptive fathers usually remain in the wings, whether they are supportive or not. While the government bodies that pronounce laws and policies controlling the movement of people on both sides of these international transactions are perceived as impersonal and masculine, the majority of social workers and counselors who are intimately engaged with adopters and birthmothers are women.[3] The situation in which a racialized woman from a less rich country has a child but is unable or unwilling to raise it emerges starkly in contrast with that of the adopter: usually a white woman from a richer country who desperately wishes to become a mother but is unable to do so biologically. Both perspectives raise philosophical, legal, and ethical issues regarding the right to parent, the reasons for wishing to do so (or not), and what it takes to prove that one can be a "good mother."

The reasons why a child may be available for adoption in Asia are frequently related to the child's gender, as well as to poverty and the cultural stigma attached to being an unmarried mother (see E. Kim "Wedding Citizenship and Culture" 56; Ochiai and Molony 49). In Korea, adoption is usually associated with relinquishment or abandonment of the child by the birth family or mother, rather than with being orphaned. It is rarely due to the "protective removal" of vulnerable minors on the part of the State, as often occurs in Western countries. Such differing norms stem from the ways in which gender difference and family genealogy are constructed and perceived in many Asian contexts, where girl children are still often seen as a burden whereas sons are considered a resource.[4] This view has been particularly prevalent in Korea, as in China, where the patriarchal male lineage has been culturally constructed as especially important because of the significance of rites of respect for the ancestors being carried out by male heirs (Peterson 28–31; Deuchler 129–178; Hübinette 30–33; S. W. Lee "Patriarchy and Confucianism").

The reasons why few healthy white babies are available for adoption in the U.S. or Canada include relatively easy access to contraception and abortion, as well as some access to social and financial support for single mothers—all changes hard-won by feminist activism (McDade; Westhues and Cohen). But the assumption that children are not available for adoption in North America camouflages the presence of many children needing homes who are considered "hard to place" for reasons involving race, class, health, ability, and age.[5] The fact that children of color, or older children, siblings, or those with disabilities, have difficulty finding homes in their own countries in North America is indicative of broader issues within the Western context concerning entitlement, privilege, and economic oppression, as well as disparities between North America and the Global South where most international adoptees are born.

The birthmothers' stories discussed below clearly illustrate how patriarchal social structures and changing attitudes to women's sexuality are central to understanding why so many Korean women have reluctantly relinquished their children (E. Kim *Adopted Territory*). Class-based economic conditions resulting from a combination of tradition and globalization, as well as media images of the West and the influence of Christianity, all intersect in these women's perceptions of their reasons for allowing their children to be adopted abroad.

NARRATIVE CONTEXTS

The published narratives are presented as "letters" addressed to the birthmothers' unknown children. They provide invaluable insight into the range of reasons for the mothers' predicaments, confirming the influence of changes in policies regarding domestic adoption, foster care, and assistance to single mothers, as well as the role of the extended family and religious institutions. The previously depersonalized and anonymous birthmothers become engaged actors, victims or heroes rather than villains, in these personal accounts. The ways in which their stories are framed and the implied reader(s) constructed play a significant role in how they are read.[6] The concept of letters to imaginary (but real) potential readers, simultaneously addressed to a range of eavesdroppers, constitutes a novel type of life-writing that raises questions about sincerity and manipulation in the depiction of self-accusation and disculpation.

At the time of my first fieldwork in Seoul in 2007 I had the opportunity to visit several maternity homes run by agencies (all of them Christian in origin and orientation although working with government agencies) that arrange both overseas and domestic adoptions. I was already aware of the first collection of "letters" edited by Sara Dorow, who grew up in Korea herself. As Dorow puts it, "the birth family's story may be inaccessible, poorly understood, or even avoided, leaving painful gaps in the adoption narrative" (*I Wish for You a Beautiful Life* 4). At the time when she was writing, this home, originally known as "House of Grace," was "one of the few organizations in Korea that provides …support both during and after pregnancy" (4).[7] Initially established in 1960 as a home for runaway girls and prostitutes by an American Presbyterian missionary, Eleanor Vanlierop, it was originally funded entirely by private donations. The director, Ms. Sangsoon Han (editor of the second volume from this source), who welcomed me there explained that it became a home for unwed mothers and their children in 1973, in response to the Korean government's desire to establish such homes. When the founder retired to the United States in 1983 the building was turned over to the Presbyterian Church of Korea and renamed *Ae Ran Won* ("Planting Love") in honour of Mrs. Vanlierop, as this was her Korean name[8]. Although it was licensed by the government and has since received 70% of its financing from the state, it still maintains its Christian mission to meet the "spiritual" needs of the women, as well as their physical, psychological, and vocational needs.

While seeking information at the best known adoption agency, Holt Children's Services, which also runs a home for "unwed mothers," I came across another less polished anthology, *To My Beloved Baby* (Holt Children's Services), based on accounts collected from birthmothers who had dealt with the Holt agency for their child's adoption. This book was available only through their office in Seoul, whereas Dorow's book *I Wish for You a Beautiful Life* and its sequel (Han) have received wider distribution, though mainly outside Korea. The latter includes seventeen "letters," framed by a retrospective narrative by the woman concerned and brief notes from the editor giving an update on the narrator's present situation.

All three volumes provide some information about how and why the "letters" were produced and published, while leaving a number of questions unanswered. Ms. Han explained to me that when the expectant mothers arrive at the maternity home and are considering relinquishing their child, they are encouraged to write in a diary about their own feelings, as well as their hopes and fears for the child's future. This practice has continued as a therapeutic exercise supervised by counsellors. With greater publicity around autobiographical accounts by adult adoptees, many of whom have returned to Korea to look for their birthparents, these reflections are sometimes formulated in the hope that the child may be among them. Many birthmothers now express the hope that they may see their child again at some point, as adoptions are becoming more open, and their desire to make a favourable impression is evident.

The "letters" all try to answer the imagined question, "Why did you give me up?" All those included in these volumes were read by staff members, if not directly solicited by them, who realized that they offer useful information about the circumstances of these women for both adoptees and adoptive parents. Many also serve as testimonials to the value of the work done at *Ae Ran Won*, and the role of Christian faith in enabling some mothers to cope with the grief of separation from their child, as well as the church's assistance in overcoming the material obstacles that led to that situation.

At the time when these narratives were originally written, the women in the maternity home shared their stories with each other, as they did the experience of being there. They wrote in their diaries in *hangul*, the Korean national script, and spoke to their imagined child in Korean. For publication, the accounts were first selected (with success stories not surprisingly predominating), then translated into English, edited, and presented in a frame that emphasizes the positive role of the agency and the fact that all proceeds from the books go to running programs for the birthmothers and their children. The introductions, prefaces, and forewords direct the reader to approach these texts in a certain way:

> We [the *Ae Ran Won* social workers] find that a helpful part of recovery for each birth mother (is) to express her feelings in the form of a letter to her child. It is my pleasure to select some of these letters from our files ...in order to share them with the adopted children and their families.... My staff and I hope that people who read these letters will better understand birth mothers [and] that the stories courageously told by some birth mothers will help other women in their journeys. (Dorow *I Wish for You a Beautiful Life* 3)

During my visit Ms. Han confirmed that the letters were not published without the writer's consent, although this aspect was not mentioned in the first volume. These books represent a new type of auto/bio/graphy: the individual speaker with her unique story becomes part of a collective "we" representing all birthmothers. The addressee, her own child, is merged with all adoptees who may read the book. These texts function as "frame stories" with one act of communication (from the birthmother to her absent and unknown child) enclosed within another, between someone representing a supervisory role in relation to the mothers and the actual readers, who speak English and may be prospective adoptive parents or adult adoptees in search of their roots. The fact that both the mothers and the agency have specific purposes in mind affects the selection of what is told and the manner in which it is narrated.

In the more recent letters (Han), some of the narrators appear to be very conscious of ambivalence in regard to their addressees and implied readers. In the earlier letters (Dorow *I Wish for You a Beautiful Life*), the context of the text's production remains vague in terms of time and place, and when asked, Ms. Han attributed this to the desire to protect the identity of the narrators. Dorow states: "the letters were translated as directly as possible and edited only to protect confidentiality" (Dorow *I Wish for You a Beautiful Life* 6). In the more recent cases, by contrast, some writers have requested that their real name (or that of the child) be used, so that their child might be more likely to find them. In the most recent volume more attention is paid to assuring the reader that the writers have consented to having their reflections edited and made public, although few of them speak or read English well enough to assess the result. The collection produced by the Holt agency (*To My Beloved Baby*) is the only one to include the letters in Korean, alongside the translation, and therefore the only one that many present-day birthmothers might be able to read. However, it is not readily available even in Korea. As well, there is considerable overlap in some of the stories in the Holt collection and the others, leading one to assume that in some cases the same person was involved.

I Wish for You a Beautiful Life includes a foreword by two American social workers, Jeff Mondloh and Maxine Walton of the Children's Home Society of Minnesota, who encourage adoptive parents to become familiar with these stories, which may allow the birthmother to become "real" and convey her "struggles, disappointments, regrets, and lost dreams" (Dorow *I Wish for You a Beautiful Life* 8). On reading the letters, however, one wonders how a child might react to the mixed messages that they convey (ranging from sorrow, guilt, and grief to relief, as well as wishing happiness for their children and the adoptive families). How easy would an adoptive parent find it to read them with a child who might want to know if any of these mothers is anything like her own? In fact, they reveal a wide range of personalities and situations, as well as raising similar issues.

I begin my analysis by looking more closely at the socio-economic and family background of some of the narrators, and how these relate to the reasons for their unplanned pregnancies, the availability (or not) of termination, and their inability (until recently) to keep their children.

BIRTHMOTHERS AS VICTIMS: UNPLANNED PREGNANCIES

None of the three volumes in my discussion includes any accounts from birthmothers of the immediate postwar period, or mothers of so-called GI babies, the period often associated with the emergence of Korea's transnational adoption program (see Hosu Kim and Grace M. Cho's chapter in this volume, "The Kinship of Violence"). No woman in these collections confesses to having lived in a Korean military "camptown" or been a sextrade worker (Duncan). During the postwar period, there were no maternity homes where pregnant women could take refuge, as the few shelters available were only for children. The earliest accounts are from the early 1980s, when some basic support for mothers, at least for the confinement and delivery of very young ones, became available. The second volume from *Ae Ran Won* (Han) dates the narratives by giving the year in which the child was born, covering the twenty-year period from 1984 to 2004. The earliest letters confirm that poverty and family breakdown made some very young women vulnerable to either sexual assault or seduction. Several narrators describe dropping out of school and running away from their parents' home at a young age to find work, because of the violent behaviour of alcoholic fathers and/or poverty due to the debts they incurred. Once alone in a rented room, they had no family members to defend their person or reputation, and several women reveal that their first sexual experience was forced on them. These stories suggest that few of the children born in this period were of mixed race, and many were the result of economic circumstances that lead to single young women living vulnerable lives alone and away from home.

Some were very young. The first narrator in the recent volume (Han), raped by a taxi driver at the age of fourteen, felt that she had to agree to move in with the perpetrator and mind his two sons from a previous marriage. She is not the only one to explain that family and friends thought that once a girl had lost her virginity, even by rape, she was obligated, in order to preserve her family's honour, to marry the man responsible or live with him although he was already married (Han 36). This narrator discovered she was pregnant after her aggressor had left her, having decided to return to his wife, and she had no one to turn to. Her situation brought such shame on her family that her brother advised her to kill herself. The neighbours gave her "bad looks" (Han 13), and though her mother would have supported her she did not dare to go against the father's wishes. She laments, "I broke my mother's heart" (Han 14), but "God took pity," and she discovered Ae Ran Won. In spite of the hardship she herself suffered at the hands of her own father, she still believes it would be terrible for the child to grow up "with no father" in Korea. The child was taken away from her immediately after she gave birth, and she was able to remake her life a few years later by accepting an arranged marriage. Ironically, unable to have any more children, ten years later she herself adopted a child whom she sees as a "reincarnation" of the one she lost.

Many details of this dramatic story are echoed in other accounts. Violent fathers are mentioned by a number of women, particularly those from poor or rural backgrounds, as well as moral support from grandmothers, mothers, or sisters who had no material resources to help them. Another narrator (Han Chapter 2) explains that she herself was almost given up for adoption at the age of three because of drunken domestic violence, but her mother went to get her back from the orphanage. On leaving home she also turned to alcohol, and she describes herself and her boyfriend as "selfish people who only thought about our own pleasure" (Han 24)[9]. She is not the only one to mention ignorance about contraception. There seems to have been a widespread assumption that it was the man's responsibility, and that if the woman became pregnant he should marry her, provide a home, or at least pay for an (illegal but nevertheless usually available) abortion. In this case, the boyfriend claimed that the child might not be his, and refused to do anything. Her mother was willing to help her to obtain an abortion, but she was already very advanced in her pregnancy.

These stories provide evidence of strong solidarity among women across generations, owing to the shared experience of being devalued in a patriarchal society. In another instance, the narrator (Han Chapter 3) was herself adopted, because of her own birthmother's poverty. She was well treated until the adoptive parents took in a relative's son to carry on the family name, according to traditional Korean custom. The boy was then favoured over her, and she was mistreated. This woman is one of those who were raped, and her birthmother contacted her to advise her not to marry the alcoholic man concerned, in spite of pressure from her adoptive family. She had been getting news of her daughter through a relative, without the girl knowing. The narrator admits that she hated her birthmother for not being there when she needed her (Han 31), and married the father so that the child would have a name and family. She was also happy at the prospect of having a blood relative of her own. Unfortunately, the father's violent behaviour forced her to take refuge at *Ae Ran Won*. Since children born to married couples were not eligible for adoption at that time (1994), she had to pretend that the child was not her husband's (Han 39). Finally she chose overseas adoption, not wishing her child to have an experience like her own as an adoptee in Korea. The note added by Ms. Han explains that the child, born with disabilities, was adopted abroad, and this woman returned to her husband after he converted to Christianity. She ultimately travelled to the U.S. to try to meet her daughter, but the adoptive parents refused a meeting, fearing that it would be too disturbing for the child (Han 42).

This story illustrates the ways in which gendered cultural norms interact with social policy and religious zeal, placing such mothers in impossible situations. Almost all the women who were not married mention the unbearable shame that becoming known to be pregnant implied not only for themselves but also for their whole family. One who gave birth in 1995 states: "To be an unwed mother in Korea is like being branded with a scarlet letter on the chest" (Han 49). Another remembers that: "the doctor told me that raising the baby would be disastrous for everyone involved" (Han 114). Several mention that they thought of suicide, and one tried to kill herself but was saved by a stomach pump (Han 49).

INTERNATIONAL OR DOMESTIC ADOPTION?

The letters reveal that once the decision was made to give a child up for adoption, a birthmother could request that her child be placed in South Korea or adopted internationally (Dorow *I Wish for You a Beautiful Life*), although not all of them know about the final location of their child. One writes: "I hoped you could be raised in Korea because then you could grow up without knowing you were adopted" (Dorow *I Wish for You a Beautiful Life* 101). In such cases the birthmother may find comfort in the fact that the child would remain in familiar cultural surroundings, and not be different in appearance from other children. One mother in the Holt collection writes: "I beg that the adoptive parents do everything for my daughter so that she does not become like me, an unwed mother." She continues: "Though I do not know whether my baby will be adopted within the country or abroad, I beg the adoptive parents that they love her and give her my share of love as well…" (Holt Children's Services 135).

The reasons given by some mothers for preferring overseas adoption are the possibility of it being open and the hope of meeting the child again (Han 28). They also believe that the child will have more opportunities abroad and live in a more accepting social context, "free from prejudice and discrimination" (Han 50). Some more recent letters, however, by women exposed to the critical accounts of some adult adoptees[10], reflect the fear that the racialized child may feel isolated and alienated, "looking for someone who looks like you among the people who look different from you" (Han 29). One expresses her disappointment on learning that the adoptive parents that she admired had divorced, just as she herself had done (Han 55).

Many of the birthmothers see themselves, rather than the child, as the victims of an impossible situation. One laments, "regardless of the wonderful opportunities my child will receive as a result of leaving this prejudiced land, I am forever guilty in the eyes of society" (Han 77–73). Nevertheless, those who record having met their child later, and in some cases also the adoptive mother, express relief and even delight. Contact through letters and photos, especially on birthdays, may be made possible through the agency. In other cases, the mother has sought her child in vain, since records were not always complete or accurate. One or two examples of correspondence with the adoptive mother illustrate a best-case scenario. As one birthmother puts it, "For a healthy adoption, I thought it would be necessary to share the facts and together fight through difficulties we would face" (Han 63).

Many of the Korean birthmothers express gratitude to the adoptive parents who are willing to raise their child. Several see the child as a "gift" to the family that desired one: "My heart aches when I think of the fact that you were given up for adoption, as I was a single unwed mother … but I should stop thinking in this way," one states, "because you were not given up but merely taken care of by different parents. I will consider you a gift to them and they will help you to grow up as a fine person" (Dorow *I Wish for You a Beautiful Life* 47). The use of the words "give" (up) and "gift" softens the guilt or irresponsibility implied by harsh terms like "abandoning" or "relinquishing" a child. It moves the birthmother into a position of choice and generosity, rather than the forced circumstances and neediness that characterize many of their narratives. Allowing the child to go to a supposedly better place is the unselfish act that redeems them and wipes out their past mistakes, making them examples of the Korean self-sacrificing mother.[11]

The artwork accompanying these texts (Dorow *I Wish for You a Beautiful Life*; Han), depicting Christian-style mother-and-child motifs (Briggs "Mother, Child, Race, Nation" 184), conveys images of what was lost but is retrieved by writing about it. Similar self-justifying emotions and reasons are stated in other letters: "I did not abandon you, I had no choice but to place you for adoption…because you were born of a mother with no husband" (Dorow *I Wish for You a Beautiful Life* 25). Another claims: "You needed to be loved by family members, and you could have that love only if you were in a family. I couldn't have given that love by myself ... adoption was my gift to you" (Dorow *I Wish for You a Beautiful Life* 37).

These explanations and justifications are accompanied by feelings of guilt and responsibility. One narrator whose story is in the Holt collection states, "In such a narrow-minded Korean society, it would be rough facing society as an unmarried mother raising a baby without a father.... She continues: "letting you go was the best choice ..." but nevertheless concludes: "I am very sorry" (Holt Children's Services 139). Another echoes the pervasive view (until recently) that the situation would be as bad for the child as for the mother: "I decided to have her adopted rather than have her suffer the misery of growing up forever taunted and labelled an outcast for being without a father and a child of an unwed mother." She adds: "I will remember that I did this for the baby's happiness and bear the pain" (Holt Children's Services 133–35). Until recently there was little or no financial or moral support for single mothers to raise a child alone in South Korea. In some cases the grandmother was ready to help, but this brought great shame on her also, as well as blame and in some cases threats of violence from her own husband. Another account in the Han collection provides a dual story, told by the grandmother of a child born at *Ae Ran Won* in 2004 as well as her daughter. The grandmother's husband left her and she raised her daughter as a single mother, only to become distraught when she discovered that the daughter had become pregnant without a husband. She blames herself and asks: "Would she have become a single mother if born into a normal family?" (Han 202). Horrified that her daughter would also suffer "the cold glare of our relatives and scornful criticism of our neighbours" (Han 203), she tells the child, "Don't feel you are the only one who was hurt" (204).

Very few of these narratives depict the father as playing an active role in the decision to allow the child to be adopted. Several narrators were expecting to marry the father, and only realized after they were pregnant that he was unfaithful, alcoholic, had many debts, or was already married (Han 85). In other cases the couple were both very young and unable to support themselves, let alone a child (Han 80). Most of the fathers who were aware of the situation expected the woman to have an abortion, and some offered to pay for it. Others simply disappeared right away. A number of women describe going to a clinic to terminate the pregnancy but being unable to go through with it, especially those who had already seen an ultrasound picture of the foetus (Han 70, 98).

Many of the writers express contradictory and shifting feelings, ranging from remorse, regret, and self-accusation to anger and resentment at
their own fate and that of the child. The desire to justify what happened
frequently emerges as a story of redemption through self-sacrifice in giving
up the child for adoption for its own good. This act, initially undertaken
under duress to ensure the mother's social survival, or because she cannot
afford to raise the child, becomes interpreted as the wisest choice since the
child would be stigmatized in Korea for having a single mother. The message most of the mothers want to send to their child is that they were not
abandoned for lack of love, but because they were loved. As one mother
puts it:

> How can I pity myself with the pain of sending you away? I
> just had to understand my future. …I had to give you up as
> soon as you were born, my lovely child, because I loved you so
> much. Maybe you will hate me. But I had to send you away
> because I was sending you to a better environment and a bet-
> ter place where you could be happy rather than live with an
> incompetent mother …it would be too cruel to raise you as
> the child of a single unwed mother in this society because of
> the way people would treat you. (Dorow *I Wish for You a
> Beautiful Life* 29)

THE ROLE OF CHRISTIANITY

Adoptions from South Korea to the United States were heavily marked,
from their start in the aftermath of the Korean War, by Christian missionary zeal.[12] About a quarter of Korea's population is currently affiliated with
some branch of Christianity, and many of the women who ended up at *Ae
Ran Won* already had contact with a church (Han 55). A number of them
mention the attendance at church services required at the maternity home
as part of a disciplined schedule to which some had difficulty adapting (Han
14, 61, 70). At least one was converted and baptized while there (71). Another, who came from a Catholic family although she herself had not been
practising the religion, was shocked when a priest refused to baptize her "illegitimate" child (165). One woman refers to a Bible story about a prostitute
being forgiven (Han 31).

One story recounts the ironic situation of a "good Christian girl" who taught Sunday school and had become a regular churchgoer in spite of her parents' opposition (Han 94-6), but nevertheless became pregnant by a fellow church member who turned out to be already married. Some church people reviled her, calling her a prostitute (98) and her child "the illegitimate trash of an equally worthless mother" (Han 102). Choi Hee An, a Korean feminist theologian, confirms in her account of Korean women's relationship with the Christian church that women who admitted to premarital sex were "disdained and treated as prostitutes" (Choi 68-69). She also mentions that some former prostitutes have been known to convert and become "aggressive, restrictive and conservative Christians" (93). While none of the birthmothers cited here fall into that category, many of those rejected by their own parents or partners find the concept of a protective and forgiving Father-God attractive. One reassures herself by writing to her child: "even though I can't be beside you and watch you grow up, I am not worried about it. I trust that God, who is always with me, will be with you forever" (Dorow *I Wish for You a Beautiful Life* 98). God may provide forgiveness and salvation, for both mother and child.

Christianity, for some of these women, has affinities with the Korean concept of *han*,[13] which has been defined as "the individual or collective consequence of being sinned against" (Clement 152). While some of the birthmothers confess that they themselves have "sinned" by being irresponsible or promiscuous, they also proclaim the fact that they were mostly sinned against, by men who deceived or let them down and a society that blamed only the women and refused to help them. As mentioned in some of the letters, the fact that some churches oppose abortion prevented many from terminating their pregnancy. Nevertheless, as Nicola Jones points out in her study of the various branches of the women's movement in Korea, Christianity initially had a liberating effect for many Korean women.

THE CURRENT SITUATION

The more recent entries in *Dreaming a World* reflect changes in the level of support provided for unwed mothers through training centres such as the one run by *Ae Ran Won*. Young mothers who give up their child are offered not only counselling and therapy but vocational training in a range of occupations, from cooking, sewing, flower-arranging, and hairdressing, to computer skills and assistance with high school completion. Some have received scholarships to continue their studies in Korea or the U.S., and a number of those selected for inclusion in the volume have gone on to contribute to *Ae Ran Won* by volunteering, becoming social workers, conducting workshops, or making financial contributions.

The biggest change is that women may now receive some government assistance to raise their child, although conditions are attached (Han 3): they must apply for the limited amount of funding available, with all the humiliation that entails, and agree to stay in a group home for young unmarried mothers, such as the one run by *Ae Ran Won*, where the number of places is very limited. According to Ms. Han, 80% of the single mothers who give birth at *Ae Ran Won* now wish to keep their child, compared to 1% in 1995 and 20% in 2000. However, since the amount of financial support they receive from the government is less than that given to adoptive parents, and terminates when the child is ten years old, the aim is to provide them with enough training to become financially independent.[14]

Other significant changes have occurred as the result of the abolition of the "male head of family" rule in 2008 (Nam). One birthmother explains in her story that every Korean previously had to be included in a family registry, and it was impossible in 1997 to register a child's birth without a father to sign (Han 87). This determined individual tracked the father down and forced him to marry her so that the child would have a name, although she never saw him again after that. Single-parent families have since become less exceptional, as the new changes to the Family Law benefit divorced women, who may now claim custody of their children, as well as single mothers.[15] Eleana Kim (*Adopted Territory* 37–38) mentions that single women may now adopt a child in Korea, and some relatively well-off individuals are doing so. The result is that far more women than ever before, single or formerly married, now live alone and may be raising children without a male partner.

The authors of the published letters from birthmothers did not benefit from the new laws, and continued with their lives as best they could. Several women who gave up their child say that they have since married and had other children. Most of them told their husband before marrying about the child they gave up, although some men have had difficulty accepting it and one such marriage ended in divorce when the mother wished to meet her child (Han 52-53). The reason for maintaining anonymity for many women, and for not publishing any accounts by others, is probably that they may have (re)married without telling their husband about the past, which they presumably are trying to forget, or fear losing their husband if attention is drawn to it. Raising children alone is financially difficult for a formerly married woman as well as for an unmarried one, and divorce used to be expensive to obtain, as explained by one determined mother who studied law in order to be able to arrange one for herself (Han 88).

For those who decide they cannot raise the child alone, for financial or other reasons, there are now more options available. Longer-term foster-care allows the mother to see the child and retain the possibility of regaining custody later, although this may be disturbing for the child and the foster family. Transnational adoptions are scheduled to be phased out, but South Korea's acceptance of the Hague Convention may lead to arguments for its continuation, if domestic placements are not available in sufficient numbers [16]. More open adoptions make reunions increasingly common. The results of such meetings, as described by adult adoptees, vary enormously. The well-documented experiences of adopters, adoptees, and birthmothers in the Korean context provide a wealth of material relevant to broader debates around the effects of transnational adoptions in general. Thus, the perspective of Korean birthmothers, through their "letters" to the relinquished child not only provides long awaited insight into the reasons for the continuation of adoptions from Korea, but also signifies the gendered role played by women in decisions involving mothering across borders.

NOTES

[1] These include Barbara Yngvesson's *Belonging in an Adopted World*, which includes India as well as Latin-American countries; Karen Dubinsky's *Babies Without Borders: Adoption and Migration across the Americas*; most recently Laura Briggs' *Somebody's Children: The Politics of Transracial and Transnational Adoption*; and Frances Latchford's edited collection *Adopting and Mothering*.

[2] For other works giving perspectives of birthmothers (U.S. and China) see: Laurel Kendall, "Birth Mothers' Imaginary Lives," in Volkman (162-85); Sara Dorow, *Transnational Adoption*; Bartholet's *Family Bonds: Adoption and the Politics of Parenting* and *Abuse and Neglect, Foster Drift, and the Adoption Alternative*. Briggs ("Making American Families" 610) points out Bartholet's connections to the neo-conservative American Enterprise Institute and successful lobbying for subsidies to white parents in the U.S. who raise children of colour. The title of Briggs' recent book *Somebody's Children* might be seen as a response to Bartholet's downplaying of the birthmothers' perspective. *Somebody's Child* is also the title of a recent collection of twenty-five personal stories by people adopted in British Columbia

(Gillespie and Van Luwen). This volume is a sequel to two collections of accounts of childlessness entitled *Nobody's Mother* and *Nobody's Father*.

3 Even more so in the past than now. Balcom traces the role of women's networks in the development of social work as a profession in North America. See also Herman, *Kinship by Design*.

4 However there is a surprising shift behind an increase in domestic adoptions of girls and international adoptions of boys in recent times in Korea, where of 1,314 children adopted domestically in 2009, 855 were girls and 459 boys. Girls, who are expected to grow up to be more docile and contribute more in the home, are preferred. See "Girls favored over boys in adoption" (*Korea Times* 11 May 2010). Web. 23 Dec. 2010. The figures for 2011 show a further increase in the disparity, with 1,066 girls to 482 boys (KCARE).

5 Briggs ("Locating Adoption"; *Somebody's Children*) challenges the assumption that international adoption in the U.S. is due to the lack of available children there.

6 My own reading adopts the approach set out by Smith and Watson in *Reading Autobiography. A Guide for Interpreting Life Narratives*.

7 Since then things have changed, and there are now around forty maternity homes.

8 The botanical image also seems to be a logical extension of Bertha Holt's *The Seed from the East*.

9 Jones (33) provides insight into this pervasive problem of violence in Korea related to the consumption of alcohol. Lee Sung-Eun also graphically describes the kind of corporate sexual culture situation that young women may find themselves in, causing them potentially to end up somewhere like *Ae Ran Won*. Also, what is more intriguing is the fact that the social workers at agencies in Canada dealing with adoptions from Korea overemphasize the use of alcohol by a few birthmothers by stating: "due [to] the changing culture in Korea, more of the birthmothers have a history of some alcohol use and smoking during their pregnancy" (Sunrise Family Services Society). The Children's Bridge website similarly warns potential applicants of the need to educate themselves as to the risks of "recreational" smoking and drinking by birthmothers, in other words to be prepared for more health problems than the record might lead them to expect. This emphasis on what is obviously deemed irresponsible behavior by the mothers, putting the health of their child at risk, echoes the images associated with "underclass welfare mothers" in the United States, as discussed by Briggs (*Somebody's Children*) in analyzing the ways in which "underclass" American birthmothers are encoded as not deserving to keep their child.

[10] Many accounts by individual adoptees, including Katy Robinson (*A Single Square Picture*; "Relative Choices") and Jane Jeong Trenka (*The Language of Blood*; *Fugitive Visions*), begin with memories of being "reborn" in the air, from the artificial womb of a plane. Others have also opted to tell their own individual story in public include works such as: *Seeds from a Silent Tree* (Bishoff and Rankin), *Voices from Another Place* (Cox) and *After the Morning Calm* (Wilkinson and Fox). The first book-length autobiographical account was *The Unforgotten War: Dust of the Streets* by Thomas Park Clement, a biracial man adopted at the end of the Korean War who became a "poster boy" for early Korean adoptees. (On Clement, see E. Kim *Adopted Territory* 80–81, 83–86, 96–97). Most accounts by those adopted later have been by women, including Elizabeth Kim's *Ten Thousand Sorrows*, Joanne Higginson's *Unlocking the Past*, and Jeanne Vance's *Twins Found in a Box*, which are all mentioned by Palmer.

[11] Korean feminist scholar Lee Sang-Wha explains the force of patriarchal control in Korea by a theoretical model showing the centrality of the family, embedded within a larger system encompassing political, military, and social institutions, organizations of production, and ideology (S. W. Lee "Patriarchy and Confucianism" 70); see also B. Y. Lee.

[12] As illustrated in the personal accounts by Bertha Holt (*The Seed from the East*; *Bringing My Sons From Afar*).

[13] See Jae Ran Kim "Scattered Seeds. The Christian Influence on Korean Adoption" (152), and Choi (4) on *han* as reflecting "the subjective experience of those who have been oppressed politically, exploited economically, and marginalized socially."

[14] In 2009 a monthly payment of $85 per child to families adopting children was introduced—about twice the allowance to single women raising their child alone. At the same time a small group of South Korean women established the first association to defend the rights of unmarried pregnant women to raise their own children. Many unmarried mothers do not apply for assistance because of the stigma still attached to their situation. A government-sponsored survey estimated that 96% of those who discover they are pregnant obtain abortions (although they are still officially illegal except in specific circumstances); 70% of those who gave birth opted for adoption, and 90% of the 1,250 Korean children adopted abroad in 2008 were born to single women. For details see Choe.

[15] "South Korea Divorce Quick and Cheap" (*People's Daily* 25 Aug. 2006). Web. 12 June 2012.

[16] For more discussion on the issue, see Bagga.

WORKS CITED

"A Generation Fights to Reform Adoption Laws." *Joong Ang Daily.* 11 Nov. 2009. Web. 29 Nov. 2009.

"Adoption Law: Nation Needs to Join Hague Convention." *Korea Times* 28 Sept. 2010. Web. 23 Dec. 2010.

Bagga, Rupa. "Perceptions and Deceptions: Perspectives of Adoptions from South Korea to North America." Diss. University of British Columbia, 2012. Print.

Balcom, Karen A. *The Traffic in Babies: Cross-Border Adoption and Baby-Selling Between the United States and Canada, 1930–1972.* Toronto, ON: University of Toronto Press, 2011. Print.

Bartholet, Elizabeth. *Family Bonds: Adoption and the Politics of Parenting.* Boston: Houghton Mifflin, 1994. Print.

Bishoff, Tonya, and Jo Rankin, eds. *Seeds from a Silent Tree: An Anthology by Korean Adoptees.* San Diego: Pandal Press, 1997. Print.

Briggs, Laura. "Mother, Child, Race, Nation: The Visual Iconography of Rescue and the Politics of Transnational and Transracial Adoption." *Gender and History* 15.2 (2003): 179-200. Print.

—. "Locating Adoption in Relation to State Processes: War, Economics, Trauma, Politics." Paper presented at the University of Michigan, May 19–22, 2005. Print.

—. "Making American Families: Transnational Adoption and U.S. Latin American Policy." *Haunted by Empire.* Ed. Ann Laura Stoler. Durham, NC: Duke University Press, 2006. 606–42. Print.

—. *Somebody's Children: The Politics of Transracial and Transnational Adoption.* Durham, NC: Duke University Press, 2012. Print.

Children's Bridge. *Children's Bridge.* Web. 12 Feb. 2012.

Clement, Thomas Park. *The Unforgotten War: Dust of the Streets.* Bloomfield, Indiana: Truepeny Publishing Company, 1998. Print.

Choe, Sang-Hun. "Group Resists Korean Stigma for Unwed Mothers." *New York Times.* 7 Oct. 2009. Web. 14 Aug. 2011.

Choi, Hee An. *Korean Women and God: Experiencing God in a Multi-Religious Colonial Context.* Maryknoll, NY: Orbis Books, 2005. Print.

Cox, Susan Soon-Keum, ed. *Voices From Another Place: A Collection of Works from a Generation Born in Korea and Adopted to Other Coun-*

tries. St. Paul, Minnesota: Yeong and Yeong, 1999. Print.

Deuchler, Martina. *The Confucian Transformation of Korea.* Cambridge, Massachusetts: Harvard University Press, 1992. Print.

Dorow, Sara, ed. *I Wish for You a Beautiful Life: Letters from the Korean Birth Mothers of Ae Ran Won.* St. Paul, Minnesota: Yeong & Yeong, 1999. Print.

—. "'China R Us?': Care, Consumption, and Transnationally Adopted Children." *Symbolic Childhood.* Ed. Daniel Thomas Cook. New York: Peter Lang, 2002. 149–68. Print.

—. *Transnational Adoption: A Cultural Economy of Race, Gender, and Kinship.* New York: New York University Press, 2006. Print.

Dubinsky, Karen. *Babies Without Borders: Adoption and Migration across the Americas.* Toronto: University of Toronto Press, 2010. Print.

Duncan, Patti. "Genealogies of Unbelonging: Amerasians and Transnational Adoptees as Legacies of U.S. Militarism in South Korea." *Militarized Currents: Toward a Decolonized Future in Asia and Pacific.* Ed. Setsu Shigematsu and Keith L. Camacho. Minneapolis: University of Minnesota Press, 2010. 277–307. Print.

Gillespie, Bruce, and Lynne Van Luven, eds. *Somebody's Child: Stories About Adoption.* Vancouver: Touchwood, 2012. Print.

"Girls favored over boys in adoption." *Korea Times* 11 May 2010. Web. 23 Dec. 2010.

Grice, Helena. "Transracial Adoption Narratives." *Meridians: Feminism, Race, Transnationalism* 52.2 (2005): 124-48. Print.

Hall, Nicola. *Gender and the Political Opportunities of Democratization in South Korea.* New York: Palgrave Macmillan, 2006. Print.

Han, Sangsoon, ed. *Dreaming a World. Korean Birthmothers Tell Their Stories.* St. Paul, MN: Yeong & Yeong, 2010. Print.

Herman, Ellen. *Kinship by Design: A History of Adoption in the Modern United States.* Chicago: University of Chicago Press, 2008. Print.

Higginson, Joanne, and Peter Kearly. *Unlocking the Past: A True Story.* Michigan: A.N.Y.O. Publishing Company, 2003. Print.

Holt Children's Services. *To My Beloved Baby: Writings of Birth Mothers.* Seoul: Holt Children's Services, 2004. Print.

Holt, Bertha. *The Seed from the East.* Eugene, Oregon: Holt International Children's Services, 1956/1976. Print.

—. *Created For God's Glory*. Eugene, Oregon: Holt International Children's Services, 1982.

—. *Bringing My Sons From Afar: The Unfolding of Harry Holt's Dreams*. Eugene, Oregon: Holt International Children's Services, 1986/1992. Print.

Holt, Harry Mrs., and David Wisner. *The Seed From the East: The Outstretched Arms*. Eugene, OR: Industrial Publishing Company/Holt Children's Services, 1956/1986. Print.

Hübinette, Tobias. *Comforting an Orphaned Nation*. Seoul: Jimoodang, 2006. Print.

Jones, Nicola Anne. *Gender and the Political Opportunities of Democratization in South Korea*. New York: Palgrave Macmillan, 2006. Print.

Kendall, Laurel. "Birth Mothers and Imaginary Lives." *Cultures of Transnational Adoption*. Ed. Toby Alice Volkman. Durham: Duke University Press, 2005. 162–84. Print.

Kim, Andrew. "A History of Christianity in Korea: From its Troubled Beginning to its Contemporary Success." *Korea Journal* 35.2 (1995): 34–53. Print.

Kim, Eleana. "Wedding Citizenship and Culture: Korean Adoptees and the Global Family of Korea." *Cultures of Transnational Adoption*. Ed. Toby Alice Volkman. Durham: Duke University Press, 2005. 81–116. Print.

—. "The Origin of Korean Adoption: Cold War Geopolitics and Intimate Diplomacy." US-Korea Institute Working Paper Series: Washington DC, 2009. Print.

—. *Adopted Territory: Transnational Korean Adoptees and the Politics of Belonging*. Durham, NC: Duke University Press, 2010. Print.

Kim, Elizabeth. *Ten Thousand Sorrows: The Extraordinary Journey of a Korea War Orphan*. New York: Bantam Books, 2000. Print.

Kim, Hyun Mee. "The Formation of Subjectivities among Korean Women Workers: A Historical Review." *Women's Experiences and Feminist Practices in South Korea*. Ed. Chang Philwa and Kim Eun-Shil. Seoul: Ehwa Womans University Press, 2005. 177–204. Print.

Kim, Jae Ran. "The Christian Influence of Korean Adoption." *Outsiders Within: Writing on Transracial Adoption*. Ed. Jane Jeong Trenka, Julia Chinyere Oparah, and Sun Yung Shin. Cambridge, Massachusetts: South End Press, 2006. 151–62. Print.

Korea Central Adoption Resources (KCARE). Domestic Adoption Statistics from 1958–2011. Web. 13 Mar. 2012.

Latchford, Frances. *Adoption and Mothering*. Toronto: Demeter Press, 2012. Print.

Lee, Bae-Yong. "Family Ethics and Women's Status Within Confucian Tradition and its Transformation." *Feminist Cultural Politics in Korea*. Ed. Jung Hwa Oh. Seoul: Prunsasang Publishing, 2005. 45–85. Print.

Lee, Sang-Wha. "Patriarchy and Confucianism." *Women's Experiences and Feminist Practices in South Korea*. Ed. Chang Philwa and Kim Eun-Shil. Seoul: Ehwa Womans University Press, 2005. 67–116. Print.

—. "The Adoption of Feminism in Korean Philosophy and Consequential Changes in the Philosophical System." *Feminist Cultural Politics in Korea*. Ed. Jung Hwa Oh. Seoul: Prunsasang Publishing, 2005. 2–44. Print.

Lee, Sung-Eun. "The Office Party: Corporate Sexual Culture and Sexual Harassment in the South Korean Workplace." *East Asian Sexualities: Modernity, Gender and New Sexual Cultures*. Ed. Stevi Jackson, Liu Jieyu, and Woo Juhyun. London/New York: Zed Books, 2008. 69–80. Print.

McDade, Kathryn. *Intercountry Adoption in Canada: Public Policy*. Ottawa: Studies in Social Policy, 1991. Print.

Moon, Katherine. *Sex Among Allies: Military Prostitution in US-Korea Relations*. New York: Columbia University Press, 1997. Print.

—. "South Korean Movements Against Militarized Sexual Labor." *Asia Survey* 39.2 (1999): 310–27. Print.

Nam, Sanghui. "The Women's Movement and the Transformation of the Family Law in South Korea: Interactions Between Local, National and Global Structures." *European Journal of East Asian Studies* 9.1 (2010): 67–86. Print.

Ochiai, Emiko, and Barbara Molony, eds. *Asia's New Mothers: Crafting Gender Roles and Childcare Networks in East and Southeast Asian Societies*. Folkestone, UK: Global Oriental, 2008. Print.

Palmer, John D. *The Dance of Identities: Korean Adoptees and Their Journey Toward Empowerment*. Honolulu: University of Hawaii Press, 2011. Print.

Peterson, Mark. "Some Korean Attitudes Towards Adoption." *Korea Journal* 11 (1977): 28–31. Print.

Robinson, Katy. *A Single Square Picture: A Korean Adoptee's Search for Her Roots*. New York: Berkley Books, 2002. Print.

—. "Relative Choices. Adoption and the American Family. Tracing my Roots Back to Korea." *New York Times* 6 Nov. 2007. Web. 6 Nov. 2011.

Smith, Sidonie, and Julia Watson. *Reading Autobiography, Theory: A Reader.* Minneapolis: University of Minnesota Press, 2001. Print.

"South Korea Divorce Quick and Cheap." *People's Daily.* 25 Aug. 2006. Web. 12 June 2012.

Sunrise Adoption and Family Service Society (Canada). 2005. Web. 20 Jan. 2005.

Sunrise Family Services Society. "Korea 1: Adoption Information" 2007 [pamphlet]. Print.

Trenka, Jane Jeong. *The Language of Blood: A Memoir.* St. Paul, Minnesota: Minnesota Historical Society Press, 2003. Print.

—. *Fugitive Visions: An Adoptee's Return to Korea.* Saint Paul: Minnesota: Graywolf Press, 2009. Print.

—, Julia Chinyere Oparah, and Sun Yung Shin, eds. *Outsiders Within: Writing on Transracial Adoption.* Cambridge, Massachusetts: South End Press, 2006. Print.

Vance, Jeanne. *Twins Found in a Box: Adapting to Adoption.* Illinois: First Book Library, 2003. Print.

Volkman, Toby Alice, ed. *Cultures of Transnational Adoption.* Durham: Duke University Press, 2005. Print.

Westhues, Anne, and Joyce S. Cohen. 1995. *Intercountry Adoption in Canada.* Ontario: National Welfare Grants, Human Resources Development Canada, 1995. Print.

Wilkinson, Sook, and Nancy Fox, eds. *After the Morning Calm: Reflections of Korean Adoptees.* Minneapolis: Sunrise Ventures, 2006. Print.

Yngvesson, Barbara. "Placing the 'Gift Child' in Transnational Adoption." *Law and Society Review* 36.2 (2002): 227–41. Print.

—. *Belonging in an Adopted World: Race, Identity, and Transnational Adoption.* Chicago: University of Chicago Press, 2010. Print.

III: East Asian Mothers Moving Toward Social Justice

13.

Reproductive Justice and Mothering

API Activists Redefine a Movement

KRYN FREEHLING-BURTON AND EVELINE SHEN

Reproductive Justice is the complete physical, mental, spiritual, political, economic, and social well-being of women and girls, and will be achieved when women and girls have the economic, social and political power and resources to make healthy decisions about our bodies, sexuality and reproduction for ourselves, our families and our communities in all areas of our lives. *A New Vision*, 2005

In 1989, a group of Asian and Pacific Islander (API) activists from the Bay Area on the west coast of the United States formed an organization to empower women to participate in their own reproductive health, challenge the hegemonic women's movement around reproductive choice, and chart new directions for communities with respect to women's reproductive lives. Today this organization is called Forward Together but many know its work under its previous names, Asian Pacific Islanders for Choice (APIC), Asians and Pacific Islanders for Reproductive Health (APIRH), and most recently the Asian Communities for Reproductive Justice (ACRJ). Forward Together was the first API organization in the pro-choice movement and is a founding member of SisterSong Women of Color Reproductive Health Collective. The organization was instrumental in the reframing of reproductive choice as reproductive *justice*. With roots in the women's health and civil rights movement, reproductive justice in API communities is situated in specific historical contexts that include a legacy of historical and contemporary anti-Asian immigration restrictions as well as the need to overcome stereotypes about Asian women and other women of color (Silliman et al. 158–164). As the organization states on their website, "The Reproductive Justice framework stipulates that reproductive oppression is a result of the intersections of multiple oppressions and is inherently connected to the struggle for social justice and human rights" (ACRJ 1).

Centering reproductive justice in a volume on mothering is critical for understanding the ways bodies of women are imagined, legislated, and restricted even before motherhood begins. Within Asian Pacific Islander communities, it is particularly critical, as there is a long history within North America of restricting and regulating the bodies of Asian women and other women of color. Forward Together keeps women of color and youth in focus, and engages in participatory action research to center the needs of specific marginalized communities. Activism conceptualized by women, in all the specificity of our various identity markers, illuminates powerful ways we can connect with the histories of body rights and mother rights in order to imagine a future where all women may freely choose if, when, and how we become mothers.

THE BEGINNING

Forward Together started in 1989 when a group of East Asian activists came together to form what was initially called Asian Pacific Islanders for Choice (APIC). APIC identified the need to mobilize when states started controlling abortion access at the state level. This particular group of women came together to promote an API voice within the larger pro-choice movement as volunteer community organizers. APIC wanted to address issues from broader and more holistic perspective than the reproductive choice movement often did.

APIC affirmed that the encompassing health and reproductive rights of Asian Pacific Islander women included abortion access but worked to de-center abortion access as API women's only or most important issue as was common for the larger mainstream pro-choice movement in the United States in the 1980s. These activists held focus groups and meetings across California with various ethnic groups within the API community culminating in a large conference where they brought everyone together and discussed the various ways in which the community's reproductive health is impacted. The founders decided to focus on addressing the root causes of reproductive restrictions and making change around these causes instead of just providing services. APIC was subsequently renamed Asian Communities for Reproductive Justice (ACRJ) to more accurately reflect the focus of the organization that was emerging as a leader within the national Reproductive Justice movement. ACRJ wrote the paper that identified for the first time the differences between reproductive health, reproductive justice, and reproductive rights and provided a definition of reproductive justice that was one of the first to be articulated.[1]

At its core, reproductive justice centers a race and gender analysis and is connected to an intersectional approach for organizing around reproductive issues within communities of color. Centering an intersectional analysis of race, class, gender, and sexuality for women of color communities led the leaders to incorporate reproductive justice in this new name. The term, reproductive justice, emerged from the experiences of women of color, and attempts to move beyond a simplistic focus on "choice," or a binary "pro-choice"/"pro-life" framework, so often employed by the mainstream reproductive rights movement. A reproductive justice approach places reproductive health issues within a larger social, economic, and political context, linking these issues to other movements for social justice. In ACRJ, the commitment to Asian leadership with that analysis was strong. Early work of APIC/ACRJ was locally focused but activists quickly realized that working at the local level, with school districts for instance, was insufficient; work also needed to be done at the state level because the communities are directly impacted by what happens at the state policy level. As the Reproductive Justice movement started to grow nationally, ACRJ began working with Reproductive Justice groups from around the country. This national work became more multiracial; coalitions and collaborations became the norm. After the paper was published, ACRJ received many requests from people and organizations wanting to work together. One result of a strategic visioning process was the realization that one of the core strengths ACRJ brought to the movement was bringing folks together. ACRJ provided spaces for groups that did not know each other but were working on a common issue or common strategy to come together[2] and be able to do things they would not be able to do as easily on their own. ACRJ wrote analyses and reports about the state of the Reproductive Justice movement, particularly addressing the connection between youth organizing and reproductive justice.

YOUTH FOCUS

In 2012 ACRJ became Forward Together, in part to recognize the local work with Asian youth from East Asia and Southeast Asia. Forward Together now includes young men and the youth are working on getting comprehensive sex education in the school district in Oakland. Recognizing from the beginning that young women play an important role in our communities and in our families, Forward Together remains committed to centering the voices, experiences, and programs of youth. Within immigrant families daughters are often the ones who provide caretaking work, taking the older family members to the doctor and providing translation. At the same time there is no place for them to talk about what they need and want to help build their empowerment as young Asian women. Listening to these young women and privileging their needs and perspectives is core to the work of Eveline Shen, the executive director of Forward Together since 1998. Under Shen's leadership, Forward Together's work has focused on strong families and innovative leadership in various iterations.

STRONG FAMILIES

The Strong Families Initiative is a long-term plan for changing the way that Forward Together supports families in the U.S. According to the 2010 census, close to 80% of households in the United States do not have a family that is the traditional nuclear family form of a heterosexual couple with their biological kids. Forward Together works toward having policies in our country reflect what our families actually look like and what these families need. At the core of Forward Together's policy work is the reproductive justice analysis and the commitment of Strong Families is that every member in every family has the opportunity to thrive, especially focusing on people who have not traditionally had those opportunities to thrive—women, girls, and queer and trans people. The idea of a strong family includes explicit connotations about equity and justice within families and making sure that conditions outside of families are supportive of this equity and justice. Forward Together focuses on families that have traditionally been on the margins, including LGBTQ families, families of color, immigrant families, single-parent families, and families who have members who have been incarcerated. The Strong Families Initiative centers these families to identify the range of issues that must be addressed in order to achieve justice, including immigration policies, marriage equality, and affordable childcare.

INNOVATIVE LEADERSHIP

Understanding how our lived experiences work and practicing an intersectional analysis contribute to innovative leadership within the organization as well as in the larger community. Work in the United States is very silo-ed; for instance, people work on environmental justice or immigrant rights or ending gender-based violence. However, Forward Together recognizes that people do not experience climate change on Monday and then health care issues on Tuesday. We are affected by all of these issues simultaneously and the innovation of our framework comes in recognizing that you cannot just work on one issue without seeing the connections to the other issues. You cannot just work on one aspect of oppression; you have to see the connections between oppressions. Someone who is a low-income queer Asian person in Arkansas is going to face very different experiences than that person if they lived in LA and so at any moment you do not know if what you are facing is due to your sexuality, your sex, or your race. These identity markers cannot be separated from one another.

One example of how Forward Together youth practice innovative leadership is their 2012 "Let's Get it On" study about Oakland School District's sex education curriculum. California has one of the most comprehensive sex education laws in the country but lack of funding prevents consistency and enforcement. These youth activists completed their own research project about the current state of sex education in the Oakland School District, found the gaps, and are working on a campaign to raise awareness, including the publication of their report, "Let's Get It On," and an intervention in the district curriculum. The research confirmed that Asian parents are supportive of sex education, even though there often is not much communication within Asian families about sex. Language and working parents are only two of a number of reasons for this minimal communication within families. This is not even necessarily specific to Asian families; parents of many kinds do not feel comfortable talking about issues about sexuality with their kids. The youths' research confirmed that the Oakland School District does attempt to follow California state law regarding offering comprehensive, accurate sex education in the schools, but the curricula is not always culturally appropriate nor does it address what the youth desire to learn. School curricula are also not the only way that Asian youth access sex education. Oakland Asian youth articulate a desire for sex education that goes beyond condoms and contraception.

Sex education has the potential to play an integral role in addressing some of the critical needs within Asian communities. How do individuals negotiate relationships and the sexual encounters that accompany these relationships? For instance, Forward Together staff and mentors note that violence is one of the top three most important issues that young Asian women face, whether it is violence on the street, domestic violence, or violence in their relationships. Comprehensive sex education can provide the tools to negotiate and navigate relationships in ways that could mitigate the violence.

IMMIGRATION REFORM

Asians are the fastest growing race or ethnic group in the United States (2012 U.S. Census). Immigration reform and immigrant rights are critical areas for API activism because so many Asian immigrants have children. They are mothers. They work in industries not addressed by those crafting immigration reform. Legislators and policy makers are focusing on opening up opportunities for immigrants with science and technology degrees (STEM), but a lot of the women Forward Together works with are working in hotels; they're doing domestic work. They are not in STEM areas so their pathways to citizenship are drastically limited. Immigrant women, and especially mothers, who have been in this country for many years do not have the same kinds of opportunities to become citizens as many men do. Family unification, accessing health care, jobs with secure wages and benefits are main priorities for Forward Together's intersectional approach to reproductive justice that includes immigration concerns, extending far beyond the standard list of contraception and abortion access.

ACCESS TO REPRODUCTIVE RESOURCES

Another area of focus for the organization is access to reproductive resources. Knowing where to go and being able to go and get the services needed is critical for reproductive justice to be achieved. Young people seeking abortions in an area without an abortion provider do not have access to the full range of options for reproductive health. Neither do people for whom the local Planned Parenthood or other clinic does not provide language specific services. Women who decide to have their babies as young mothers face particular societal pressures and expectations that can differ greatly in their family or cultural understandings. In some cultures within the Asian communities being a young mother is valued but the stigma towards young parents in the United States and the accompanying policies or lack of policies that protect young parents prevent these young mothers from accessing reproductive justice. It is not justice when young women who want to keep their babies and become mothers and also stay in school are kicked out of school. Many of these young mothers are tracked to alternative high schools, denied excused absences to take their kids to the doctor, or do not have access to child care. Forward Together works to support young mothers by addressing these issues and advocating the creation of policies that help them rather than stigmatize them.

MAMA'S DAY CAMPAIGN

Asian motherhood is so often stigmatized and targeted. Education, ending gender-based violence, immigration rights, young mothers, mothers who are in relationships where there is violence, and resisting rhetoric about anchor babies are critical pieces of reproductive justice. Forward Together's Strong Families Initiative is shifting the ways society sees mothers who are often invisible, targeted, or stigmatized. The aim of this campaign is to humanize these mothers.

The Mama's Day Campaign suggests that mothers need more than flowers and chocolates once a year. We need access to health care, clean drinking water, and reproductive health. We need to sleep free from violence and earn a living wage. Forward Together captures the invisibility of Asian mothers in our communities and makes their faces visible in a celebratory way through the "Mama's Day Our Way" campaign. Through a series of blogs that link to specific policies that Forward Together and other organizations are working on right now this campaign connects motherhood to larger social change. In addition to changing policy, the organization aims to shift culture so that all mothers are recognized whether or not they are documented, regardless of their sexual orientation, their age, their ability, etc. The heart of the Mama's Day Campaign is a series of e-cards that people can send to their mamas and others directly from the webpage to honor mothers in our lives on Mother's Day (and beyond). Social change artists created original art that makes visible the wide range of mothers in our society. The images feature lone moms, incarcerated mothers, lesbian mamas, fathers who mother, other mothers, and more. These are moms that deserve to be honored and celebrated who are not often recognized in the mainstream society. People sent more that six million e-cards last year. Mobilizing around Mother's Day can shift people's thinking around supporting all different kinds of moms and standing in solidarity with them.

CONCLUDING THOUGHTS

The Mama's Day campaign is just one of the many tangible examples of Forward Together's work for reproductive justice. The importance of Forward Together in the national reproductive justice movement cannot be understated. From its inception and its involvement in the earliest of conversations about reframing notions of choice for women of color, to its contemporary campaigns today, Forward Together keeps a race and gender analysis at the core of its work. An intersectional approach informs their research, policy development and analysis, and grassroots activism. Their sex education research and policy recommendations, for example, demonstrate this intersectional approach by the use of community-based, youth participatory work. Forward Together's commitment to reproductive justice cannot be separated from how we negotiate power in relationships, the language barriers we encounter, or the particular realities of young Asian women in their families and communities. This integration of reproductive justice with realities API mothers face is confirmed by the research conducted by youth themselves about what they and their peers were learning and wanted to learn about sex education in school. The organization supported teens in the research design and the subsequent reporting of the results to the Oakland School District but proudly recognize and present the work as the youth's contribution to the movement. This report entitled, *Let's Get It On*, is available on the website (http://forwardtogether.org/youth-organizing/youth-organizing-campaigns).

Working with multiracial and multi-ethnic communities, Forward Together expands its influence beyond Asian Pacific Islander communities through the multiple coalitions and collaborations maintained since the 1990s. The lived experiences of individuals inform the organization's work. To humanize those mothers most at risk (including young mothers, immigrant mothers, queer and trans mothers, disabled mothers) we all must be free from violence, have access to reproductive health care, clean drinking water, living wages, affordable childcare, and secure immigrant status. Forward Together uniquely positions itself with those on the margins of society in order to advance security and justice in our daily lives. Those most invisible, targeted, and stigmatized find voice and space to contribute to conversations and policies that help individuals and families from API communities. Mothers are supported best when the fullness of our experiences is recognized and supported. Forward Together makes this support real.

Explore Forward Together at forwardtogether.org. SisterSong can be found at www.sistersong.net. Many thanks to the staff of Forward Together.

NOTES

[1]See this definition at the beginning of this paper. This definition, though formalized by ACRJ, reflects the work of many activists who began collaborating in 1994 when the phrase reproductive justice was coined at a Black women's caucus.
[2]Some of the groups who benefitted from working in connection with one another include Casa Atabex Aché, SisterLove, MoonLodge, and the National Asian Women's Health Organization.

WORKS CITED

Asian Communities for Reproductive Justice. "A New Vision for advancing our movement for reproductive health, reproductive rights and reproductive justice." *Forward Together* 18 July 2013. Web. 2005.

Silliman, Jael, Marlene Gerber Fried, Loretta Ross, and Elena R. Gutiérrez. *Undivided Rights: Women of Color Organize for Reproductive Justice.* Cambridge: South End Press, 2004. Print.

14.

For the Family

Filipino Migrant Mothers' Activism and their Transnational Families[1]

VALERIE FRANCISCO

In March of 2007, a Filipino domestic worker named Felisa "Fely" Garcia was found hanging from her closet in her rented room in the Bronx, New York City. The New York Police Department (NYPD) officers who came to assess the crime scene found four suicide letters after they collected her body. One letter stated that Garcia sustained abuses and harassment from her erstwhile employer, Werner Oppenheimer; she noted that she had apologized for something that offended Oppenheimer to no avail and that this conflict was one of the main reasons for her death. Although the letters left gaping questions about the conditions under which Garcia chose to take her own life, the scene of the crime led the NYPD investigators, and later the New York Philippine Consulate, to cease any further investigation on Garcia's case, specifically her situation with her employer. After the NYPD's autopsy report was released stating that there was "no foul play, rape or physical abuse" found on Garcia's body, Consul General Edgar Badajos reiterated the finding in an official statement urging Garcia's family, friends and the public to focus on the repatriation of her body (Villadiego).

Garcia's landlord, the person who found her, and Garcia's roommates were devastated at the tragedy, and were confused as they attested to Garcia's jovial disposition in the days and even night of her suicide. Moreover, they were infuriated that there would be no further inquiry from the state or the consulate about Garcia's troubled relationship with Oppenheimer. Without any contact information for Garcia's family in the Philippines, two

Filipino immigrants who rented rooms in the same house as Garcia decided to look for some community support to demand further investigation into Garcia's case. Within the ethnic enclave of Filipino businesses, groceries, and organizations in the Roosevelt neighborhood in Queens, they found a Filipino community center called Philippine Forum that housed an organizing program called *Kabalikat* (literally translated as "shoulder to shoulder") Domestic Workers Support Network. This small and nascent group of fifteen Filipino domestic workers, only formed a couple of months earlier around offering computer classes to domestic workers, suddenly found a full-blown campaign on their laps.

It took *Kabalikat* members—who were not trained community organizers or seasoned activists—about five minutes after hearing Garcia's story to sign up to take on the campaign as their first real project. In the hour-long meeting with Fely's roommates, *Kabalikat* members immediately referred to Fely as *Ate*[2] Fely with an honorific reserved for older sisters in Filipino, and they asked about her family in the Philippines and her job situation in New York. Garcia's friends gave them the little details they knew about Fely's life and the sparse information about her four children. Joan, a new member of *Kabalikat* who had only been to the community center twice, said:

> *Naku, anong mangyayari sa mga bata? Yan talaga ang ki-nakatakutan ko, kung maymangyari man sakin, God forbid. Ang iniisip ko parati ay ang mga anak ko, paano na sila kung hindi ko sila mapadalhan. Anong mangyayari sa mga anak niya?*
>
> Oh no; what will happen to her kids? That's exactly what I fear, if something happens to me, God forbid. All I think about is my children, what'll happen to them if I can't send money back. What will happen to her kids?

Immediately after Joan made this comment, a flurry of side conversations exploded with each *Kabalikat* member talking about their own families and their fears about something tragic like this happening to them. With their own families in mind, they felt the urgency in Ate Fely's case in that her body was still languishing in a morgue in the Bronx. In bewilderment, they also identified the Philippine consulate in New York as accountable to at least notify Ate Fely's family and, at best, to offer financial support to repatriate Ate Fely back to her family in the Philippines. They talked about how sad it would be if Ate Fely's family would not be able to see her again, even in death. They commented that culturally, Filipinos hold the ritual of a wake, a funeral and prayers with high regard; how then would Ate Fely's family move forward without her body?

At the end of the meeting and with the help and suggestions of staff organizers at the Philippine Forum, they decided on three forms of action: holding a community town hall meeting at the community center in Queens; starting a petition to demand further investigation of Ate Fely's death and her employer; and organizing a grassroots fundraising campaign to demand the consulate to pay for the costs of Ate Fely's repatriation back to her home in Batangas, Philippines. As a volunteer at Philippine Forum with the *Kabalikat* program and a researcher in my early years of graduate school, I saw Filipina migrants' instantaneous agreement to help Garcia, basically a stranger to many *Kabalikat* members, and I wondered, what did they see in Ate Fely that moved them to find an affinity towards her life, and more importantly, her death? What about Ate Fely did *Kabalikat* members relate to so much so that they volunteered their days off and after-work hours to help repatriate her body? How did these seemingly disconnected women come together under such intense conditions to fight for a dead woman they did not know? With these thoughts in mind, the more sociological question I have come to are: Under what conditions do migrant Filipina domestic workers join together to form bonds of solidarity and political mobilization? And, what processes of identification and political subjectivities were activated to unite for the Justice for Fely Garcia campaign?

In this chapter, I explore the different political subjectivities migrant domestic workers use as resources for political mobilization in their migrant destinations. Deepening literature on domestic worker mobilization, I use evidence from my research to highlight that domestic worker organizing not only hinges on the political subjectivities of migrant and domestic workers but also experiences as women and mothers. A majority of migrant domestic workers in my study are transnational mothers, many separated from their young children for an extended amount of time. I find that they draw on their new meanings of motherhood, produced through both imagined and material familial relations and responsibilities, to activate political organizing and mobilization for one another. Following literature on activist mothering, especially activist mothers with absent, disappeared, or extracted, children and families, I argue that migrant mothers are using a similar basis of motherhood to address material abuses and exploitation they face daily even without their children in proximity. I provide evidence that Filipino domestic workers, specifically around the case of Fely Garcia in 2007, use their experiences of separation from their families in the Philippines as a resource for solidarity and mobilization around common issues. Lastly, I highlight the role of neoliberal globalization in producing transnational families and the exploitative conditions under which migrant domestic workers live, thereby calling into question the viability of a political economic structure that reduces families into aggregate profitable units while simultaneously discarding and devaluing familial obligations.

METHODS

From 2007 to 2011, I conducted qualitative research with Filipino domestic workers in New York City and their families left behind in Manila, Philippines. This multi-sited research was conducted through interviews, group interviews, participant observation and field notes as primary methods for data collection. My project was inspired by principles of participatory action research wherein participants took part in the construction of interview guides, data collection (particularly in group interviews) and data analysis (Torre et al.; Fine). In New York City, I interviewed 40 domestic workers, half of whom were members of *Kabalikat* and the other half were contacts made from snowball sampling strategies. In Manila, I interviewed 25 family members left behind including children, husbands, siblings, best friends, and parents. However, for the purposes of this paper I draw mainly from the interviews and group interviews held with Filipino domestic workers in New York City and my ethnographic notes during my research there.

I draw from the scholarship on women's activism globally and in the U.S. to situate the gendered political subjectivities that infuse *Kabalikat*'s local activism in New York. I highlight analyses of maternal activism that center the family, social reproductive labor, and children (disappeared, disenfranchised and imprisoned) as points of unity for women who organize and mobilize around the conditions that impinge on these sacred parts of women's lives. Instead of dwelling on conditions that could frame them as victims (Mohanty), *Kabalikat* women use their conditions of dispossession to create new forms of social solidarity.

MOTHERHOOD AS A POLITICAL RESOURCE: ACTIVIST MOTHERING

Scholars studying women's community based activism and feminist organizations argue that examining the role of families is key in understanding the development of women's political consciousness, organizing, and mobilizing (Bookman; Naples). Women have been making claims for change on the basis of their gendered experiences. In what Kaplan calls "female consciousness," she argues that women's ascribed roles in gendered division of labor provides women a motive for political action (Kaplan). Naples expands this notion of activism based on gender, through the term "activist mothering" arguing that motive for action is not solely based on gender, rather women's activism is informed by the "interacting nature of labor, politics and mothering" (112). The latter definition interests me the most in thinking about the members of *Kabalikat* finding their initial affinity to organize around Fely's case through the inter-subjective identity as a mother, working away from home to support her family. This simultaneity of political organizer, mother, and migrant worker urge us to examine how these identities are intertwined, informing one another. For the mothers in *Kabalikat*, their circumstance of mothering from afar is structured by the fact that they had to migrate to find work. Thus, they draw on this commonality to relate to one another and forge ahead with campaigns to help fellow domestic workers and mothers.

Hondagneu-Sotelo and Avila argue that motherhood is a historically specific and socially constructed practice and that migrant motherhood is a redefinition of the meaning and roles of mothers as they and their families sustain long-term separation over long distances. I marry their definition with Naples' conceptualization of activist mothering and argue that motherhood shaped by political and economic conditions also produces a basis for motherhood for political action. In the past, mothers have emerged as political activists in response to political conditions and their experience of motherhood was shaped by ideologies of resistance for change (Bouvard; Mellibovsky; Gilmore "Pierce the Future for Hope"). I argue that the political economic conditions, critique of the state, and processes of identification shape the ways in which migrant mothering becomes a basis for grassroots mobilization.

After the military coup of 1976 in Argentina, the political phenomenon of the Madres of the Plaza de Mayo ushered in a different image of the political activist (Mellibovsky; Sepulveda; Bouvard; Low). Under the fascist

military dictatorship of Jorge Rafael Vidale, the Madres demonstrated at
the Plaza de Mayo in front of the presidential palace in Buenos Aires as a
form of protest against the disappearances of their children who were il-
legally abducted and detained for criticism of the dictatorship. At a time
when people curtailed their opposition for fear of torture and disappearance by the government, the Madres' battle for human rights and equality
stood as a firm testament against the inhumane crimes of a military regime.
In this example, these women claimed their motherhood as their strongest
weapon. The Madres of Plaza de Mayo challenged the social and political
milieu by redefining the political potential of motherhood.

Despite the social values of machismo, or a strong and aggressive sense
of masculine pride, that otherwise held women in their roles as mothers in the private sphere, the Madres took their responsibility as women
and mothers to the public sphere which is historically codified as a male-
dominated public. By carrying their children's photographs, they pulled
their filial obligation out of their homes into the streets, embracing the duties ascribed to them, their womanhood and their motherhood, and turned
it on its head by exposing the contradictions of the state in disappearing its
citizenry. Bouvard writes that the Madres of Plaza De Mayo "... asserted the
claims of motherhood against the state during the time of military junta"
(15). In this way, although the Madres were defiantly taking to the streets,
they pushed the boundaries of the socially accepted role of womanhood
and motherhood by expanding that definition towards a maternal activism.
Bouvard states, "they challenged and transformed traditional interpreta-
tions of maternity by redefining it in a collective and political manner: they
described themselves as mothers of all the *disappeared*" (15). Madres blurred
the line between private and public spheres on the platform of their maternal obligations to their children as they clung to their disappeared children
as a form of mothering out in the open. In a way, under very different conditions, *Kabalikat* mothers also cling to photos of their children from afar
to transform their definition of motherhood towards activist mothering.

In a discussion of the Madres' activism, Gilmore states that the activism sparked by the murder and disappearance of children in Argentina
"transformed individual grief into politics of collective opposition" ("Pierce
the Future for Hope" 26). In Gilmore's work she writes about another
set of mothers who pushed the boundaries of private domestic sphere by
transforming motherhood into political ideology. The multi-racial group
of mothers called Mothers Reclaiming Our Children (Mothers ROC) organized around the increased frequency with which young people were be-

ing locked into the California prison industrial complex in the Los Angeles County (Gilmore, *Golden Gulag*). Mothers ROC used informational campaigns, leafleting, regular meetings, protest actions and mere presence in federal institutions and halls, under the principle of "educate, organize, empower," to bring together hundreds of mothers whose children were taken by the state. Because many families were pulled into the labyrinthine criminal justice system in California without much support around understanding the legal processes and steps to fight for their family members, Mothers ROC provided a space for mothers to learn how the system operated. Gilmore argues, "They come forward, in the first instance, because they will not let their children go" ("Pierce the Future for Hope" 27) The imprisonment of the children of members in Mothers ROC—that is, the corporeal extraction of bodies from their homes and community—enabled the political organizing of these women. However, their unity did not just end with motherhood as ideology, instead Mothers ROC's critique of the prison industrial complex is situated in a complex analysis of race and class. They qualified their unity as mothers by analyzing that racism and poverty produce an individuating process that leaves their children vulnerable to the criminal justice system. As Gilmore puts it, "As a community of purpose, Mothers ROC acts on the basis of a simple inversion: We are not poor because our loved ones are in prison; rather our loved ones are in prison because we are poor" ("Pierce the Future for Hope" 29). Refusing the "naturalness" of crime and the criminal justice system is a critique of the retreat of the welfare state. Mothers ROC fills up that space with radical motherhood; this is an attempt to reclaim children and expand the bounds of motherhood from the private to public sphere. Here it is important to note that the politicization of motherhood has an inherent critique of systematic forces of oppression. This critique of racialized political economic conditions also reverberates for *Kabalikat* mothers who analyze their motherhood as produced in and through immigration and globalization.

Under different political economic conditions, mothers in Harlem, New York were facing a different type of war, the War on Poverty. As antipoverty programs were developed originating from the Lyndon B. Johnson administration in the early 1960s, there had been much doubt about the efficacy of "Community Action Programs" or CAPs—programs aimed to provide jobs for low-income residents. The objectives of these programs were to instill the principle of community organization in poor neighborhoods and perhaps change the culture of poverty in those areas. Naples' research examines the oral histories of low-income women who are employed in CAPs in their neighborhoods in Harlem. She argues opposite from the state rhetoric that urban neighborhoods lacked in organization. In fact, the women employed in CAPS were continuing the community work that they traditionally practiced in the past through different community institutions like churches, schools, hospitals, and recreation centers.

In her study, Naples argues that "activist mothering" expanded the scope of mothers to include their surrounding neighborhood and community. Women in poor neighborhoods "built political houses...for the benefit of the collectivity rather than as an individual possession" (Naples 3). She draws on Hill Collins idea of "othermothers" to examine how mothers have built up community institutions for the welfare of their own families and those of their neighbors. For poor African American, Latina, and a few white and Asian women in Harlem, their paid work in CAPs was an extension of the activist mothering that considered the other poor people's families as their own. Disproving the idea that poor communities lack a sense of community organization, the women highlighted as "grassroots warriors" proved that organization and coordination have already always existed through strategies of community caretaking (Stack). Dynamics of interracial relations undoubtedly complicate this situation but the significant thing to note here is that the blanket effect of the retreat of the state on these neighborhoods pushed mothers in the community to rely on one another as fictive kin to raise children and maintain their families. Similarly, in what Gilmore calls "social mothering," she notes that mothers in Mothers ROC, "stay[ed] forward, in the intensified imprisonment of their loved ones, because they encounter many mothers and others in the same locations eager to join in the reclamation project" ("Pierce the Future for Hope" 27). The horizontal relationships built between mothers in Mothers ROC made room to care for the hardship and often isolating manner of advocating for someone on the "inside." In this way and across the board from the Madres to Mothers ROC to grassroots warriors, the politics of motherhood is not just about reclaiming children but also radicalizing care in local communities, all while holding together a critique of the state and political economy.

For *Kabalikat* mothers, a critique of the retreat of the state begins in the Philippines where poverty is rampant and going abroad is often the only option for livelihood. Many of the migrant mothers who find themselves and one another in a city like New York understand that their migration is fueled by the lack of jobs in the Philippines. Although their families do not live with them in their neighborhoods in Queens, they understand the sacrifice of each mother in leaving her children and family behind in the Philippines. In the case of *Kabalikat* members, 'othermothering' and social mothering did not involve the physical labor of taking care of other children as with mothers in Harlem and Los Angeles. Rather, taking care of one another was a way to take care of children and families left behind in the Philippines.

From these examples of activism and the analysis of scholars who studied the activist work of mothers, I discuss not only the bravery of mothers' activism but also the differing socio-political economic conditions under which motherhood is transformed into a basis for action. For *Kabalikat* mothers, migration in neoliberal globalization is the condition under which traditional ideas of motherhood change, but it is also the condition under which ideas of motherhood can transform into political unity and action. Above, the hostility of dictatorship, the violence of incarceration, and the abandonment of the welfare state have been conditions under which women and mothers found courage and intrepid solidarity with one another. In these often hopeless circumstances, the space of domesticity that seems constrained and limited expands into the public realm and towards a politics of collective opposition. This analysis and critique of structures of power becomes the anchor under which mothers challenge the legitimacy of the existing social order. In the case of *Kabalikat*, an analysis of the Philippine state's labor export policy and its consequential phenomenon of forced migration follows the critique of macro systems that permeates the above examples of activist mothering. As I will show later, a radical critique of how migrant motherhood is produced becomes a key aspect that sparks political unity among Filipino migrant workers in New York.

Moreover, I point to these particular mothers' activisms because they were fueled by the loss and absence of their children and their families. Although the loved ones they fought for were not within reach, they did not fail to remind governments, neighborhoods and, more importantly, one another that their motherhood was defined by the relationships with their children—deceased or alive, disappeared or present, imprisoned or free. Activist mothering in the aforementioned examples blossomed through absence of loved ones and was fortified by the emergent "conscientization" (Freire) of motherhood (Gilmore, "Pierce the Future for Hope"). In New York, I found myself amidst children-less migrant mothers and mother-less migrant daughters whose family members were thousands of miles away from them. And even if they had not seen or been with their families for years on end, *Kabalikat* members emerged as activists to reclaim their motherhood and their relationships with their families as impetus for action. Transnational families were definitely not within arms' reach but they were in the scope of justice that was activated during campaigns and organizing in *Kabalikat*. In this way, the conscientization of motherhood applies to migrant mothers even if they do not have their children and families near.

KABALIKAT MOTHERS

On May 7, 2007 at the Greenwich Village Funeral Home in lower Manhattan, *Kabalikat* Domestic Workers Support Network organized a community wake for Ate Fely. The memorial hall was bursting at its seams with over 100 visitors and community members from the metro New York area who came to pay respects to Ate Fely's life. During the wake and in keeping with Philippine burial customs, *Kabalikat* members found a Filipino priest to preside over the service, prayed rosaries for Fely's life, served snacks and refreshments to visitors, and welcomed people who had never met Ate Fely, counting on their prayers to move Ate Fely's spirit into the great beyond. Outside of honoring Ate Fely, the wake had two special guests, Gabriel and Gliff, who were flown in from their home in Batangas, Philippines in large part paid for by the grassroots fundraising efforts of *Kabalikat* members. *Kabalikat* members organized Ate Fely's wake aligned with Philippine mourning customs and without Ate Fely's family members in the room, the final goodbye would not have been right. In a standing-only room, the wake began with a prayer from Father Sancho Garrote, the chaplain of the Jacobi Medical Center, where Garcia's body had been recently released. His solemn prayer was followed by a reading of a poem called *Misteryo ng Hapis* (Mystery of Sorrow),[3] written for Fely Garcia by an award-winning poet and University of the Philippines professor Maria Josephine Barrios. Then, leaders and members of the New York Filipino community organizations offered their remarks to the audience and Ate Fely's family. Shirley Cayugan-O'Brien of *Kabalikat* spoke first by delivering a poem entitled "Mother," wherein she remarked at the great sacrifice of mothers from giving birth and giving life to their children. Some organizations criticized the Philippine Department of Foreign Affairs (DFA) for not notifying the Garcia family about Ate Fely's death until two weeks after her body was found. Others underscored the sacrifice migrant mothers often make as they are forced to choose to work abroad for their families' survival because of the lack of jobs in the Philippines, influenced by structural adjustment programs and the state's investment in a migrant industry of remittances.

Lastly, Ate Fely's eldest son made sure that he told his mother's audience of strangers *cum* friends about the person she was in his eulogy:

> *Mabuting siyang tao, pinalaki niya kaming lahat na mga anak niya sa mabuting paraan. May pinag-aralan, titser siya sa high school noon sa Batangas at nag trabaho din sa office of the Mayor sa amin.*

> She was a very good person, she reared all of us in a very good manner. She was educated, and worked as a high school teacher in Batangas as well for the our Mayor's office.

Fely Garcia immigrated to New York City in 2003 to work and support her four children in the Philippines, some of whom were attending college. Garcia received her first job as a domestic worker upon her arrival to the U.S. through the network of Filipino friends she met prior to coming to New York. She continued to find work when necessary through the same networks. She kept in constant contact with her family in the Philippines. Although she was never able to return physically to her home and family, her presence was felt through her regular financial remittances and long distance communication through phone and information computer technology. During Ate Fely's memorial services, her roommate and close friend, Amy, said:

> Ate Fely didn't leave much for her own personal spending every month. What she didn't remit back to the Philippines, she saved up in a box under her bed for when she returned home. She wanted to buy a big house for her whole family to live in. (Field notes, May 2007)

In this way, Ate Fely was a lot like the members of *Kabalikat*; they all similarly gambled on a chance to work abroad to sustain their families with hopes to return one day. It was this common desire or what they continually termed "sacrifice" that unified *Kabalikat* members to this stranger, who was not so strange after all, Ate Fely.

In the moment of death and abandonment, repeated in similar cases in the next years,[4] *Kabalikat* members forged solidarity based on their identities as mothers, daughters, sisters and aunts to mobilize politically around the issue of the repatriation of a fellow migrant mother. For example, Joan, a *Kabalikat* member, stated "She is a mother, I am a mother. We're both feeding our family from far away. We have to help her because we are not different." Joan's quote illustrates two points about the historical, political economic, and mutual construction of motherhood and political mobilization. One, migrant women identify their migration as part of their expanded definition of motherhood, that then becomes a salient point of solidarity. Their migration and subsequent separation has a driving objective: providing for and sustaining their transnational families. Their families then becomes a resource for engagement in local campaigns, in this case of Fely Garcia, because they hold this sacrifice as one of the most decisive reasons for their current situations.

Scholars argue that "transnational motherhood" is produced by the political economic systems that demand migrant women of color to work as domestics around the globe (Hondagneu-Sotelo and Avila; Arat-Koc). Migrant women's right to stay in their homeland and care for their families in physical proximity is essentially constrained by the structural forces of labor migration in globalization. Given these redefined terms of migrant motherhood, the women of *Kabalikat* have transformed their ideas of motherhood to include migrating to become breadwinners for their transnational families. Therefore, although these mothers are separated from their family, those very components of their family form shape the maternal activism they activate to stand in solidarity with one another. They come together under the political subjectivity of "mother," even if their motherhood is narrated by long-term separation because they understand that the meaning of mother has completely changed given the social conditions that forced them to migrate to work as domestics abroad. This political potential relies dually on the objective daily conditions that migrant women experience as waged domestic workers abroad, securing the financial welfare of their families in the Philippines. Referring to Ate Fely's situation, Lallie from *Kabalikat* says:

> *Kahit ako naintindihan ko naman eh. Anong hirap ng trabaho dito. Ang malayo sa pamilya. Tapos siyempre nagtitiis ka dito 'diba na mapalayo sa pamilya mo kahit na yung asawa ko nga laging sinasabi hanggang kailan siya magtitiis. Sabi ko naman pareho naman tayo nagtitiis sige lang. Darating din ang araw na basta makakapiling din natin sila, magdasal ka lang.*

> Even I understand her. The struggle of working here (in New York City). Being far from the family. And of course, you just try your best right, that you have to stay away from the family

when even my husband asks how long will they have to endure separation. What I say is, that we are the same in suffering and enduring this, we keep going. The day will come that we will be with them again, just have faith.

Lallie expresses the dual nature of her solidarity with Ate Fely, the hardships of working as a domestic and migrant coupled with what those conditions mean for her marriage and motherhood. She unpacks her shared positionality with Ate Fely as she recounts the struggles she faces as migrant worker as a form of sacrifice and obligation to her family. Although local struggles like Ate Fely's death take on primacy in bringing women together and conscientizing them into political action, motherhood, in all of its redefinitions, unites women to commit to a collective like *Kabalikat*.

In the above examples, migrant women have demonstrated that the meaning of motherhood has changed. Migration and work as domestics is seen as an extension of motherhood. These two lived experiences are intertwined. Although they are very different identities, lived distinctly in a migrant domestic worker's everyday life, they are bound up in one another. Women migrate for a better future for their children. They take care of others' children, sacrificing their ability to take care of their own, to provide for children left behind. This shared experience becomes more pronounced when cases like Ate Fely's surface because it reminds one and all about the gamble that migrant women make by extending their motherhood in this way. More importantly, it galvanizes the sacrifice of migration, along with their daily sacrifice of separation, into a politically charged experience that can then be used as a resource for organizing and mobilization.

A MOTHER'S CRITIQUE OF THE PHILIPPINE LABOR BROKERAGE STATE

Transnational motherhood, constructed as a sacrifice, does not stand alone as the force for mobilization for *Kabalikat* members. In the four-month long campaign to repatriate Ate Fely's body back to the Philippines, *Kabalikat* mothers deconstructed just how their migration and separation from their loved ones was a *situated* circumstance produced by the labor export policy in the Philippines. Robyn Magalit Rodriguez characterizes the Philippine state as a "labor brokerage state" explains the migration industry in the Philippines as an institutionalized management and regulation of Filipino labor migration to the world. Instead of developing national industries and job opportunities, the Philippine state invests in a sophisticated and aggressive labor brokerage of Filipinos that begins with global market research, bureaus to sell Filipinos to the labor demands of different countries globally, and then the institutionalized training and sending off of Filipinos to the world. She argues that because migrants keep the national economy afloat from the US$18 billion dollar annual remittance industry that returns to the Philippines, migration management is unequivocally a top national priority.

Migrant workers echoed the labor brokerage analytic when they identified the reasons for their migration as an extension of globalization and the neoliberal retreat of the Philippine state in providing sustainable jobs and livelihood for Filipino citizens, which included themselves, their husbands and children. They pointed out the "modern day hero" rhetoric (Rodriguez), lauding migrants as the saviors of the nation, within which women's migration in the name of the family is specifically acclaimed as courageous. And then, as they witnessed Ate Fely's body languished at a morgue for more than two weeks, they integrated that analysis to reframe Ate Fely's case as a betrayal of the "modern day hero" trope narrated by the Philippine state. The critique and analysis of the Philippine state's abandonment buttressed the political unities of *Kabalikat* around motherhood for Ate Fely. This critique, coupled with their shared identities as mothers abroad, transformed into political articulation of why the Philippine state needed to disburse funds to repatriate Ate Fely back to her home and her family. And in the end, this critique, alongside consistent organizing and people power, was the effective framing to push the Philippine consulate in New York City to finance Ate Fely's final trip home.

In a *Kabalikat* meeting strategizing how to leverage financial support from the consular office in New York, the political analysis of migrant remittances as central to the Philippine national economy emerged. Helen, a *Kabalikat* mother who left her six-month old daughter to migrate to Kuwait in 1993 and was jailed three times after being caught escaping abusive employers before she came to New York, stated:

> *Noong kailangan ko ng tulong mula sa gobyerno, wala ibinigay. Ngayon, kailangan ni Fely. Saan sila? Philippines is like a sinking boat, at tayo ang kanilang lifesaver. Kahit na mamatay tayo di talaga sila kikilos?*

> When I needed help from the government, they would not give me any. Now, Fely needs help. Where are they? The

Philippines is like a sinking boat, and we are their lifesavers.
Even if we are dead, are they really not going to move?

When Helen was imprisoned in Kuwait, neither the Philippine state nor
the consulate office offered her assistance. She sympathized deeply with
Ate Fely's vulnerability and invisibility. And now here was a woman worse
off than she who received the same treatment. Helen's expectation that
the Philippine state assist migrant workers is high since it is a well-known
fact that migrant remittances keep the country afloat. In her comment, she
expects some form of aid from the Philippine government given the role
of migrants in the national economy. Further, upon migrants' departure
from the Philippines, they are required to pay large fees to government
institutions like the Overseas Worker Welfare Agency (OWWA) and the
Philippine Overseas Employment Administration (POEA) that promise assistance to migrants in the time of need. The betrayal Helen expresses in
her comment links to lack of protection and advocacy from the Philippine
state even though migrant remittances are integral to the national economy.
Moreover, her anger towards the state comes from the abandonment she
felt in her own migrant experience and, then again, in Fely's situation.

The migration industry in the Philippines is carried by a gendered cultural logic that puts the Filipino family at the center of why women should
migrate to work abroad (Guevarra). Scholars argue that the systematiza-
tion and management of Philippine labor migration relies on a gendered
logic to encourage Filipino women to take up migration as an answer to the
global demands in the domestic industry (Rodriguez; Guevarra; Francisco).
The brokering of migrant labor by the Philippine state, scholars posit, is a
venue for the Philippines to secure a position in the global order of neoliberal globalization. *Kabalikat* members expressed their intimate knowledge
of the state "modern day hero" rhetoric in their discussion of Ate Fely in
their meetings:

> In our group discussion days before the action in front of the
> consulate, leaders of *Kabalikat*, Joan, Helen and Rita led a
> discussion about the reasons why the consulate should fund
> Fely's repatriation. Rita commented that they should not treat
> *mga bagong bayani* or modern day heroes in this way. She
> asked, rhetorically, "Where's the honor in this?" In which Joan
> replied with a statement on how the Philippine government
> so easily spends money to training programs for Filipinas to

become better domestic workers like in the Supernanny Program. She continued talking about how the government is so quick to send mothers away from their families through these programs, as if they are helping the women who are leaving, but refuse to spend a percentage of remittances to bring them back when the time comes. Helen replied to her with a note on the percentage of migrant remittances in the current Gross Domestic Product of the Philippines. Sarcastically, she asked how much money does the Philippine government need to justify thousands of daughters without mothers. (Field notes, April 2007)

In my observations during the campaign, it was clear that *Kabalikat* members understood how the Philippine state relied on a gendered logic, for migrant mothers in particular, to speak to the filial piety embedded in Filipino family values. Further, they noted state initiatives and economic statistics to back their knowledge of the political economy of migration of the Philippines. The knowledge of these institutional policies was juxtaposed by their experiences as mothers away from their families. In this meeting, mothers made clear how the migration industry of the Philippines is intricately bound up in shaping the contemporary Filipino family. They stated this shift in the family form, engineered by the labor export program in the Philippines, as a significant reason for the Philippine state to take responsibility for its migrant citizenry. In this discussion, the mothers' analysis of motherhood as shaped by the political economy of a nation-state became a sharp tool with which to craft the demands for repatriation fees from the consular office.

In an online petition, authored in consultation with members in community discussions, *Kabalikat* members agreed on the following language that exacts a sharp critique of the Philippine migration industry as well as the gendered logic under which it operates:

> We, the undersigned, express our sincerest sympathies for the loss of Felisa "Fely" Garcia, 58, found dead in her closet by her landlord last 14 March 2007 in the Bronx, New York. Garcia had left four suicide letters in an envelope in the kitchen for her landlord to find. In one of the letters, Garcia describes she faced "abuse and harassment" from her employer, who remains unnamed.

3,000 Filipinos leave the shores of the Philippines daily, Filipino overseas contract workers, largely women, are being deployed to different countries around the world to work as domestic workers, nannies, elderly caregivers, among others. On the global stage, our people are exposed, generally, with no rights to protect them.

As the Philippine economy fails to improve under a system reeking with corruption, we can expect that this aggressive outmigration, touted as an economic solution to our homeland's troubles and downturns, will produce more cases like Fely's that will not be handled properly because the orientation of our consular offices abroad is not to help migrants with their basic problems, but help them remit their earnings back to the Philippines.

Justice For Fely Garcia Online Petition, April 2007[5]

In this petition, in their conversations and in their actions for Ate Fely, *Kabalikat* members exhibit their politics of collective opposition informed by the redefinition of motherhood, both from below—in their daily lives and practices—and from above, constrained by the logics of the Philippine labor brokerage state in an era of neoliberal globalization. Thus, *Kabalikat* activist mothering also draws from a critique of the state and globalization as it is shaping the transnational family.

CONCLUSION

The years of organizing and field research I conducted with *Kabalikat* led me to ask questions about the sociopolitical conditions and the intersubjective processes under which a group of domestic workers united and mobilized for a fellow migrant in need. In this chapter, I identified that the conditions that produce such vulnerable identities are that of migration under neoliberal globalization. I argue that the very vulnerabilities that are presented to women who live their lives as migrant, mother, and worker become galvanizing points of unity. I build on the scholarship of activist mothering to add the case of *Kabalikat* mothers and *titas* to the growing and inspiring list of women who are taking on difficult situations and crafting responses to answer the problems that confront them. Migrant women in this case study use their transnational families as a resource for social justice and action. They draw inspiration from their sacrifices—migration and separation—to champion their rights as mothers. Even if their families are absent from their daily lives, migrant mothers claim their redefined motherhood to inform a politics of collective opposition.

In this chapter, I also presented data that describes how migrant mothers use a critique of the state and the political economy of migration to bolster their political organizing. Following other scholars of women's activism, it is important to note that the deployment of motherhood as political ideology is not solely based on a gendered experience of transnational families. Rather, *Kabalikat* mothers demonstrate that the form of motherhood they are experiencing is a product of forced migration from a developing country further debilitated by neoliberal globalization.

In theorizing my work with *Kabalikat*, I understand that even as migrant mothers may be conscientized in remarkably creative ways, they choose which types of struggles they take up. *Kabalikat*'s transnational engagement with the Philippine state means that their local engagement with struggles for better work conditions for domestic workers in New York City was thin. Although there were vigorous mobilizations for the Domestic Worker Bill of Rights around and after the same time as Ate Fely's campaign launch, *Kabalikat* mothers felt more connected to lobby the Philippine government for rights of migrant workers. I continue to think through the dynamic between local and transnational political mobilization for *Kabalikat* mothers and ask, in what ways do Filipino migrant women see themselves a part of the American political schema? How will they approach inter-ethnic solidarity with other domestic workers to fight for change around standardizing labor rights for the domestic work industry in the U.S.? The answers remain to be seen.

Migrant women are drawing from their experiences as transnational mothers and domestic workers to fight for their inalienable right to be with their families, even in death. Ate Fely's case and *Kabalikat*'s response to her unexpected demise tell an important story of unity under complicated conditions. The conscientization of motherhood in this case study highlights the formidable force in women's lives and experiences. Although the commoditization of domestic labor and devaluation of women's work is en vogue in the current moment of neoliberal globalization, it is my hope that women continue to find their strength in one another and continue to rupture the circumscribed lives they live.

NOTES

[1] A version of this chapter appears in a forthcoming anthology called In the Dark: Family Rights and Migrant Domestic Work edited by Glenda Boni-facio and Maria Kontos.

[2] *Ate* is a Tagalog word, a prefix to the names of older women as a sign of respect and familiarity.

[3] *Misteryo Ng Hapis* Para kay Fely Garcia, domestic worker sa New York na diumanoy' nagpatiwakal. By Maria Josephine Barrios.

 Nakabitin siyang
 Natagpuang patay,
 Anong misteryo ng hapis

 Ang tanging sinisiwalat
 Ng pantali sa kanyang leeg
 Ay sanhi ng pagkamatay,
 Di nito maibubulalas
 Ang hapdi ng kaluluwa,
 O ang dalamhating inipon sa dibdib.

 Ang ipinagluluksa natin
 Ay di ang katawang walang buhay,
 Di isang numero sa statistiko
 Ng mga manggagawang nangibang-bayan
 Di lamang si Fely, ang mahal nating si Fely,
 Kundi si Huli, lagging si Huli,
 Katulong na bayad utang,

 Lahat tayong inaakalang
 Aliping bayad utang.

 Tanging ang kanyang pagkamatay
 Ang misteryo.
 Ang kairapang nagtutulak sa pagluwas
 Ang trahedya na nakasakmal sa ating mga leeg,
 At tayo'y nakikibaka, bawat saglit nakikibaka
 Para sa bawat hiningang walang pangamba,
 Para sa luwalhati

Ng kaunti man lamang pag-asa.

The Mystery of Grief For Fely Garcia, a domestic worker who allegedly committed suicide in her New York apartment. By Maria Josephine Barrios.

> She hung there
> Dead in the closet,
> A mystery of grief.
>
> All we learned from
> The rope round her neck
> Was the cause of her death
> Say nothing of the
> Soul's suffering or the
> Anguish in her heart.
>
> We mourn
> Not the lifeless body,
> Nor a figure in the statistic
> Of our workers sent abroad
> Not only Fely, our beloved Fely,
> But also Huli, in all ways Huli,
> The maid who died for debt,
>
> For all us they count as
> Maids and houseboys to die for debt.
>
> Her suicide the only
> Mystery.
> The poverty that drives us from homeland is
> The tragedy that holds fast round our necks,
> We struggle, in every moment struggle
> For each breath we dare steal from fear
> For the hard-won glory
> Of the smallest hope.

[4]In 2008, *Kabalikat* members launched a similar repatriation campaign for Putli Asjali who died at her workplace in Bridgeport, Connecticut ("Gov't Urged to Pay for Repatriation of Pinoy Aneurysm Victim in Connecticut"). In 2010, *Kabalikat* was also involved in assisting the family of Maitet

Romero who committed suicide; they supported her newly immigrated teenage son by placing him in a home and setting up employment for him.
[5] http://www.petitiononline.com/J4FG2007/petition.html

WORKS CITED

Arat-Koc, Sedef. "Whose Social Reproduction? Transnational Motherhood and Challenges to Feminist Political Economy." *Social Reproduction: Feminist Political Economy Challenges Neo-Liberalism*. Montreal: McGill-Queen's University Press, 2006. 75–92. Print.

Bookman, Ann. *Women Politics And Empowerment*. Temple University Press, 1987. Print.

Bouvard, Marguerite Guzmán. *Revolutionizing Motherhood: The Mothers of the Plaza de Mayo*. Rowman & Littlefield, 1994. Print.

Fine, Michelle. "Working the Hyphens: Reinventing Self and Other in Qualitative Research. Handbook of Qualitative Research." *Handbook of Qualitative Research*. Ed. Norman Denzin and Yvonna Lincoln. Thousand Oaks, CA: Sage, 1994. 70–82. Print.

Francisco, Valerie. "Moral Mismatch: Narratives of Migration from Immigrant Filipino Women in New York City and the Philippine State." *Philippine Sociological Review* 57 (2009): n. pag. Print.

Freire, Paulo. *Pedagogy of the Oppressed*. Continuum International Publishing Group, 2000. Print.

Gilmore, Ruth Wilson. *Golden Gulag: Prisons, Surplus, Crisis, And Opposition in Globalizing California*. University of California Press, 2007. Print.

—. "Pierce the Future for Hope: Mothers and Prisoners in the Post-Keynesian California Landscape." *Global Lockdown: Race, Gender, and the Prison-Industrial Complex*. Ed. Julia Sudbury. Psychology Press, 2005. 231–254. Print.

Hondagneu-Sotelo, Pierrette and Ernestine Avila. "'I'm Here but I'm There': The Meanings of Latina Transnational Motherhood." *Gender and Society* 11.5 (1997): 548–571. Print.

"Gov't Urged to Pay for Repatriation of Pinoy Aneurysm Victim in Connecticut." *ABS-CBN News*. N. p., 4 Sept. 2008.

Guevarra, Anna Romina. *Marketing Dreams, Manufacturing Heroes: The Transnational Labor Brokering of Filipino Workers*. Rutgers University

Press, 2009. Print.

Kaplan, Temma. "Female Consciousness and Collective Action: The Case of Barcelona, 1910-1918." *Signs* 7.3 (1982): 545–566. Print.

Low, Setha M. "Symbolic Ties That Bind: Place Attachment in the Plaza." *Place Attachment.* Vol. 12. New York: Plenum Press, 1992. 165–185. Print.

Mellibovsky, Matilde. *Circle of Love over Death: Testimonies of the Mothers of the Plaza de Mayo.* Willimantic, CT: Curbstone Press, 1997. Print.

Mohanty, Chandra Talpade. "Under Western Eyes: Feminist Scholarship and Colonial Discourses." *Feminist Review* 30.1 (1988): 61–88. www.palgrave-journals.com Web. 11 June 2014.

Naples, Nancy A. *Grassroots Warriors: Activist Mothering, Community Work, and the War on Poverty.* Psychology Press, 1998. Print.

Rodriguez, Robyn Magalit. *Migrants for Export: How the Philippine State Brokers Labor to the World.* Minneapolis, MN: University of Minnesota Press, 2010. Print.

Sepulveda, Emma, ed. *We, Chile: Personal Testimonies of the Chilean Arpilleristas.* Trans. Bridget Morgan. illustrated edition. Azul Editions, 1996. Print.

Stack, Carol B. *All Our Kin: Strategies for Survival in a Black Community.* unknown edition. Basic Books, 1997. Print.

Torre, Maria et al. "Critical Participatory Action Research as Public Science." *APA Handbook of Research Methods in Psychology.* Ed. H. Cooper and P. Camic. Washington DC: American Psychological Association, 2012. Print.

Villadiego, Rita. "Consulate to Repatriate Caregiver's Body to RP." *Filipino Express* 9 Apr. 2007.

15.

Asian American Mothering as Feminist Decolonizing Reproductive Labor

Four Meditations on Raising Hapa Boys

MELINDA LUISA DE JESÚS, PATTI DUNCAN, RESHMI
DUTT-BALLERSTADT, AND LINDA PIERCE ALLEN

INTRODUCTION

The creative nonfiction pieces presented here emerged from our April 2013 roundtable entitled "Anti-Imperialist Grrlz Raising Feminist Hapa Boyz" at the annual Association for Asian American Studies conference in Seattle. Our objective was to explore the intersections of Asian American feminist mothering and activism: namely, how we as women of color academics, feminists, and mothers theorize the nature of our reproductive labor in raising hapa[1] boys from within the belly of the empire itself. Some of the questions that structured our discussion included the following: despite the very heated and sexist discourse surrounding hypergamy and Asian American women's out-marriage rates, our experiences as Asian American academic feminist mothers raising hapa boys have been largely ignored. Why has this been the case? What does this silence signify in terms of our work and its relationship to community? Why the silence overall about feminist parenting in discussions of Asian American cultural activism? How do Asian American feminist moms contribute to the process of decolonization? How is the act of raising hapa feminist boys in hegemonic heteropatriarchal white America a political act? How do we deal with the stereotypes placed upon our mixed race children by others? And how does globalization impact our experiences of confronting and resisting whiteness, cultural nationalism, hegemonic masculinities, and hegemonic white motherhoods?

Why is this such an important topic? Beyond the media fascination with Asian American parenting styles as reflected in the recent "Tiger Mom" phenomenon (discussed elsewhere in this volume), a quick look at the most recent census tells the story. As reported in *The New York Times*, "Among American children, the multiracial population has increased almost 50 percent, to 4.2 million, since 2000, making it the fastest growing youth group in the country" (Saulny). Moreover, since 2000, the white and Asian population grew by about 750,000—an increase of 87%, second only to the white and black population which grew by more than one million and increased by 134% in the same period (United States Census Bureau).

America, your future is here, and it is clearly multiracial. So how do we as Asian American feminists and moms intend to address the issues of identity, family and community, let alone the ideologies of nation and state, within this new twenty-first century framework? As we have seen from the racist responses to the "Just Checking" Cheerios ad that dared to feature a multiracial family, many adults have a lot of work to do.[2] But we can take one positive thing from this incident: kids who viewed Cheerios ad and were told about the controversy were completely surprised by the outcry. They didn't understand why a mixed race family should be a cause for concern[3]. We have much to learn from their wisdom and worldview.

The four pieces below explore our experiences of mothering through reflections on culture, identity, heredity, language, body, privilege, and consciousness. We hope our stories serve as springboards for further discussions regarding the diversity of experiences in mothering hapa boys.

MEDITATION ONE: MELINDA LUISA DE JESÚS

Anti-imperialist grrl raising a hapa feminist boy:
a peminist mom's progress
For Zacarias Jose Roberto, a.k.a. Stinson

Motherhood was something rejected
at first.
I resisted being reduced to just

my body, mere biology—
my nature, as my dad called it
my duty, according to my mother.
Any cow can have a calf! was my retort.
I wanted the room of my own
I had so much to learn.

Then, at 40, motherhood humbled me profoundly
I have never loved my brown body more
As I grew and then birthed my son early, at 34 weeks
no drugs
Stinson unaware, feeling nothing
Secure in his watersack until the last moment.
Clasping his tiny fingers and toes
I was in awe of him
So beautiful, so fragile.

"But he's so white!" his dad's mother couldn't help exclaiming
        when she saw the first pictures
"We're sure he'll brown up right away!" his dad answered.
And so, on my baby's very first day
The lines are drawn.

I miss the simplicity of pregnancy
The baby swimming inside me
Of me, of my own body,
protected.
This little boy has my face
But his light skin means that somehow
He can't really be mine.
The difference between our skin colors
Is the only thing people can see.

We always thought of you as white! Stinson's grandmother
        told me some 15 years ago
Like it was the highest compliment she could ever give me—
Because somehow I had overcome my tiresome cultural bag-
        gage?
Because I'd somehow managed to emulate my colonizers and

fully deracinate myself?
I bristled with the ridiculous absurdity of it
Caught between my class privilege and my brown-ness
What could I say?

*I'm so damn white the racist neighborhood kids tried to burn
down our house. Twice.*
*I'm so damn white my siblings tried to lighten their faces with
baby powder before we went to school.*
*I'm so damn white my 5th grade nickname was "The Oriental
Coffee Bean."*
*I'm so damn white I created a note system in 4th grade where
I was fucking Scarlet O'Hara!*
*I'm so damn white I was never taught Tagalog or Ilocano—
languages my parents spoke.*
*I'm so damn white my dad told me that there was no culture
in the Philippines until the Spanish arrived—and I
believed him.*
*I'm so damned white I learned to swallow my confusion and my
anger, eat it down, pounds and pounds of heartache.*

I was so deracinated I was in graduate school when I finally
learned the history of my own people
Of our resistance
Of my family's role in Philippine independence
Of our colonial mentality
And suddenly my childhood made sense—
And my journey into my own history and identity began.

Decolonization
Is the legacy
I must pass along to my son
As I raise him deep in the belly of the imperialist beast
To resist erasure and whitewashing
To know his roots
Claiming Pin@yhood is our greatest gift and challenge

My mom's slow slide into the darkness of Alzheimer's drives
this urgency.

She's the last tie to our homeland
She, who taught Filipino literature, Tagalog and Philippine
      folkdance—
things she denied me and my siblings because we didn't "need
      them"
Her memories, our family history, slip away
And the mom I once knew disintegrates before my very eyes.
As she travels backwards, away from us,
Will Ilocano and Tagalog become her final languages, just like
      Grandma?
None of us will be able to reach her
And I can only watch, horrified,
as that long, frayed thread snaps…

But what will Stinson need?
He can pass, the mestizo dream—
And still
He seeks reassurance from me:
"We have the same skin, mom, right? The same hair.
I look like you!"
Yes, you do, son.
We have the same love for books and music and dance
For bibibingka and pinsec,
Polvoron, adobo, and fried rice.
The same energy and emotions,
(To the chagrin of your father!)

I've surrounded you with books about the Philippines, about
      Filipino American culture
But I worry—will it be enough?
Can it be enough?
What do I have to give you except
My writing
This family history
My own story of becoming Pinay[4].

I want you to feel proud to be Pinoy
In your own place and time

In your own way.

And so we walk this road together,
holding hands
Our journeys so different
Yet forever intertwined.

MEDITATION TWO: PATTI DUNCAN

Growing up mixed race, I never imagined one day sitting on an academic panel talking about being mixed race, talking about raising a hapa son, and what that means in terms of some of the issues that come up with feminist mothering, racialized masculinities, histories of colonialism, and my own identity as I think through recent shifts in representations of mixed race people. When I was a child, mixed race Asian Americans were largely invisible, and when we were represented, we were often represented as isolated and somewhat tragic. We were generally seen as victims of war, militarism, and colonialism. As Laura Kina and Wei Ming Dariotis suggest in their introduction to *War Baby/Love Child*, a collection on mixed race Asian American art, these depictions centered around stereotypes of Amerasians or mixed race Asians as "war babies"—"children of war, at war with themselves, forever infantilized by their public image as the children of U.S. soldiers and hypersexualized Asian and Pacific Islander women" (12). As such, these mixed race subjects were always structured by racialized gender, and positioned as "illegitimate." Recently, however, there's more of a celebratory tone in contemporary U.S. discourse about mixed race or multiracial people. More public figures are claiming their mixed race identities, and somehow the mixed race subject "has been transformed subversively into a positive (but still stereotypical) image of mixed race people as harbingers of racial harmony—even as 'racial saviors'" (Kina and Dariotis 13). And of course both of those representations are problematic for various reasons, and I'm curious about the shift in discourse, and how it affects us and our children as mixed race subjects.

Elsewhere I have written about representations of mixed race Asian Pacific Americans in recent narrative and documentary films.[5] Reflecting on my own experience as a mixed race subject, I wrote: Growing up mixed race in America meant being interrogated regularly about my racial and ethnic heritage: "Where are you from?" or "What *are* you?" people would ask. When my childhood responses didn't satisfy, the questions became more aggressive: "Well, how did your parents meet?" "What's your nationality?" or "Can I guess your background?" Growing up mixed race meant enduring the constant scrutiny of the non-mixed, who never tried to hide their feelings of superiority, illustrated by comments like, "It must be so hard to be mixed," or "You must feel caught between two worlds," and other, more insidious remarks: "Mixed race people are so exotic." I learned to live with ambiguity as I was frequently subjected to such contradictory statements and assumptions. Growing up mixed race meant feeling invisible, always having to justify my existence and my identity. It meant apologizing to one community or another, for never being *enough*. Sometimes it meant passing, or being passed over by those who needed to categorize or quantify my racial identity for their own comfort. It meant feeling different, other, *wrong*. At other times, I was accused of "selling out" one race or the other. Frequently, it was implied that I was not "Asian enough" or "white enough." When I was very young, my (Asian) mother was occasionally mistaken for my nanny. When people found out my (white) father had served in the U.S. army, stationed in South Korea, they sometimes asked if my mother had been a prostitute. Always, growing up mixed race meant constant assumptions about who I am, who my parents are, and what my experiences must be.

In my origin story, as the child of a U.S./Korean camptown encounter—and subsequent marriage—mixed race signaled "bad" blood, marked by war, violence, colonialism, and the U.S. military occupation of South Korea. But for my son, who's two, almost three, being hapa functions differently, especially within this context that I mentioned earlier, where multiraciality is frequently celebrated as progress and imagined as an answer and antidote to racism, or even a signifier of a "post-racial" society. My son is really young, but I wonder how he will experience his racial identity. What will it mean, for him, to "look white" or "look Asian"? How will he identify? What are the politics of visibility and visuality for Asian Pacific Americans and other people of color, particularly those of us who are mixed race? As he grows older, will he feel invisible (as I sometimes did)? Will he feel pressured to pass?

What strategies of feminist parenting will effectively intersect with the work of decolonization, with the kind of radical decolonizing efforts that Melinda brings up in her introduction? How will my son experience and interpret racialized gender, and his place in the hierarchy of racialized masculinities, and what lessons can I impart, especially within the context of white supremacist U.S. society, where race is commonly understood only in terms of binary opposition? Finally, when is our reproductive labor—as the mothers of mixed race sons—simply normative, reproducing not only heteronormativity (and repronormativity), but also racial(ized) norms and hierarchies, and when can we resist? When might our acts of resistance perform what M. Jacqui Alexander and Chandra Mohanty refer to as "a radical, decolonizing function?" (24). As I consider my son's future, I take inspiration from Maria P. P. Root's "Bill of Rights for Racially Mixed People." "I have the right," she asserts, "not to justify my existence in this world…" This is what I hope for my son: that he will grow up with a sense of community and belonging, taking pride in all the parts of who he is, and that he will know that we are whole—just as we are—and that we need never apologize for or justify our mixed race identities.

At the same time, I want my son to develop a critical consciousness about race, particularly as it intersects with gender, class, sexuality, national belonging and citizenship, and other categories of identity. I believe this is part of my work, in terms of feminist antiracist mothering or parenting, to help him locate and comprehend his experiences within a larger context, and to be able to recognize forms of privilege as well as oppression that he may experience.

MEDITATION THREE: RESHMI DUTT-BALLERSTADT

While I am myself not hapa, raising my mixed race son has allowed me to both observe and theorize the state and stakes of raising a hapa boy in America.

In our household we have three different nationalities and citizenships. I am East-Indian and now have an American passport. My husband is a German citizen and a U.S. Resident Alien. Our son was born in Oregon and is an American. Like most first generation immigrant parents we are also learning about America through our son's lens, experiences that neither I, nor my partner has experienced. Yet, our struggle has been less with understanding the interiors of the American culture, and more with a desire and a struggle to transfer to our mixed raced son our native languages (Bengali and German).

Let me start with a small anecdote on language to frame this dialogue about mothering, raising a hapa son and the self-conscious ways in which my own politics of race, nationality, colonialism or rather anti-colonialism, ethnicity, and gender are transmitted. Also, by framing a dialogue with an autobiographical narrative of raising a mixed raced hapa boy, I may subconsciously be producing a counter-narrative of South Asian motherhood by being more critically aware of my own self-confusions and contradictions, self-justifications, and a self-conscious exploration in positioning myself as a mother of a hapa boy—a position that no one in my immediate family can identify with.

Long before I had my son, I was critical of first generation South Asian immigrant parents who either refused to, or were defensive when it came to speaking their mother-tongue to their children. I had seen first-hand my British born cousins unable to speak their mother tongue, Bengali, and hence their struggle to fit and adjust when they visited our grandparents and relatives in India during their summer or Christmas vacations. This was in the 1980's in Britain when Margaret Thatcher with her anti-immigrant and nationalist policies made it impossible for any South Asian, or any other immigrants, to promote a cultural consciousness other than that of the (white) English. As a result, my cousins and their generations were Jhumpa Lahiri's "Gogols" of England—misfits of sorts, brown bodies speaking the Queen's English. My grandmother for one, was not pleased to see her grandkids that looked Indian but could not speak their mother tongue Bengali. For her the paradox was both simple and ironic, as she often said, "Two hundred years of British rule didn't make us British or forget our language, and only a few years in England have made you more British than the British." Although my grandmother's words may have seemed accusatory toward her own children for not passing down to her grandkids their "mother tongue," the anxiety was elsewhere, i.e., in an inability to carry on daily conversations in her "broken" English with her grandchildren. She experienced a gap in translating her deep love and emotions toward her grandchildren in a language that was not her own, and where meanings were often lost in translations.

Growing up in India, the politics of language, or rather the ability to speak one's mother tongue and its relationship to an "interior" belonging was deeply embedded in my consciousness. Naturally, I didn't want my son to be in the same position as my British cousins, or for that matter, myself to be accused of becoming too Americanized and forgetting my past, my motherland. More so, maybe both my grandmother and I subconsciously made deep links between the ability to speak one's mother tongue to one's state of belonging to one's motherland. Yet, when I think about it now, this link troubles me, since India is not my son's motherland. In fact to make it worse, legally, it is no longer mine either. When I took U.S. citizenship, my Indian passport was "cancelled without prejudice"—a troubling symbolic gesture of canceling my past.

Irrespective of this complexity of where I *really* belonged, or whether my past was really cancelled, I was determined to speak in Bengali when my son Ronan was born. Interestingly enough, Ronan is neither an Indian nor a German name, but shares roots in the Irish tradition. Unlike my cousins who are cultural hybrids, my son is also a racial and a global hybrid, and this hybridity requires that I honor both his East Indian and his East German heritage. While my husband quite organically speaks in German with our son, I have found myself in a position to force myself to speak Bengali. Even this forced determination has been challenged quite harshly by my own lack of persistence in continuing to speak the language when my son is hesitant in speaking the language back to me.

By the time my son was two years old and could speak, I realized that I was having a monologue. I would ask him a question in Bengali, and he would ignore me. So, I would ask him the question in English and he would reply. This continued and became a pattern. I began to give up, perhaps out of anger, perhaps out of humiliation of being defeated by a mere two-year-old in matters of language transmission. Perhaps I was giving it up too soon. I justified my "giving up" by convincing myself of the reality of my own colonial upbringing, where I went to English medium schools and studied English as my first language, and my own mother-tongue Bengali as a "second language." India's preoccupation with the English language as a marker of one's status continues, where knowing "good English" is the road to status and upward mobility.

So I shifted strategies. Instead of speaking the language, I began singing to my son in Bengali. Every night I sang to him some Bengali lullabies with my invented lyrics. Then one fine day as I tried to put him to sleep, he sang back to me in Bengali, a lullaby. Beautiful and clear Bengali words came out of his mouth. I really couldn't believe my ears! I asked him if he would sing it to me one more time and he did. Was I proud? Was I relieved that my instructions were finally paying off? It was not until David Miller, while interviewing me for the *Oregon Public Radio* regarding a chapter in my book, *The Postcolonial Citizen: The Intellectual Migrant* on second generations and stakes of belonging, asked me, "So why this obsession with language? Is it because you fear that *if* your son doesn't speak your mother tongue he will not understand you, your history, your past, your people?" David had finally nailed my fear. He nailed my uneasy and insecure position in raising a hapa boy—a boy that doesn't look East Indian, and hence my self-conscious ways in which I wanted to mark him as a half South Asian subject by injecting language. And this desire to give him a language was not just an emotional response to my own heritage, but was deeply rooted in my intellectual postcolonial consciousness about the link between one's language and heritage. Frantz Fanon in *Black Skin White Masks* writes: "A man who has a language consequently possesses the world expressed and implied by that language" (18). I, too, wanted my son to be a part of his Indian heritage and experience this shared belonging. Other studies also have indicated correlations between language proficiency and racial/ethnic identity. I wanted my son to be able to access his South Asian identity not through his ethnic outfits and visits to India, but through *language*.

So one day, while talking to my son during dinner I asked, "Ronan, do you know that you are half Indian and half German? That's why you are 'Dutt-Ballerstadt.' " In response, my son said, "I am not *this* and I am not *that*. I am a boy." I insisted, "Ronan, yes, you are a boy. But you are an Indo-German boy." To this he said, "I don't like that. I told you I am a boy."

So one thing became clear to me. My son, at his young age had a clear conception of his gendered identity, but was clearly ambiguous about his mixed ethnic identity. Yet this ambiguous ethnic identity rather than making him an "anxious hapa" makes him what Kina and Dariotis in their book, *War Baby/Love Child* calls a "Happy Hapa"—a shift from a generation of mixed Asian children who were assumed to be either "by-products of war or of illicit free love" (12). According to these authors, "the Happy Hapa is the flip side of the tragic Eurasian. No longer the worst of both worlds, the Happy Hapa embodies the 'best' of two imaginaries, living blissfully in a bubble of racial uniqueness, sealed away from complicated histories" (14).

I teach postcolonial literature and theory, and realize more than ever before the complex space and intersection of racial hybridity that my son will have to navigate as he grows up. During our trips to India, I am reminded of the still colonized mentality of members of my own family and folks on the streets. People young and old come and shake hands with my young son and address him as "hello sir." Within my own family, some of my aunts and uncles endearingly calls him *"Ronan Sahib"*—Sahib, a term used formerly as a form of respectful address for a European man in colonial India. These categories of racial identification (of my son being White) shifts when my son visits Germany, where he is dislodged from his status of the "little Sahib" to an ethnically "other" subject. In Germany he looks more Turkish with his dark hair and light skin, rather than German (like his own father who is white and blue eyed).

Within America, he too one day will have to check a box to mark his identity, and I doubt that this box will be one representing the "Happy Hapa" category. So the challenges will remain for me and others of my generation as to how we pedagogically and critically transfer to our mixed raced sons this vexed space of their legal belonging within America as a "hapa" where they will resist any homogeneous category of racialization that does not take into account their hyphenated reality, and yet will enjoy their privileged male subjectivity, where their hyphens will not matter. How do we make them understand the structure of patriarchal domination and its relationship to imperialism and control, while teaching them their own histories and alliances to forms of global oppression and colonialism of which they are byproducts? And of course for me, the question of language still returns—will my "giving up" of teaching my son Bengali rob him of ever understanding his South Asian identity?

MEDITATION FOUR: LINDA PIERCE ALLEN

Reflecting on Patti's and Reshmi's experiences alongside my own, I cannot help but to think about their future grandchildren. If Chance or Ronan partners with—and I don't want to assume heterosexuality, but hypothetically—if they partner with a white American woman, and the children are not racially marked at all, what identifies their grandchildren as Korean, as Indian, as Indo-German? At what point does racial identification become a choice, or ethnicity become whitewashed, and what is the responsibility of the parent to prevent that generational whitewashing? Moreover, I know Melinda and I share the experience of having parents who intentionally did not transmit the Philippine language to their children; in both of our cases, this withholding was purposeful. So, if both racial identity markers and language are out of the equation, what then is the marker for ethnic identification? That is the question on which I focus my meditation.

For me, the question of mothering a hapa son is complicated in part because my own family's immigration story is not a traditional one, and in part because of the politics of my current location (which I will discuss more later). My mother immigrated to the States in 1970, just after what is known as the first quarter storm of Marcos' second term as Philippine President. She had been a Filipina movie star, one of the darlings of Fernando Poe, Jr. Productions, and a former "Junior Miss Philippines," but there was never any question that she would one day leave her homeland behind and stake her claim in America. Her emigration was a foregone conclusion because her father was an American soldier who married her Filipina mother just after the passage of the War Brides Act near the end of the Second World War. Because my mother is herself a *mestiza*, and the daughter of an American but also a first-generation immigrant to the U.S., her experience does not adhere to many of the standard tropes of the traditional immigrant narrative. The dual citizenship with which she had been born would expire once she turned twenty-one, so the plan had always been to emigrate to the infamous homeland of her father in order to claim her rightful inheritance.

Just a few months after she immigrated to the States she met my father, a white American military man with suppressed Cuban ancestry, at a Halloween dance held at the Filipino American community center in Miami. They married and had three mestizo children: the first one tall, dark and handsome and then two more who could pass for white. Her American born children share many of the traditional experiences of first-generation children of immigrants, but this doubled exogamy ("out-marriage") also altered the lens through which we viewed our developing identities. After my older brother, whose marked racial status often leads strangers to question "what are you?" I came along and was not what anyone had expected. When my mother's family went to the baby nursery at the hospital to get a glimpse of their first Pinay grandchild born in the U.S., they completely overlooked me as they skimmed the faces of the newborns lying behind the glass window (the way they used to display them in the early '70s). They scanned back and forth, repeatedly skipping me because, after knowing my older brother, they dismissed the possibility of a pale-skinned, red-headed baby girl. Finally, they began to squint to read the name cards, and only then did they realize their baby Pinay was a redhead (at least for the first couple years of my life).

Throughout my life, although I have always felt my Pinay sensibilities keenly, I had to announce them in order to make them known in unfamiliar spaces—and of course the choice and opportunity to make such an "announcement" is wrought with both personal and political complexities. By and large I knew who I was: much of the foundation of my identity was heavily influenced by my experiences as the daughter of an immigrant woman, and my identity often located me politically and informed my epistemologies in significant ways.

When I took a job in southern Mississippi, I wondered whether I would find a Pinay community in the Deep South. I did, but it is largely a "pen pal" community, quite different from my experiences in Oakland, where I was born, and Seattle, where I was raised. Exogamy and hypergamy practically define most of the marriages, and the mestizo children live with the complexities of the contemporary "mail order" bride relationship. Nevertheless, I found kinship across these diverse experiences of Pinayism, and made my home in this space. When I ended up marrying a blonde-haired, blue-eyed, wonderfully gentle soul who was born and bred in Mississippi, my mother held her breath, hoping her dream for a blue-eyed grandchild would finally be realized. One of the movies in which my mother had starred in one of the lead female roles in the Philippines was the infamous "Captain Philippines and Boy *Pinoy*," and we had long appropriated the "Boy *Pinoy*" title for many of the baby boys in the community. We had anticipated the arrival of my own Boy *Pinoy* but, with strong hues considerably more pronounced than those of his own mother, this Boy *Pinoy* was a ginger. When I had Ash, with his blaze of red hair, porcelain skin and sparkling blue eyes, my mother declared him the most beautiful baby she had ever seen; as soon as they laid eyes on him, my Mississippi Filipina community concurred, naming him "their dream baby." They searched his features and ultimately declared that he "still has the Filipino nose," but one Até noted that it "might not stay," indicating that her *mestiza* daughter's Filipina nose had changed as she grew.

The raising of a ginger Boy *Pinoy* begs several questions: since racial categorization has long been debunked as a biological fiction, but a social construction steeped in visibly marked identifiers of difference designed to protect and preserve whiteness, what makes my son Pinoy? I began with this brief autobiographical narrative because in order to answer that question, I had to consider what makes me Pinay, but the answers to those two questions are very different. In many ways, my Pinay identity feels essential: I am the daughter of a Filipina immigrant woman, and my development has been informed by the quotidian manifestations of that experience for the past four decades. Although my racial status is not immediately discredited, my sensibilities discredit me at every turn. My sensibilities began essentially, and were honed critically as my education progressed. I have a Cuban heritage on my father's side that, while I have never denied it, I have also never really claimed, because it was "historical fact" more than experientially present. My father's grandparents refused to pass on or teach any of their children Spanish and purposefully repressed their native culture, because they wanted their children to assimilate to find success in America. Three generations later, my father's connection to any supposed Cuban identity was ancestral at best, questionable at worst. All of this tells me that for my son, the Pinoy Ginger, his hapa identity *must* be constructed if it is to be preserved instead of being whitewashed entirely with three generations of exogamy. And while, of course, he will be the most important agent in his late- and post-adolescent identity construction, my role seems crucial in his developmental years.

So, the question that I've been grappling with is how do I model Pinoy identity for my white, multiracial son? Language seems so crucial, and we don't have that tie; I don't speak Tagalog so I cannot pass it on to him. If language is not there, you're left with things like food and, while a lot of people have written convincingly about its significance in culture, when you're trying to talk about the construction of identity, food seems very superficial. The attempt to construct identity absent any particular marked status or linguistic tie depends entirely on an understanding, an intellectualization, that is different from an essential cultural experience. My son is not going to have the experiences that I had growing up as the daughter of an immigrant woman, an "ESL" speaker. That's not necessarily a bad thing, but where does my parental responsibility come in if I wish to preserve our cultural heritage, and what kind of intervention should I be thinking about as I guide my son in the development of his ethnic identification? Other than my own intellectualization of identity construction, one thing I've done in Mississippi is try to link Ash's experience to the Filipino/a community, to make sure he knows his Titas and understands the culture. The other thing I have done is to make him a little traveler, because the Mississippi Filipino community, even though they've really embraced me and I love them, is not the Filipino community experience that is my experience. And so we're part of that one at home; we come to Seattle and see Grandma and we're part of one there; Great-Grandma is still alive in Oakland (or at least she was at the time of this conference; she has since passed, but we still have many Titas, Uncles and cousins in the bay area), so we join that community as well. Yet, while I value our family ties to our culture, I am reticent to rely solely on travel for cultural connection; wary of identity tourism, the challenge of my son's identity construction looms large for me. I'm sorry I only posed questions and not answers, but I'd love to begin conversations with others to explore more potential answers.

CODA, JUNE 2014

In rereading these narratives, we are struck by the realization that we moms are at the very beginnings of this journey. Our children are *little boys* right now, but the bigger, scarier challenges of their negotiating identity, masculinity, sexuality, and power are just around the corner. As they approach adolescence and adulthood, how will our sons' relationships to their white/Anglo fathers impact their own sense of identity and power? Will they reject the brownness of their mothers for the whiteness their fathers inhabit? Is there a third or even fourth space for them to claim as hapa young men?

In the aftermath of the horrific murders of six U.C. Santa Barbara students by a troubled self-described Eurasian male, never has our Asian American feminist mothering of hapa boys seemed so crucial. Clearly our interrogations of racialized sexuality, mixed race masculinity and power in white supremacist, patriarchal America must continue if we are to raise healthy, critically conscious and empowered feminist hapa men.

NOTES

[1] *Hapa* is the term many Asian Americans use to describe people who are mixed race—"half" white and "half" Asian. The word originates from the Hawai'ian term *hapa haole* (or half white) and suggests both a history of colonialism and a shared set of experiences among mixed race Asian Pacific Islanders with some white heritage. For more context, see Kip Fulbeck's *The Hapa Project* and *Part Asian, 100% Hapa*, as well as Folen and Ng's "The Hapa Project: How Multiracial Identity Crosses Oceans." See also: http://www.mixedracestudies.org/ "Scholarly perspectives on the mixed-race experience."

[2] http://www.nytimes.com/2013/06/01/business/media/cheerios-ad-with-interracial-family-brings-out-internet-hate.html

[3] http://www.today.com/news/angry-over-what-kids-react-mixed-race-cheerios-ad-new-6C10658002, Kids React video by the Fine Bros: http://www.youtube.com/watch?v=VifdBFp5pnw

[4] "Pinay" is the Filipino American term for Filipino women. Pinoy is the term for Filipino men.

[5] Duncan, Patti. "In Search of Other 'Others': Exploring Representations of Mixed Race Asian Pacific Americans." *Women's Lives: Multicultural Perspectives*, ed. Gwyn Kirk and Margo Okazawa-Rey. Mountain View, CA: Mayfield Publishing Company, 6th edition, 2012. 145-151. Print.

WORKS CITED

Alexander, M. Jacqui Alexander and Chandra Talpade Mohanty. "Cartographies of Knowledge and Power: Transnational Feminism as Radical Praxis." Amanda Lock Swarr and Richa Nagar, eds., *Critical Transnational Feminist Practice*. Albany, NY: State University of New York Press, 2010: 23–45. Print.

Dutt-Ballerstadt, Reshmi. *The Postcolonial Citizen: The Intellectual Migrant*. New York: Peter Lang, 2010.

Fanon, Frantz. *Black Skin, White Masks*. New York: Grove Press, 2008. Originally published 1952. Print.

Folen, Alana and Tina Ng, "The Hapa Project: How Multiracial Identity Crosses Oceans." University of Hawaii at Manoa. Spring 2007. Web. 1 June 2014.

Fulbeck, Kip. *Part Asian, 100% Hapa*. San Francisco, CA: Chronicle Books, 2006. Print.

—. *The Hapa Project*. Seaweed Productions. 2011. Web. 22 June 2014.

Lahiri, Jhumpa. *The Namesake*. New York: Houghton Mifflin Harcourt, 2003. Print.

Nakazawa, Donna Jackson. *Does Anybody Else Look Like Me? A Parent's Guide to Raising Multiracial Children*. Cambridge, MA: DaCapo 2004. Print.

Kina, Laura & Wei Ming Dariotis, eds. *War Baby / Love Child: Mixed Race Asian American Art*. Seattle: University of Washington Press, 2013. Print.

Root, Maria P.P., ed. *Racially Mixed People in America*. Thousand Oaks: Sage Publications, 1992. Print.

Saulny, Susan. "Census Data Presents Rise in Multicultural Population of Youths." *The New York Times*. 24 March 2011. Web. 1 June 2014.

United States Census Bureau. "2010 Census Shows Multiple-Race Population Grew Faster Than Single-Race Population." 27 September 2012. Web. 1 June 2014.

16.

Kite

FIONA TINWEI LAM

He runs into the wind—
the kite rises. Swerves
against it—the kite dives.
Soon, the park is
festooned with colour:
streamers, planes, butterflies.
He runs on amid zig-zags
of sprinting children,
dragging it along the battered grass
until moribund bird
becomes stubborn dog.
For a few metres, it whoops up
like a miracle, then
plummets. We try again.

A year ago, buffeted by wind,
he stood on a mound of sand and logs
by the beach. How he brimmed
sky and sunlight, first kite
soaring.

How I want that back.
Despite my warnings, he runs
between two gnarled trees,

wind behind him. The kite
sags, then snags.
I sigh, lecture, berate,
tug the kite one way, then the other,
finally break the string,
tangling both of us up
in that twisted, blunted tree.

He crouches pondside,
all glory flatlined.
One more time, I say.
He won't hear me.
My son and I, grounded
beneath vacant skies.

17.

Snowman

FIONA TINWEI LAM

Everyone praises my son
for the snowman on our front lawn:
porkpie hat, pebble smile,
the raised twig eyebrows slightly amused.

Silent, my son looks away.
How he toiled, rolling those balls of snow
all around the lawn. Finally,
he enlisted my help. I stacked them,
brushed off soil and leaves,
rounded off corners, packed
fault lines, fussed and shaped
to sculpt a face, adorn the head.

I offered him the eyes—
he shoved in the stones
and left. He was building
a mound he called a stage,
fifteen feet away. Room for one.

Two years ago, a wooden train set.
I spent an hour laying track
to form criss-crossed loops on the coffee table.
Anything he'd try to lay down

I dismantled, pleading
for patience. When
I was done, he'd lost
interest. For weeks, that track lay there,
a masterpiece of devotion.

My son approached it once,
unsmiling, to connect a snaking line
of engines, cars, cabooses that derailed
on a corner going up a bridge.
He cried. I rushed over
with solace, advice. Only
when it crumbled away
could he create again,
without me.

18.

Bringing Visibility to East Asian Mothers in Prison

ANITA HARKER ARMSTRONG AND VICTORIA LAW

Writer Jenji Kohan was recently criticized for her portrayal of women of color in prison in the popular series, *Orange is the New Black*, based on the experiences of Piper Kerman, a well-educated middle class white woman who was incarcerated following a drug trafficking conviction. Critics have charged Kohan with the offense of lazily relying on stereotypical representations of women of color, specifically invoking the image of the "quiet and submissive token Asian" woman (The Feminist Griote 1). Kohan may be guilty as charged but she would likely cite the dearth of understanding about the experiences of Asian women in prison in her defense. For example, although the Bureau of Justice Statistics (BJS) gathers statistics on the Asian female population in general, they fail to distinguish the number of East Asian women vs. South Asian women in prison. Indeed, writers are left with few sources to turn to when tasked with representing East Asian women in prison; however, it is no excuse to default to stereotypes that serve to perpetuate their marginalization.

In this chapter, we seek to combine current literature on incarcerated mothers in general to help map out important considerations and projections for future research about East Asian women more specifically in an effort to foster social justice for this vulnerable and largely invisible population. We approach this topic together, from our respective positions, with an understanding that this area of research is significantly underdeveloped. As a sociologist and mother, Anita's interest in the topic stems from previous work where she attempted to better understand the reentry process from the perspective of mothers. As an East Asian American woman who was once entangled with less-than-lawful activities, Vikki Law is now an activist and social justice advocate for women in prison. Through Vikki's connections we were able to make contact with one East Asian mother in prison, whose correspondence we share in excerpts to contextualize the current literature and research.

UNMET NEEDS OF WOMEN IN PRISON

The needs of the female prison population have shocked a system that has traditionally been focused on incarcerated men (Thomas 2, Women's Prison Association 2003a). Sensitivity towards the specific needs of women, and mothers in particular, has failed to surface on a large scale (Kruttschnitt and Gartner 287; Britton 2). The physical and mental health needs of women in prison have not been adequately met. For example, women in prison report having experienced more physical and sexual abuse than both men in prison and women in the general population (Wright et al. 1616). Yet, greatly needed counseling services in prison are severely lacking. Moreover, while research has shown that substance abuse is a larger problem for women, the availability of drug rehabilitation programs, while woefully inadequate, is still greater for men (Pollock 2002). As well, unmet physical and emotional needs of women in prison is patently clear given that in twenty-nine states, the dangerous practice of shackling incarcerated women during labor, delivery, and postpartum recovery continues. In the twenty-one states that do have anti-shackling legislation, it is not rigorously enforced (Baker 1, see Birthing Behind Bars)

GENDERED ATTITUDES AND PATTERNS OF CRIMINALITY

Public perceptions of people who commit crimes continue to be deeply gendered. Kellor (679) illustrates the historically held double-standard for men and women, in reference to criminal activity:

> It is a prevailing opinion that when women are criminal they are more degraded and more abandoned than men. From the observation of the two sexes, this seems due rather to the difference in the standards which we set for the two sexes. We say woman is worse, but we judge her so by comparison with the ideal of woman, not with a common ideal. For instance,

> I have included swearing and use of tobacco as bad habits among women; among men, we should not consider them in the same light.

One hundred years later, women are still dealing with sexist attitudes that somehow it is not as bad for men to be criminals as it is for women—*especially* women with children. This sentiment is echoed in the words of a thirty-eight-year-old woman who was being detained in an urban jail:

> It's like we are all used to the brothers [men] getting locked up. But no one has any sympathy for us when we go down [go to prison]. It's like we are somehow supposed to not get caught up [involved in illegal activity] the way they do. But it is getting just as bad ... no it is worse for us now. There is no way to make it without running the streets to support yourself. Plus, the cops are now looking more for women than for the brothers. It's like they are after us now. And they get us good! But folks don't realize that (Richie 383).

Indeed, in comparison to men, women have surpassed the growth rate of men by 1.5 times on a yearly basis, having increased by 592 percent between 1977 and 2001 (Women Prison's Association). The majority of crimes committed by women are non-violent in nature and drug-related (Richie 373, Sharp and Eriksen 121). By the end of 2012, there were over 108,000 women in state or federal prisons, and an additional 102,000 women in local jails (BJS). These numbers do not account for those who find themselves under the custody of the U.S. Immigration and Customs Enforcement (ICE) agency in detention centers across the country following their release, due to lack of citizenship status. Although the percentage of women in prison is still comparatively small (currently at seven percent) the dramatic increase in female incarceration rates is disturbing (Sharp and Eriksen 119); and their increasing presence is found throughout the criminal justice system.

MOTHERS IN PRISON

With the increase of women in the prison population in recent years, more and more children are left without fathers, mothers, and at times, both. In 1976, mothers of an estimated 21,000 children on any given day were absent from the home due to incarceration (Travis and Burkhead 85). By

1998, the number of women in prison had risen to 84,427 (Mickey and Warner-Robbins 6). This is a great concern as an estimated two-thirds of women in prison in the early 2000s were mothers of minor children (Petersilia 2; Women's Prison Association). Between 1991 and 2007, the number of mothers in prison increased by 122%, compared to fathers at a rate of 76% (Schirmer, Nellis and Mauer 2). According to a Bureau of Justice Statistics Special Report, as of 2007, 744,200 fathers and 65,600 mothers were incarcerated in the United States, resulting in 1,706,600 children under the age of 18 whose parent(s) were housed in either State or Federal prisons (BJS 2). If we widen this scope to include parents in local jails, an estimated 2.7 million children under the age of 18 (which translates to 1 in 28 children) are waiting for their parents to be released (Owens 2).

Fathers who are incarcerated usually have the option of leaving their children with the mother during their separation (Sharp and Eriksen 125, Stanton 36). In fact, many men do not live with their child(ren) prior to incarceration. Women offenders are more often unmarried, and are alone in their responsibilities to care for their children (Stanton 37). Of the mothers in state prisons, over half reported that their children lived with a grandparent, while an additional 25 percent indicated that other family members were caring for their children (Sharp and Eriksen 2003). Whether extended family members are in the position to care for additional children is questionable. They typically already experience financial strain, heightened by the new additions to the household. Of these caregivers, 95 percent are single females themselves and 90 percent are also recipients of public assistance in some form (Petersilia 7). About 10 percent of the children of mothers in state prisons were instead placed in foster care (Petersilia 6). Mothers, in fact, were five times as likely as fathers to report that their children were in foster care (BJS).

The most common scenario for children whose mothers are facing incarceration is to reside with grandparents or other family members during their mothers' sentence (Sharp and Eriksen 125; see Mumola). But this can be problematic given that over 60 percent of women in prison have histories of sexual or physical abuse as children (Sharp and Eriksen 126; see Greenfeld and Snell); and during incarceration, their children often live in the homes where their own abuse originated. Again, this is largely due to the fact that many mothers face no good alternative for their children's placement during their incarceration, and do not wish to risk losing their children to the state, especially given the increasing length of sentences. As well, the likelihood of a grandparent with a history of violence becoming the caretaker of children is the same likelihood as that of a nonviolent grandparent (Sharp and Eriksen 123). Sharp and Marcus-Mendoza discovered that 11 percent of American women in prison indicated that the place of their children's current residence was with family members who had histories of violence (Sharp and Eriksen 124). Overall, foster homes appeared to be safer places for children of incarcerated parents; but the thought of losing one's children is often too much to bear for incarcerated women.

"MODEL" MINORITIES AS "MODEL" WOMEN IN PRISON?

Visibility and understanding the specificities of the experience of incarcerated East Asian women is lacking; but we can assume that just like their cellmates, many of them also have children. Taking what we do know about mothers in the criminal justice system, we can extrapolate and theorize about the potential unique aspects and/or barriers that East Asian mothers in prison might confront. Given the prevalence of the "model minority" stereotype of Asian Americans (Chou and Feagin 3), it appears to be a natural extension that Asian women might also be expected to be "model" women in prison. Or, that is, she may be stereotyped as such. While conceptualizations of what it means to be a "good" mother have fluctuated with historical periods, cultural contexts, and geographic locations, one universal element seems to cut through in terms of identifying what a "good" mother is *not*—that is, a "good" mother is *not* in prison. She is present. She is devoted. She is selfless. So, what can we expect from a "model minority" who has become a "bad mom"? This juxtaposition of a racial category that has, at least in the west, been linked to "hyperfeminine" characteristics (Pyke and Johnson 35; see Espiritu) is in tension with hegemonic conceptualizations of "bad" mothers.

SOSON'S STORY

As indicated earlier, during the course of gathering information for this chapter we were privileged to be connected with an East Asian mother currently serving time in prison. Her name is SoSon, and she has generously consented to sharing her story with us for publication in this book. At the time of our correspondence in 2013, SoSon had been spent approximately eight years in prison (half of which were in a remote maximum security institution), with three years ahead of her before coming up for parole. While SoSon's experience is singular, this intimate glimpse provides a promising first step towards informing future research endeavors that will take seriously the consideration of what has been a neglected and vulnerable group of women—indeed, a group that has been largely invisible.

SoSon was born in a small town in South Korea to an abusive father and a mother who left the marriage but was not allowed to take her daughter with her. Instead, SoSon was passed around her father's family, and her father continued his violence. At the age of twelve, SoSon left for the United States with her mother who was finally able to gain custody of her and her new step-father, an American. In SoSon's words, "it was like a fairy tale." She was back in her mother's home, and headed to a land of hope and new beginnings. Interestingly, SoSon was careful to qualify her mother's relationship with an American man, explaining in some detail how it was that they came to be in a relationship, because as she puts it, "when I mention my mom and step-dad most people assume my mom was some kind of loose Asian whore who was looking for an American to score and she is far from that." From this statement, we might assume that SoSon has lived a life patterned by the weight of negative stereotypes and culturally-based misinterpretations.

While SoSon had initially viewed this escape from her abusive father to live with her mother in America as a "fairy tale," she quickly encountered difficulty with conforming to the demands of all that comes with transitioning to a completely new culture. Speaking of school, she shared that she

> struggled because ...I DIDN'T SPEAK the language. So I lost interest quick...I began to hang out with the "wrong crowd"—dropped out in 9th grade. Fast forward I'm 16 ...I meet Steve[1]. He was 18—I was in the middle of my full teenage rebellion. Mad at the world—my mom and I bumped heads so much because she wanted to raise me in that strict Asian ways—her and I both brand new in the States—I was going through puberty and seeing all the American kids hanging out and having fun! So I decided to get married . . . I got pregnant shortly after.

Things progressively got harder for SoSon, who became a young mother in a "rocky" marriage that would end when her baby was just five months old. For much of those early years of Sarah's life, SoSon described herself as "young and wild" and running "around all over the United States doing all the wrong things." Steve ended up taking custody of Sarah, and she was two and half years old the last time SoSon saw her. Around this time, So-Son "shot two individuals four times each with 9mm hollow tip bullets," explaining that she "felt at the time [she] had nothing to lose and didn't care about [herself] or anybody else." She "left them for dead," and was later arrested.

Having spent many years in prison at the time of our correspondence, SoSon had clearly also spent much time reflecting. Reflecting, and mourning—mostly the loss of her daughter. SoSon explained that connecting with Sarah has been difficult, not surprising given what we know about mother and child relationships while in prison more generally. The distress experienced when trying to maintain relationships with children while in prison is typically a heavy burden on both parties. The situation is made even more difficult by limited visiting opportunities and economic hardship (Richie 372).

LIVING WITH REALITIES

From the perspective of the child, the stigma of having a parent in prison is coupled with emotional distress (Golden 25). While this pain is apparent, little response has been made in the way of programs to abate the suffering experienced by mothers who long for a connection with their children (Richie 373; Ferraro and Moe 10). Sadly, few parents and children have the privilege of regular visits. Many barriers impede the likelihood of visitation including a lack of transportation, inconvenient visiting hours (often during the day, disrupting working hours), poor relationships with the child's current caregiver, as well as geographical distance (Enos 15). In fact, the possibility of children visiting is much less likely for mothers as opposed to fathers. In addition to the aforementioned barriers, the majority of women in prison are housed over 100 miles from where they lived prior to their imprisonment. In the federal system, over half of the women are housed over 250 miles from their homes, and another 30 percent are over 500 miles from home (Sharp and Eriksen 125; see Ekstran, Burton, and Erdman). Essentially, since there are fewer women's prisons, the distance those prisons are from family is typically greater. Of those children that are able to visit under positive conditions, fears concerning their parents' well-being are often calmed and their parents' love for them reconfirmed. This can greatly aid the adjustment process and increase the likelihood of successful reentry for parents upon release (Wright et al. 1622, Brown and Valiente 2).

When visits are not a possibility, contact is generally maintained through mail. Mumola (2000) found that about two-thirds of mothers in state prisons reported receiving mail from their children on a monthly basis (Sharp and Eriksen 127; see Mumola). And for SoSon, this was indeed the primary way she communicated with Sarah, writing her a letter "every week for four years." What is less than ideal is the fact that many children of imprisoned parents are very young and unable to read and write without the help of an adult. The comfort provided by mail is significantly less for these young children (Sharp and Eriksen 127). This was certainly the experience SoSon and Sarah lived through in the sense that they both spent years with little to no connection. Although Sarah is now older, she is theoretically able to gain more through written contact, but this connection is still tenuous given the early limitations to their communication. SoSon explained that her ex-husband's sister "was the only one who sent me pictures of Sarah." She further explained that she's "not angry [and does not] hold it against them for keeping Sarah from me—but I pray [Sarah] doesn't hold it against them when I am back in her life. I do all I can but it is tough to deal with not having her in my life. It's been 10 years—and I don't even know what her voice sounds like."

While phone calls can be common for some, for various reasons, they were not possible for SoSon and Sarah. To provide some context, the expense accrued by regular use of prison telephones is very large. Connection fees alone cost $1 to $3. Most prison policy requires incarcerated people to make collect calls. Although the costs of long distance phone calls have decreased for the general public, it continues to increase for incarcerated people. A call that last only fifteen minutes "can cost more than thirteen dollars" (Sharp and Eriksen 129; see Sharp and Marcus-Mendoza). In addition, calls are often broken up by regular recordings. For example, in California "calls are interrupted about every 20 seconds by a mechanical robotic voice, which comes on the line and says, "This is a call from a California prison inmate" (Petersilia 45). For an incarcerated person attempting to rebuild and/or maintain positive familial relationships, this constant reminder would likely be a large distraction and hindrance to constructive communication. In addition, caregivers for prisoners' children who are already burdened by the increased costs of raising a child, are further bombarded by the expense of covering the cost of collect calls. This may help explain why phone calls were not a valid option for SoSon, and many other mothers.

And so, while she was unable to hear her daughter's actual voice, she took every opportunity to make her voice known to Sarah, and she took comfort in believing that Sarah's voice would be familiar to her when she could hear it. She explained,

> All I can imagine is she's probably a lot like me ... I've done several "messages projects" they offer here ... One thing that upsets me in here is some mothers living their lives like they don't care—about their children—I believe everything I do and I don't do is connected with Sarah. In those messages I've sent to Sarah, I always made a point to let her know she is loved—and for her to know who she is. I tell her she's half Korean and if she is anything like me, she would be outgoing and adventurous. I encourage her to be herself and not be afraid of who she is.

From this passage, it is clear that SoSon's status as a mother, and her racial identity as an East Asian, is integral to her sense of self. She elaborates on this in the following terms,

> Now, my identity as an Asian influences me greatly in my incarceration because especially here in [the Midwest], the last 10 years in prison I've only seen one other full Korean and handful of mixed women—but none who has actually grew up in Asia and are accustomed to their culture and language. Many people do have the misconception I grew up in a "good" home but my childhood was really bad—which have contributed to my rebellion.... I'm not sure if it's just [here] or all over United States—many believe Asia is a country. I usually have to explain how "Asia" is a continent—and that I am Korean—and there is a difference between North and South and ... really give a quick geography lesson.

As a postscript to her letter, SoSon added that

> [j]ust the other day my unit manager mentioned how he talked about me in some kind of class. He said about me—being the ONLY Asian in prison here [in the Midwest]—I'm sure that might be the truth. I gave him a funny look—he said he was using that as an example of "Ethics of Asians" and why there are so few of them in prison.

To situate SoSon's experience this within the larger framework, of the in-carcerated parent population, two thirds are nonwhite. To put this in per-spective, 1 in every 15 black children, 1 in 42 Latino, and 1 in 111 white children have a parent in prison, although we do not know the breakdown between how many are mothers versus fathers (Schrimer, Nellis, & Mauer 2009). Statistics on Asians in prison are available, but are insufficient. The differ-ence between South and East Asian is not identified, nor are they separated by gender and parental status. According the Bureau of Prisons, about 1.6% of the prison population in the U.S. is Asian. As a point of reference, the State of New York Department of Corrections reported a total of 14 Asian women (or 0.6% of the women's population) were under custody in 2011.

Whether SoSon is the only East Asian woman in the geographical area in which she is housed is perhaps less important to verify than the fact that she has *experienced* her incarceration as the only East Asian woman in prison. The complexities faced by "tokens" (be it on the basis of gender, race, ethnicity, sexuality, and so forth) have been documented in several ar-eas of research, and the concept was originally theorized in Rosabeth Moss Kanter's seminal work, *Men and Women of the Corporation*. It is com-pelling to read SoSon's descriptions of her experiences through the lens of tokenism, understanding that rather than viewing women as tokens (as was the case in Kanter's work), we can easily extrapolate this concept to fit other social identities. As in, the experience of *one* East Asian mother in prison, surrounded by people who use stereotypes to inform their understanding of what it might be like to be SoSon (or someone like her). With this in mind, we share SoSon's experience as a token, so to speak, in her own words:

> Okay—I'm going to write the truth as it comes to me—people mostly react to what they can physically see. And I say this humbly—I am an attractive person. And being Asian I get a lot of attention whether I want it or like it or not. What helped me along to do the right thing was when I first came to the [maximum security prison] as a young woman, I was still acting out—the chaplain woman called me into her of-fice and had a little talk with me. "You know there are only .004% Asians in prison." Yeah. "It's time to represent Asians right—even in prison. Right?" Ha ha. So, I get a lot of peo-ple thinking that I'm stuck up or conceited because I don't associate with too many people. I am very confident and se-cure in who I am so that intimidates a lot of women, even per-

haps some staff members also. I've been told (matter of fact just yesterday) several times that I am the prettiest woman on the compound—but I don't care about those things. Many asks me when they find out I can speak Korean, "say something!" I just want to roll my eyes but I don't want to be rude. I do eat things that "normal Americans" don't—like mackerels. I try to make food that somewhat reminds me of home. It's hard. My mom did teach me many things—really back then it sounded like nagging but I see why she did . . . I am singled out time to time because I do what's right (most of the times)—prison, prison, prison—filled with insecure, codependent and CRAZY women—I've had ones who doesn't really know me (new on the yard) see me and wink then find out I don't like women—I have ones who have known me for years—from the distance and then given the opportunity confess their long time crush—I have staff members (men) giving me the funny eye or flirt because the idea of an ASIAN woman. I do feel like I have favor and on their "good" side. I would like to believe it's how I carry myself but I'm sure being an Asian has something to do with it.

She continued by explaining that,

To note, I've changed and matured. When I came to prison and my last 8 years I'm I guess you can say "a model inmate" but that was a choice I had to make because it would have been easy to be sucked into a life style typical to so many women in prison; relationships, drugs, and rebellion. I have built myself a reputation of someone who doesn't get in trouble . . . I'm used to sharing my story—I've been somewhat of a poster child in the prisons. I do believe certain responsibility does come with standing out physically and mentally. It's like you are a leader whether you like it or not because you choose to do the right thing. It's crazy.

From these descriptions of SoSon's experience it is easy to see that her life in prison has been shaped by the expectations put upon her to represent her racial and ethnic identity. The way this expectation influences East Asian women in prison warrants further exploration. While SoSon appears to have internalized this from a motivating perspective, it is possible that it could be a polarizing interaction in the sense that women East Asian mothers may be demonized for their failure to live up to both stereotypes of "model minorities" and "good mothers."

Finally, one additional factor that potentially complicates the experience of East Asian mothers in prison is in regards to citizenship status. So-Son shared her thoughts on this possibility.

> As far as me, being an "East Asian" woman—at this point I do not know if I am going to be deported back to Korea. I am adopted and as I've mentioned earlier, I've only met one other Korean. Week before she discharged she was put on ICE hold [U.S. Immigration & Customs Enforcement]—facing deportation to Korea. She had no idea what was going on. She left home when 14 so she hasn't spoken to her mother since then—had to get in touch with her only to find out she is full Korean brought to here as an infant and adopted. She hired a lawyer and avoided deportation. I am not terribly worried since I am adopted. It's a possibility that I might face deportation also. Then I am worried I won't be back to the States and not see Sarah again unless she comes to Korea. However, I pray that is not the case.

While SoSon is not actively worried about deportation, it still remains in the back of her mind as a possibility. To provide some context, the number of actions that qualifies one for deportation have skyrocketed since the *Anti-Terrorism Effective Death Penalty Act* and the *Illegal Immigration Reform and Immigrant Responsibility Act* were passed in 1996. This means that it is much more common for individual's lacking citizenship status to be held in immigrant detention pending deportation upon release from prison. Now, this is something that both men and women alike, regardless of parental status, may face, no matter what the circumstances of them having to leave their country of origin were. Arguably, the complexity of this issue increases for mothers, who more often were the primary caretakers of their children prior to their incarceration, as they are forced to choose between bringing their children back into what may be very unstable or dangerous situations in their home country, or essentially leaving their children in the United States, which they will not be able to reenter.

FOUNDATIONS FOR FUTURE RESEARCH

This chapter draws attention to a category of the incarcerated population that has thus far been overlooked and who are "invisible." SoSon's story gives voice and visibility into the intimate experience of *one* East Asian mother in prison—a life patterned by abuse, misconceptions, responsibilities, and isolation. Our understanding increases; however, there remains much unknown about the *generalized* experience of this group of women. But we do at least have ideas about where to begin.

Future research points to exploring what it means to be a model minority, what it means to transgress that identity in a very tangible sense, and how motherhood complicates that experience. For instance, are East Asian mothers more or less likely to have familial networks to care for children during their incarceration? Understanding the reentry process and how it may or may not differ for these women in terms of resources available and/or expected stressors is additionally important to understand. The development and implementation of informed policies and programs to support these women upon release hinges upon our understanding of specific barriers East Asian women face. But because of the inadequacy of current statistical reporting practices on race and ethnicity in the prison population, coupled with the incentives for mothers to withhold information about parental status to prevent potential termination of parental rights, we also must first make steps towards understanding exactly *who* is in prison. Furthermore, the additional impact of invisibility and isolation experienced during incarceration should be more fully explored—not only from mother's perspectives but for the children they leave behind. In this way, such research brings urgently needed visibility and contributes to social justice for this population.

NOTES

[1]Pseudonyms of SoSon's partner and child have been used to protect their identity.

WORKS CITED

Incarceration Facts. Aid to Children of Imprisoned Mothers, Inc. March 2004. Web. 6 June 2014.

Baker, Katie J.M. Most Prisons Still Shackle Female Inmates While They're Giving Birth. *Jezebel.* October 2012. Web. 20 June 2014.

Britton Dana M. *The Gender of Crime.* Lanham: Rowman & Littlefield, 2011. Print.

—. *At Work in the Iron Cage: The Prison as Gendered Organization.* New York: New York University Press, 2003. Print.

Brown, Ely and Alexa Valiente. *Babies Born, Raised Behind Bars May Keep Mothers From Returning to Prison.* Nightline. February 2014. Web. 18 June 2014.

Glaze, Lauren E. and Laura M. Maruschak. *Bureau of Justice Statistics Special Report, Parents in Prison and Their Minor Children.* March 2010. Web. 18 June 2014.

Chou, Rosalind S. and Joe R. Feagin. *They Myth of the Model Minority: Asian Americans Facing Racism.* Boulder: Paradigm Publishers, 2008. Print.

Cuomo, Andrew and Marc Fisher. "State of New York, Department of Corrections and Community Supervision. Under Custody Report: Profile of Inmate Population Under Custody on January 1, 2011," 2011. Print.

Enos, Sandra. *Mothering from the Inside: Parenting in a Women's Prison.* New York: SUNY Press, 2001. Print.

The Feminist Griote. *Orange is NOT the New Black.* August 19th, 2013. Web. 11 June 2014.

Ferraro, Kathleen J. and Angela M. Moe. "Mothering, Crime, and Incarceration." *The Journal of Contemporary Ethnography,* 32.1 (2003): 9–40. Print.

Kanter, Rosabeth Moss. *Men and Women of the Corporation.* New York: Basic Books, 1977. Print.

Golden, Renny. *War on the Family: Mothers in Prison and the Families they Leave Behind.* New York: Routledge, 2005. Print.

Kellor, Frances A. "Psychological and Environmental Study of Women Criminals, II." *The American Journal of Sociology,* 5.5 (1990): 671–682. Print.

Kruttschnitt, Candace and Rosemary Gartner. "Women's Imprisonment." In *Crime and Justice, A Review of Research,* Vol 30, edited by Michael Tonry. The University of Chicago Press: Chicago, 2003. Print.

Law, Victoria. "In US Since Age 10 But No Dream Act for Young Activist." *Fire Next Time.* Jan 5, 2013. Web. Feb 27, 2013. Print.

Mickey, L. Parsons and Warner-Robbins, Carmen. "Factors that Support Women's Successful Transition to the Community Following Jail/Prison." *Health Care for Women International* 23.6 (2002): 6–18. Print.

Owens, Michael Leo. "2.7 Million Children Under the Age of 18 Have a Parent in Prison or Jail—We Need Criminal Justice Reform Now." *The Guardian.* August 19, 2013. Web. 18 June 2014.

Petersilia, Joan. "When prisoners return to the community: Political, economic, and social consequences." *Sentencing & Corrections: Issues for the 21st Century, No. 9, Papers from the Executive Sessions on Sentencing and Corrections.* Washington, D.C.: National Institute of Justice (2000): 1–8. Print.

Pollock, Jocelyn M. 2002. *Women, Prison & Crime,* Second Edition. Belmont: Wadsworth Thomson Learning, 2002. Print.

Richie, Beth E. "Challenges incarcerated women face as they return to their communities: Findings from life history interviews." *Crime & Delinquency* 47.3 (2001): 368–388. Print.

Schirmer, Sarah, Ashley Nellis, and Marc Mauer. "Incarcerated Children and Their Parents: Trends 1991–2007." *The Sentencing Project, Research and Advocacy for Reform,* 2009. Print.

Sharp, Susan F. and M. Elaine Eriksen. "Imprisoned Mothers and Their Children." In B. H. Zaitzow & J. Thomas (Eds.), *Women in Prison, Gender and Social Control* (119-36). Boulder: Lynne Rienner Publishers, 2003. Print.

Stanton, Ann M. *When Mothers Go to Jail.* Lexington: Lexington Books, 1980. Print.

Thomas, Jim. "Gendered Control in Prisons: The Difference Difference Makes.: In B. H. Zaitzow & J. Thomas (Eds.), *Women in Prison, Gender and Social Control* (1–20). Boulder: Lynne Rienner Publishers, 2003. Print.

Travis, A. Fritsch and Burkhead, John D. "Behavioral Reactions of Children to Parental Absence due to Imprisonment." *Family Relations* 30.1 (1981): 83–88. Print.

Wright, Emily M., Patricia Van Voorhis, Emily J. Salisbury and Ashley Bauman. "Gender-Responsive Lessons Learned and Policy Implications for Women in Prison: A Review." *Criminal Justice and Behavior* 39 (2012): 1612–1632. Print.

19.

Motherhood and the Race for Sustainability

MARIE LO

Among the 2011 "Word of the Year" possibilities considered by Geoff Nunberg, linguist and commentator on the radio program *Fresh Air*, "Tiger Mom" was a contender, only to be beaten out by the word, "occupy," as in the broad-based collective protests of the Occupy Wall Street Movement.[1] It is both fitting and ironic that a term that has become shorthand for ambitious and overbearing parental stress on individual achievement should be pitted against a term that embodies the power of collective politicization and protest. Though diffuse in its object of critique and in its organizational structure, the Occupy Wall Street movement mobilized people through its critique of globalization, corporate greed and the ever-widening gap between the 99% and the 1%. Amy Chua's *Battle Hymn of the Tiger Mother*, in contrast, reads like a primer on how to be a part of the 1%.

The controversy surrounding Chua's book—the instigatory and sensationalized *Wall Street Journal* excerpt titled "Why Chinese Mothers are Superior" not withstanding—seems somewhat overblown if we consider it in the context of other Asian American narratives on mothering. We need only to recall Maxine Hong Kingston's Brave Orchid in *The Woman Warrior: Memoirs of a Girlhood Among Ghosts* or any of the mothers in Amy Tan's novels for literary predecessors. Chua herself acknowledges these works when she notes how authors like Kingston, Tan and Jung Chang of *Wild Swans* "beat her to it" in writing their mother-daughter stories (33). Furthermore, Chua's emphasis on parenting and Asian American academic success is not unique. Consider for example, *Top of the Class: How Asian Parents Raise High Achievers—and How You Can Too*. In fact, Chua's parenting does not seem that dramatically different from the phenomenon of helicopter parenting among certain middle- and upper-middle class families.

Despite Chua's unabashed codification of this style of parenting as "Chinese" and her simultaneous critique of the mediocre, lax form of parenting that is "Western," the supposed twist here is that the second-generation assimilated daughter has become a mother, and she is unapologetic about embracing the first-generation's methods of strict parenting. Updated for the new millennium, the "Tiger Mother" is a no-holds barred model minority equivalent of Sarah Palin's "Mama Grizzly." Tiger Mom has all of Mama Grizzly's instinctive fierce protectiveness, but instead of strangers (or liberals), her energy is directed towards preparing her young for a tough and competitive future. As a *Time* reviewer notes, "The Tiger Mother's cubs are being raised to rule the world, the book clearly implies, while the offspring of the 'weak-willed,' 'indulgent' Westerners are growing up ill equipped to compete in a fierce global marketplace."

Many have noted that the controversy generated by Chua's memoir needs to be contextualized in relation to U.S. anxieties regarding both the strength of China's economy and international influence and the decline of the U.S. educational system.[2] As reviewer Nancy McDermott points out, some critics see in Chua's text "every Western prejudice and fear" they may have about China:

> Chua's daughters may be virtuosos but, rest assured, as cowed Chinese automatons they could never actually *compose* music. Chinese parenting, we're told, is why China has so many human-rights abuses. Conversely it is why China is kicking America's butt, economically. Others say that there's nothing Chinese about Chua at all—she is simply taking intensive, over-invested American-style parenting to its ugly extreme. Janet Maslin, also writing in the *New York Times*, called her book 'one little narcissist's search for happiness.' The reaction seems all the more over-the-top when you consider that Chua's book is a memoir.

The range of these arguments about parenting, Orientalist stereotypes as well as generic conventions and expectations also evoke elements of the controversy generated by Kingston's *The Woman Warrior*.[3] However, if we understand the controversy around the Tiger Mom against the backdrop of the Occupy Wall Street movement, what emerges are not only competing narratives of parenting, race, nation and academic performance, but also how these narratives are animated by class differences and competing responses to the effects of globalization on the environment. In what follows, I expand this binary construction between an authoritarian Chinese-style of mothering versus a lax and indulgent western-style to take into account another point of reference for examining the Tiger Mom controversy, one that emerges out of a concern for the environmental impact of globalization and unfettered capitalism.

My other point of reference is a contemporaneous figure that has also captured the public imagination—the "Femivore." Most visibly aligned with the renewed interest in urban homesteading, canning and backyard chickens, this other mother is an updated version of the earth mother. A highly educated woman, she has chosen to leave her career to be a stay-at-home mom, embracing her decision to raise her children as a way to counteract the excessive consumption, materialism and environmental impact of industrialization and globalization. The "Femivore," coined by Peggy Orenstein, is a feminist farmer mom in the mold of Michael Pollan's *Omnivore's Dilemma*, in which raising children, recycling and eating local are intertwined political acts. Her more radical counterpart, the "Radical Homemaker" may or may not homeschool her children, and is more explicit in rejecting the regulatory conformity of public schools and other kinds of public or civic institutions.

In this article, I explore how the broad contours of these dominant narratives of motherhood and ecocriticism emerge to displace other forms of Asian mothering that are also engaged with issues of sustainability. More specifically, I examine the Tiger Mom in relation to the Femivore or the Radical Homemaker to demonstrate how mothering becomes a racialized site for competing narratives of sustainability. While Orenstein implies that Femivores are all women, it should be noted that "Radical Homemakers" are not specifically women nor are "Chinese moms" specifically Chinese. But rather, in both cases these terms reflect the gendering and racialization that give these identities their differential and relational value and cultural currency. Indeed, the media valorization of the Femivore over the Tiger Mom is less about parenting styles so much as it is reveals the extent to which "sustainability" discourse is a crucial site of class and gendered racial formation, both erasing the conditions which produce and necessitate "sustainability" and circumscribing the limits of what counts as "sustainable."

I wish to mark my use of the term "sustainability" in my discussion of ecocriticism and motherhood for a number of reasons. The term "sustainability," as Leerom Medovoi points out, has become a ubiquitous part of environmental discourse but its critical implications and reach remain under-examined. Moreover, sustainability implies a futurity that is often at the heart of our ideas about parenting, motherhood and the world that we want our children to inherit; what is "sustained" is, presumably, being preserved for future generations. Drawing on Medovoi's work, I argue that the racialization of motherhood privileges a particular vision of sustainability, political action and environmental consciousness aligned with white liberalism, implicitly designating Asians and Asian Americans as model minorities apathetic to environmentalism at best or environmentally destructive at worst. Sustainable practices, therefore, become figured as a sign and the domain of white, middle-class motherhood, thus rendering unintelligible the environmentalism of Asian North American women. And it is through recourse to the particular configurations of the Tiger Mom that the contours of white radical homemaking and its discursive effects become most visible.

I take "radical homemaking" from the title of Shannon Hayes' book, *Radical Homemakers: Reclaiming Domesticity from a Consumer Culture* to refer to a set of parenting styles and practices that constructs the home as the "center for social change" (18). This reclaiming of the domestic arts as a politicized practice is reflected in the recent surge in the popularity of memoirs of urbanites moving to farms, how-to-books and blogs that re-center home life as an active site for the promotion of sustainable practices.[4] Magazines such as *Mother Earth* and *Grit*, which for years have served niche markets, have suddenly become more mainstream. There are not only countless blogs on moving off the grid but also ones that focus on city gardening, permaculture, farmers markets, and community-supported agriculture (CSA). There is also a resurgence in all things handmade, such as knitting, sewing, canning and preserving, which have been given a hipster spin with publications such as *Made Magazine*, *Ready Made Magazine* (now defunct), *Stitch Nation* and *Handmade Nation* Crafting is no longer just a hobby, but "craftivism," endowed with ethical force for social change.

This shift towards homemaking as a political act seems to involve a shift in traditional gender paradigms. The return to homemaking is not represented as a return to the gendered division of labor and the domestic/public split that had animated second wave feminist struggles. Rather, the turn towards homemaking is both figured as a choice over working in the corporate world as well as an attempt to create community through supporting one's local economy and promoting equitable sustainable forms of living in the face of increasing industrialization, globalization and rapacious capitalism.

According to Kristen Williams, this "back-to the basics" movement affirms the individualism that is celebrated in the American pastoral tradition and is traceable to the "gentleman farmers" of the early colonial period. Popular contemporary terms like the "urban homestead" or the "backyard homestead" resurrect the notion of the pioneering spirit of self-sufficiency and independence. What is conveniently neglected, however, is the devastating impact the Homestead Act of 1862 had on Native American sovereignty and tribal land claims. Just as this romanticized return to the "homestead" is based on white settler experiences, the argument that reclaiming domesticity and homemaking are political acts is similarly premised on the construction of homemaking in terms of white middle-class women's experiences. According to Orenstein, "Femivorism is grounded in the very principles of self-sufficiency, autonomy and personal fulfillment that drove women into the work force in the first place." The emphasis on self-sufficiency, autonomy and personal fulfillment as opposed to financial considerations as the motivating factor in women's participation in the work force reinforces the values of the neoliberal subject decontextualized from the financial exigencies that drove many poor women and women of color to work long before the rise of second wave feminism.

The focalization and re-evaluation of the experiences of white middle-class women as basis for this new radical form of homemaking is even more explicit in Haye's work, which relies heavily on Betty Friedan's *Feminine Mystique* to explain the contemporary disavowal of homemaking. Hayes draws on Friedan's characterization of the "housewife's syndrome" to both explain women's initial entry into the work force and the current failures of the work force to provide women with the sense of fulfillment they were looking for:

> Friedan argued that the root of both feminism and women's frustration lay in the emptiness of the housewife's role, because "the major work and decisions of society were taking place outside the home." However, at this point in history, the work to heal our ecological wounds, bring a balance of power into our economy and to ensure social equity starts with our choices about what to eat, what to buy (or more importantly,

what not to buy), what to create, and how to use our time and money. Indeed, the major work of society need to happen *inside* our homes, putting the homemaker at the vanguard of social change. (45-46)

Despite Haye's initial argument that a radical homemaker need not be a woman, the slippage here between "housewife" and "homemaker" suggests that rather than challenging the gendered division of labor, radical homemaking merely re-values women's work within the same heteronormative model of the nuclear family and does little to disrupt the structures of value that have historically rendered women more financially vulnerable because their labor is non-wage labor. Furthermore, the solution to our "ecological wounds," social injustice and economic imbalance hinges on a neoliberal subject whose consumption choices—whether it be about "what to eat" or "what to buy"—remains the domain and currency of social change. Given that Friedan's book has been viewed by many as a catalyst and manifesto for the white, heterosexual middle-class women's movement, its function within *Radical Homemakers* serves to enforce a genealogy of radicalism that, in fact, shores up a white, heteronormative middle-class neoliberal subject.

The sense of fulfillment that Hayes notes is missing from contemporary homemakers' lives is the larger sense of social purpose that "radical homemaking" provides. Central to radical homemaking is the language of personal responsibility and a developmental narrative of self-actualization, a three-stage process that involves 1) renouncing consumer society; 2) reclaiming and rediscovering previously devalued homemaking skills: and 3) rebuilding to create a community and life that affirms the principles of radical homemaking. According to Hayes:

> In a life-serving economy, we individually accept responsibility for creating our own joys and pleasures. We do not rely on corporate America to sell us these things. We take personal and collective responsibility for supplying many of our needs. …In the life-serving economy, the political spectrum fades away, particularly as Americans discover that the majority of us share many of the same values. (59-60)

Rejecting the materialism and values of corporate America, the proposed alternative of a "life-serving economy" still draws on the neoliberal belief in the free market as the means by which the ideals of personal choice and individual responsibility can find their fullest expression. Merely a shift in scale, the reach of corporate America is substituted for a more localized economy, which is invested with the ability to transcend difference and neutralize political dissent. This flattening of difference in the promotion of a neoliberal subject is, ironically, as many have argued, one of the effects of globalization—not a panacea against it.

Against the contours of this movement are the representations of Asian Americans, who are figured as antithetical to sustainability. Since their arrival in the 19th century, the recurrent representations that fueled many of the anti-Asian legislation hinge on their excessive or over-consumption of scarce resources, whether it be employment opportunities, land or other forms of property.[5] In contemporary media representations, the impact of China's rapid industrialization is often cited as a chief contributor to climate change.[6] Not only are Asians and Asian Americans cast as central agents of environmental degradation, but they are also understood in terms of capital accumulation. As Christine So notes, "Asian Americans have overwhelmingly been imagined through the rhetoric and logic of economics, defined as agents of vast economic profit or loss" (5), whether they be an untapped market share or perceived as unfair competitors. In the controversy surrounding Chua's memoir, the representation of Asian Americans in terms of economics crystallizes a particular form of motherhood, reproduction and model minority discourse that becomes inseparable from the anxiety and racial discourse surrounding Asian labor and economic competition. In other words, the anxiety about Asian motherhood and its reproduction of model minorities reflects the anxiety regarding Asian capital and economic competition and the environmental effects of Asian industrialization.

The gendering of Asians in North America in terms of over-consumption that is at the expense of environmental concerns is caricatured in a Hennessy Cognac ad which features two women, one white and the other Asian. The white woman, draped in a white dress that barely covers her back, is in the foreground, looking away from the viewer. Her hair is long and flowing, and the combined effect of her loose hair and dress suggest an innocence and natural beauty that needs no enhancement. Under her, is the label "vegetarian." The Asian woman, on the other hand, is putting on lipstick. Dressed in a black dress with her hair severely pulled back, her gaze is directed at us as if she is fully aware of her seductive powers. Unlike the white woman's natural beauty, she is wearing heavy make-up. Under her, the copy reads "man-eater." In the bottom right, the copy states, "mix accordingly," an invitation for the male viewer to taste, tame and enjoy.

In this male fantasy of inter-racial lesbian sex, what each woman eats is indicative of particular forms of racialized sexuality, and their consumption habits reveal how these forms are inseparable from narratives about the threat and encroachment on the resources of white patriarchy. It is the tag, "man-eater" that gives "vegetarian" its sexual innocence and its nurturing, life-affirming qualities for the binary opposite of "vegetarian" is "meat-eater," not "man-eater." The slippage between "meat-eater" and "man-eater" casts the Asian woman as the stereotypical predatory and emasculating Asian dragon lady. But in this scene about sexuality, race and consumption, her man-eating ways represent a direct threat to not only white masculinity but also to the resources and conditions of life. The alignment of white womanhood with vegetarianism refigures ethical concerns about the environment, animal rights, and over-consumption as the natural domain of nurturing white women who are also "more natural." In contrast, the Asian woman embodies an unnatural and manufactured sexuality whose excessive appetite is both emasculating and indistinguishable from the threat it poses to the environmental resources of a white patriarchal order.

If we read Chua's work as yet another example of excessive or unnatural consumption, then the controversy surrounding *Battle Hymn of the Tiger Mother* becomes no longer simply about extreme parenting styles but rather how Asian motherhood inculcates a mode of consumption that is both unnatural and accelerates environmental degradation. Early on, the book reproduces stereotypes about the "exotic" eating habits of Asians by equating being Chinese with indiscriminate and voracious appetites. Chua notes how her daughter Sophia "eats all kinds of organs and organisms—duck webs, pig ears, sea slugs" as evidence of how her kids are just like "Chinese kids" (56). She explains that while "in the West dogs have long been considered loyal companions, in China they're on the menu. This is so upsetting that it feels like an ethnic slur, but unfortunately it's true" (66). Chua disavows this practice because she loves Lassie, "one of her favorite literary characters" (79). While written in a tongue-in-cheek tone, Chua's reference to dog eating nevertheless replays the mainstream Western horror that the boundaries between food and family are blurry in Asian societies.[7]

Despite Chua's distaste for dog eating, the possibility that the Tiger Mother may potentially "eat dogs" which, from a western perspective can also mean, "eat her own" is enabled by the analogy that Chua makes between her children and her Samoyed, Coco, who is also subject to Chua's "Chinese parenting" (79). As a Tiger Mother, Chua's voracious appetite for competition, status, and prestige also extends to the "hopes and dreams" she has for dog. While her inclusion of her expectations for Coco is meant to be a humorous moment of self-realization of her extremism, these scenes nonetheless reiterate the specter of cannibalism found in the Hennessy advertisement. However, unlike the ad, the Tiger Mother's voracious appetite can lead her to potentially turn on her young.

In fact, the topic of how she treats her children seems to constitute the bulk of the criticisms against Chua. Many reviewers have noted her insults, her threats to burn their dolls and her rejection of their hand-made cards as examples of her exacting and competitive standards. In the coda to her book, Chua notes one of the possible book titles suggested by her daughter, Lulu, the younger child against whom Chua clashes: *The Perfect Child and the Flesh-Eating Devil*. While Lulu's suggestion of the "flesh-eating devil" is in contrast to her sister, the obedient one who is "the perfect child," throughout the memoir, Chua comments on how similar she and Lulu are. Their conflict is borne out of their similar obstinate personalities. Furthermore, the "quasi-cannibalistic" quality has a particular resonance when considered in relation to the model minority stereotype that Chua perpetuates, in which the first-generation parental desire for upward mobility creates the possibility that they can potentially turn on their young, leaving their children to identify with food.[8]

Crucially, the Tiger Mother's "Chinese parenting" privileges a kind of individualism and middle-class mobility that ironically parallels the femivores and radical homemakers' choice to return "back to the land"—they are two sides of the neoliberal coin. While the carbon footprint of Chua's intense parenting—driving back and forth between New Haven and New York for weekend music lessons with teachers at Julliard—would make her environmental counterparts cringe, their respective emphasis on individual choices and mobility in response to racial and environmental injuries respectively downplay or erase the structural conditions that produces these wounds in the first place. The "ecological" wounds described by Hayes are, in Chua's text, presented as racial injuries that are healed by the upward mobility enabled by Chua's strict parenting approaches. In one scene, Chua proudly lists the various countries she and her children have traveled before they were nine as an example of the importance of cosmopolitanism. When her children were young and mocked foreign names, she offered this cautionary tale about the dangers of provincialism: "My parents had accents—I had an accent. I was thrown into nursery school not speaking word of English. Even in third grade, classmates made fun of me. Do you know where those people are now? They're janitors, that's where" (86). Here, "provincialism" is posited as the reason for these third-grade bullies' lack of economic advancement, and their moral failings, racism and ignorance explain their blue-collar jobs. Not only are they not jetting around the world, but they are also trapped in thankless jobs that presumably they did not choose. In other words, they are not in professions that provide—in the terms of Peggy Orenstein and Femivores–"autonomy, self-sufficiency or personal fulfillment" and deserve their place in the economic ladder.

Chua's assessment of mobility as being enabled by individual achievement, in turn, puts into relief the economic mobility that Femivores and Radical Homemakers possess. Many households do not have the financial security to support a stay-at-home parent nor the employment opportunities to move out of cities to escape the higher costs of living. Furthermore, these "radical" models not only necessitate a two-parent household, potentially reaffirming heteronormativity, but the decision to move "back to the land" obscures the conditions and distribution of land ownership that have been founded on stolen lands, broken treaties with indigenous peoples and laws that prevent people of color from owning land. Access to property and affordable housing are presupposed in these narratives, and the individual choices that femivores and radical homemakers describe are bolstered by a set of invisible privileges that facilitate those choices.

If *Battle Hymn of the Tiger Mother* reinforces dominant assumptions about Asian Americans as the model minority, Chua's characterization of and emphasis on individual achievement as the source of healing racial injuries also parallel the femivore and radical homemakers' turn toward individual responsibility and the domestic sphere to heal ecological wounds.[9] In explaining why certain Asian American narratives receive so much traction in mainstream media, David Palumbo-Liu argues that these narratives, which highlight individual transcendence of racial injury, are rendered intelligible through a discursive matrix, which he calls model minority discourse, that valorizes the domestic rather than the social and political as the site for healing. According to Palumbo-Liu, model minority discourse is essentially a discourse of political containment, in which the emphasis on individual healing circumvents or forecloses a critique of the structural systems of injury under racial capitalism. In reading radical homemaking through the matrix of model minority discourse, what becomes visible is the extent to which the turn towards the domestic is not only still a precarious site of political action, but also that it is easily co-opted by neoliberal discourses. Thus, if the argument—that "Tiger Moms" need not be Chinese and "Radical Homemakers" need not be women—is a discursive as opposed to a descriptive one, then "Model Minorities" need not be Asian Americans either. Reworking Helen Heran Jun's claim that Asian Americans "have come to embody the ideal neoliberal subject" (132), we might want to also consider how, in these instances, neoliberal subjects are turned into "Model Minorities."

The apparent dichotomy reflected in these two dominant narratives of middle-class motherhood, one which casts Asian American motherhood as a threat and a drain on the environment and the other which casts white motherhood as its savior, potentially erases another narrative of Asian American motherhood, one that troubles the ethical value imputed to "sustainability" and the neoliberal values of choice, agency and economic freedom embedded in the dominant narratives of middle-class motherhood. Despite a growing body on ecocriticism of color, there is comparatively little critical engagement with Asian North American literature, with the exception of scholars such as Shiuh-Huah Serena Chou, Robert Hayashi, Julie Sze, Janice Tanemura, and writers such as Ruth Ozeki, Karen Tei Yamashita, David Mas Masumoto and Rita Wong. In part, the invisibility of Asian North American works in ecocriticism may have to do with the perception that Asian North American literature is primarily concerned with issues of immigration and assimilation. Robert Hayashi in "Beyond Walden Pond: Asian American Literature and the Limits of Ecocriticism" argues that ecocriticism's emphasis on wildlife preservation and environmental justice's focus on environmental hazards and degradation have often occluded Asian American and Asian Canadian texts from consideration. In fact, Asian Americans were often "the very engine of environmental change … They were the land's miners, railroad workers, farm hands, and fishermen: its workers" (65). Though he approaches Asian American ecocriticism at the intersection of labor and landscape, I wish to turn to texts that have been analyzed primarily in terms of mother-daughter relationships, immigration and assimilation—notably, Kingston's *The Woman Warrior*, *Obasan* by Joy Kogawa, and *Bone* by Fae Myenne Ng—to demonstrate how the representation of immigration and assimilation can put pressure on one the key terms of the mainstream environmental discourse: "sustainability."

In "A Contribution to the Critique of Political Ecology: Sustainability as Disavowal," Leerom Medovoi argues that environmentalism's embrace of "sustainability" also entails a disavowal of the injurious conditions created by neoliberal capitalism responsible for the need for "sustainability" and "sustainable practices" in the first place. By tracking the word's etymology, he notes that the word "sustain" also means "to undergo, experience, have to submit to (evil, hardship, or damage; now chiefly with injury, loss as objective, formerly also sorrow, death); to have inflicted upon one, suffer the infliction of" (131). Thus, the dominance of sustainability in environmental discourse necessarily disavows

> the "structural cause" of its own emergence—the serious injury of capitalism that wreaks on the very social and natural systems upon which it depends—while also seeking to deny this causality, so that capitalism can save the day, if not by healing the damage, at least by reducing it to a level that can be endured. (138)

If we apply Medovoi's formulation to the values embedded in radical homemaking, we can see that the "ecological wounds" that radical homemaking is supposed to heal, in fact, derives its belief in the curative powers of a neoliberal economy. This return to the homestead and to homemaking necessarily erases U.S. colonial genocidal policies of allotment and the construction of property ownership as the basis for liberal individualism and citizenship.

Drawing on Medovoi's analytic to examine Asian North American literature, I want to propose 'sustaining acts' as an analytic and a set of practices that indexes a foundational contradiction. Recalling Lisa Lowe's "immigrant acts" as a contradiction that is both dialectical and critical, in which immigration is both the "locus of legal and political restrictions of Asians" and simultaneously the site of "critical negations of the nation-state of which the legislations are the expression" (8), "sustaining acts" names a similar contradiction. "Sustaining acts" both points to how the economic, racialized and gendered marginalization of Asian Americans is a "necessary and 'sustaining' feature of capital accumulation" (Medovoi 143), which in turn gives rise to acts of survival necessary to sustain against and endure that on-going injury. Such acts, however, have been rendered invisible within contemporary sustainability discourse precisely because they are not free-floating "choices" but necessary acts of survival.

In Kingston's *Woman Warrior*, the narrator's mother is described as someone who does not waste anything, whose life is "powered by Necessity": "She plants vegetable gardens rather than lawns; she carries the odd-shaped tomatoes home from the fields and eats food left for the gods" (6). In

Obasan, the whole Nakane clan is described as attentive gardeners in living in tune with nature. They have a:

> vegetable garden, flowers, a lawn, and a chicken coop with several chickens … Sweet peas climb the wire-covered wall of the chicken coop … Through the seasons, we trace and retrace the woodland mazes, harvesting the wilderness. Dog-eared mushrooms are here and there like hidden treasures, scattered over the spongy earth. (164)

The narrator's mother in *The Woman Warrior* could be described as an early adopter of the "food not lawns" movement. And the Nakanes not only have a backyard that a Femivore could love, but their foraging in the wilderness reads a like a chapter out of *The Omnivore's Dilemma*. But, what is significantly different are the circumstances under which they employ these sustainable acts. For the narrator's mother in *The Woman Warrior*, having lived through a famine in China only to confront the disenfranchisement and downward mobility of being an immigrant in the U.S., growing a vegetable garden and eating misshapen tomatoes is an economic necessity. The Nakane's garden is located in Slocan, one of the many ghost towns where they and over 21,000 other Japanese Canadians were interned during World War II. For them, living off the land is not a choice, but the result of institutional racism powered by xenophobia and resentment towards Japanese Canadian economic success. It is the only way they can survive and endure the deprivations of internment.

In *Bone*, what registers as sustainability is inseparable from the difficult economic conditions that one must sustain oneself against. Leila, the narrator, describes a childhood scene in which the blurry lines between family, pet and food are an intertwined function of economic circumstances and motherly love. Pigeons (discovered by Leila in adulthood to be squabs) purchased at the butcher, were "a good meal at forty cents a bird." However, the children treated them like their "baby dove birds," only to return home one day to find them cooked:

> Mah said they were a special, nutritious treat. She filled our bowls high with little pigeon parts: legs, breasts, and wings. She let us take our dinners out to the front room to watch *I Love Lucy*. Mah opened up a brown bag for the bones… But Mah always sat alone in the kitchen sucking out the sweetness

of the lesser parts: the neck, the back, and the head. "Bones
are sweater than you know," she always said. She came out to
check the bag. "Clean bones." She shook it. "No waste." (30-
31)

In Sau-ling Wong's ground-breaking work, *Reading Asian American Literature: From Necessity to Extravagance*, she argues that the alimentary
images in Asian American literature symbolize "Necessity," "all the hard-
ships, deprivations, restrictions, disenfranchisement, and dislocations that
Asian Americans have collectively suffered as immigrants and minorities in
a white-dominated country" (20). In this scene, the bones become a con-
densed symbol of necessity in which "no waste" is the primary goal. But,
if we consider these acts of producing "no waste" as not simply functions
of economic necessity or essentialized immigrant frugality but the effects of
social, economic and political constraints of being a racialized immigrant,
then "no waste" becomes a marker of their endurance and of their abilities
to sustain themselves in the face of their marginalization. Rather than affirming a neoliberal individual decontextualized from the material circumstances that give it form, Mah's actions demonstrate how sustainable acts
can link ecological practices to the material effects of immigration and assimilation. In other words, sustainability acts are acts of survival under a
white neoliberal project.

When economic exigencies and necessity are judged against the privileged notion of "choice," sustaining acts become reduced to mere survival
while "choice" becomes the key word that presumes to give sustainability
its moral force and oppositional power. In an interview with Amy Spencer,
Betsy Greer, one of the leaders of "craftivism" explains that "craft has taken
on a revolutionary role. Instead of knitting, weaving or sewing because we
have to, with all the technology that is available, people are *choosing* to. It
is this choice to spend one's leisure time making something that could be
easily purchased where [sic] there is resistance" (emphasis in original). It is
notable that Greer points out not only choice but also leisure time as conditions for resistance. In the case of Mah, who works as a seamstress during
the day, and sews dresses for her daughters at night, such actions are not recognized as "subversive" but rather explained as the inevitable consequences
of being an immigrant, a woman, a mother and of being poor.

In my brief examination of these texts, I want to make clear that I
do not want to romanticize economic hardships and the difficulties of ek-
ing out a living as "more progressive" than other ways of living. Nor am

I against preservation practices or environmentalism, or trying to downplay the extent to which China's rapid industrialization has impacted the climate. Rather I am critical of how the current narrative of environmentalism has become inseparable from a white, middle class form of motherhood, one that participates in the disavowal of sustainability's costs and erases questions of what constitutes sustainable and whose lives are being sustained. The invisibility of Asian North American literature as ecocritical also reflects the dangers of equating "choice" with political action and of poverty with environmental apathy. In this formulation, frugality becomes both a function and an essentialized feature of poverty and "the immigrant experience" such that gardening, recycling, repurposing and reusing are only intelligible as environmentally friendly practices when they are a "lifestyle" choice and the structural conditions of marginalization are taken out of the equation.

Whether or not the terms "Femivore" and "Tiger Mom" will continue to resonate beyond their particular moments is debatable. However, the structuring logic of these representational figures exceeds the moment of their historical emergence. What I would suggest is a reworking of the interpretive frameworks that not only persistently cast Asian North Americans as apolitical model minorities but also the neoliberal subject that both underwrites "political action" and determines its intelligibility. By shifting the focus of sustainability from choice to one that highlights the structural conditions responsible for sustainability's emergence, we might consider the political acts of Asian American motherhood as 'sustaining acts' in the ambivalent and contradictory sense, one that is constrained by the material effects of marginalization, disenfranchisement and deprivation, and yet produces a set of practices leading to a smaller carbon footprint. Paying attention to everyday sustaining acts enables us to track, in the words of Robert Hayashi, how the "historical link between the social and natural realms" connect to the process of immigration, assimilation and motherhood.

AUTHOR'S NOTE

I would like to thank the editors for their insightful comments, in particular, Patti Duncan, whose encouragement and guidance enabled this piece to materialize into a readable form. Thank you to Maria Sarita See, who knows what I think before I do and who suggested this title.

NOTES

[1] As indication of its popularity, in the short time since its publication, Chua's memoir has already spawned a number of other texts, some only available in digital form: *My Tiger Mom and Me* by Angela Tung; *Battle Hymn of a Tiger Daughter: How one family fought the myth that you need to destroy childhood to raise extraordinary adults* by Cynthia Holquist; *Tiger Mother: Son of a Bitch* by Derek Lin; and *Tiger Babies Strike Back: How I was Raised by a Tiger Mom but Could Not be Turned to the Dark Side* by Kim Wong Keltner.

[2] The latter was confirmed by when the Program for International Student Assessment (PISA) released its results in 2010. Out of a total of countries, U.S. Students scored 17th overall in categories such as reading, science and math. Students in Shanghai scored first place in all three categories.

[3] See Sau-ling C. Wong's "Autobiography as Guided Chinatown Tour?" for an examination into this controversy and how the politics of race and representation intersect with genre expectations.

[4] Notable memoirs include: *The Dirty Life: Memoir of Farming, Food and Love* by Kristin Kimball; *Farm City: The Education of an Urban Farmer* by Novella Carpenter; *Animal, Vegetable, Miracle: A Year of Food Life* by Barbara Kingsolver; and *The Accidental Farmers: An Urban Couple, A Rural Calling, And a Dream of Farming in Harmony with Nature* by Tim Young. Popular how-to-books include *The Backyard Homestead: Produce All the Food You Need on Just a Quarter Acre!* By Carleen Madigan and *The Urban Homestead: Your Guide to Self-Sufficient Living in the Heart of the City* by Kelly Cloyne and Erik Knutzen.

[5] For example, in the 1878 report to the California State Senate on *Chinese Immigration: Its Social, Moral and Political Effect*, Chinese labors are cast as "cheap labor" that threatens "white famine" and "the starvation for our own laborers, [and] a gradual, yet certain depletion of the resources of our State" (63).

[6] In a series of *New York Times* articles that examines the intersection of parenting and the impact of China's pollution on children, Edward Wong notes the high incidences of childhood respiratory problems. The photo, which accompanies the article, "In China, breathing becomes a childhood risk," depicts a young boy wearing a face mask while playing in his bedroom. Only in the corrections did the newspaper note that the photo was staged and that the boy did not wear the mask in his home. Both the head-

line and the photo naturalize pollution as a normalized feature of current life in China and possible future life in the United States if China doesn't address its pollution problem.

[7] This shift between Asian and Chinese in this section is both to mark the specificity of Chua's comments about Chinese culture and to signal how her comments are also part of a broader Orientalist discourse that often characterizes Asians as into eating dogs.

[8] See Sau-Ling C. Wong and her examination of "quasi-cannibalism" and the model minority thesis in *Reading Asian American Literature: From Necessity to Extravagance*

[9] Thanks Maria Sarita See for helping me develop this argument.

WORKS CITED

Abboud, Soo Kim and Jane Y. Kim. *Top of the Class: How Asian Parents Raise High Achievers—and How You Can Too*. New York: Berkeley Publishing Group, 2006.

Carpenter, Novella. *Farm City: The Education of an Urban Farmer*. New York: Penguin, 2010. Print.

Chinese Immigration: Its Social, Moral, and Political Effect. Report to the California State Senate of its Special Committee on Chinese Immigration. New York: Jerome S. Ozer, 1971. Print.

Chua, Amy. *Battle Hymn of the Tiger Mother*. New York: Penguin, 2011.

—. "Why Chinese Mothers are Superior," *The Wall Street Journal*. 8 January 2011. Web. 1 February 2013.

Chou, Shiuh-huah Serena. "Pruning the Past, Shaping the Future: David Mas Masumoto and Organic Nothingness." *MELUS* 34.2 (2009): 157-174.

Coyne, Kelly and Erik Knutzen. *The Urban Homestead: Your Guide to Self-Sufficient Living in the Heart of the City*. Port Townsend: Process Media, 2008. Print.

Keltner, Kim Wong. *Tiger Babies Strike Back: How a Tiger Mom but Could Not raised me be turned to the Dark Side*. New York: William Morrow, 2013. Print.

Kimball, Kristin. *The Dirty Life: A Memoir of Farming, Food and Love*. New York: Scribner 2011. Print.

Kingsolver, Barbara with Camille Kingsolver and Steven L. Hopp. *Animal, Vegetable, Miracle: A Year of Food Life*. New York: Harper Perennial, 2007. Print.

Kingston, Maxine Hong. *The Woman Warrior: Memoirs of a Girlhood Among Ghosts*. New York: Vintage, 1989. Print.

Kogawa, Joy. *Obasan*. New York: Anchor Books, 1994. Print.

Hayes, Shannon. *Radical Homemaker: Reclaiming Domesticity from a Consumer Culture*. Richmondville: Left to Write, 2010. Print.

Hayashi, Robert T. "Beyond Walden Pond: Asian American Literature and the Limits of Ecocritcism." *Coming into Contact: Explorations in Ecocritical Theory and Practice*. Ed. Annie Merrill Ingram. Athens: UP Georgia, 2007. 58–75. Print.

Holquist, Cynthia. *Battle Hymn of a Tiger Daughter: How one family fought the myth that you need to destroy childhood to raise extraordinary adults*. Llanerch Publishing, 2011. Digital.

Jun, Helen Heran. *Race for Citizenship: Black Orientalism and Asian Uplift from Pre-Emancipation to Neoliberal America*. New York: New York University Press, 2011. Print.

Lin, Derek. *Tiger Mother: Son of a Bitch*. Monex Publishing, 2011. Digital.

Lowe, Lisa. *Immigrant Acts: On Asian American Cultural Politics*. Durham: Duke University Press, 1996. Print.

Madigan, Carleen. *The Backyard Homestead: Produce all the Food You Need on Just a Quarter Acre!* North Adams: Storey Publishing, 2009. Print.

Masumoto, David Mas. *Epitaph for a Peach: Four Seasons on My Family Farm*. New York: HarperCollins, 1995. Print.

—. *Four Seasons in Five Senses: Things Worth Savoring*. New York: W. W. Norton, 2004. Print.

—. *Harvest Son: Planting Roots in American Soil*. New York: W. W. Norton, 1999. Print.

—. *Wisdom of the Last Farmer: Harvesting Legacies from the Land*. New York: Free Press, 2009. Print.

McDermott, Nancy. "Who's Afraid of the 'Tiger Mother'?" *Spiked Review of Books*. 28 January 2011. Web. 1 February 2013.

Medovoi, Leerom. "A Contribution to the Critique of Political Ecology: Sustainability as Disavowal." *New Formations* 69 (2010): 129–143. Print.

Ng, Fae Myenne. Bone. New York: HarperPerennial, 1993. Print.

" 'Occupy': Geoff Nunberg's 2011 Word of the Year." *Fresh Air*. WHYY-FM, Philadelphia. 7 December 2011. Radio.

Orenstein, Peggy. "The Femivore's Dilemma" *New York Times Sunday Magazine* 14 March 2010. Web. 1 February 2013.

Ozeki, Ruth. *All Over Creation*. New York: Penguin, 2004. Print.

—. *My Year of Meats*. New York: Penguin, 1999. Print.

Palumbo-Liu, David. *Asian/American: Historical Crossings of a Racial Frontier*. Stanford: Stanford University Press, 1999. Print.

Paul, Annie Murphy. "Tiger Moms: Is Tough Parenting Really the Answer?" *Time Magazine*, 20 January 2011. Web. 1 February 2013.

Spencer, Amy. *DIY: The Rise of Lo-Fi Culture*. New York: Marion Moyars, 2005. Print.

So, Christine. *Economic Citizens: A Narrative of Asian American Invisibility*. Philadelphia: Temple University Press, 2007. Print.

Sze, Julie. "Boundaries and Border Wars: DES, Technology, and Environmental Justice." *American Quarterly* 58. 3 (2006): 791–814. Print.

Tanemura, Janice. "Race, Regionalism, and Biopower in Yokahama, California." *Discourse* 29.2 &3 (2007): 303-329. Print.

Tung, Angela. *My Tiger Mom and Me*. Hyperink Tiger Children's Books. Digital. 2011.

Williams, Kristen. A. "'Old Time Mem'ry': Contemporary Urban Craftivism and the Politics of Doing-It-Yourself in Postindustrial America." *Utopian Studies* 22.2 (2011): 303–320. Print.

Wong, Edward. "In China, Breathing Becomes a Childhood Risk." *New York Times*, 22 April 2013. Web. 7 June 2014.

Wong, Rita. "Watersheds." *Canadian Literature* 204 (2010): 115-117. Print.

Wong, Saul-ling Cynthia. "Autobiography as Guided Chinatown Tour? Maxine Hong Kingston's *The Woman Warrior* and the Chinese American Autobiographical Controversy." *Multicultural Autobiography: American Lives*. Ed. James Robert Payne. Knoxville: University of Tennessee Press, 1992. 248–279. Print.

—. *Reading Asian American Literature: From Necessity to Extravagance*. Princeton: Princeton UP, 1993. Print.

Yamashita, Karen Tei. *Through the Arc of the Rainforest*. Minneapolis: Coffee House Press, 1990.

Young, Tim. *The Accidental Farmers: An Urban Couple, a Rural Calling and a Dream of Farming in Harmony with Nature.* Elberton: Harmony Publishing, 2011.

About the Contributors

Linda Pierce Allen is an associate professor of English at the University of Southern Mississippi, where she specializes in Filipina American studies and multiethnic American literature. Her research appears in publications such as *Pinay Power: Peminist Critical Theory*; *Whiteness: Feminist Philosophical Reflections*; *Ethnic Heritage in Mississippi: The Twentieth Century*; and the forthcoming *Growing Up Asian American in Children's Literature*. Her co-edited textbook, *Global Crossroads: A World Literature Reader*, is now in its second edition.

Anita Harker Armstrong completed a postdoctoral fellowship at Utah State University's Center for Women & Gender in 2013 where she taught her first course on the Culture & Politics of Motherhood. Currently she teaches Sociology at Whatcom Community College in Bellingham, WA. Her research interests include examining the intersections of work and motherhood; gender and incarceration; and most recently, the experiences of couples in mixed-orientation marriages.

Rupa Bagga-Raoulx completed her Ph.D. in 2012 at the Centre for Women's and Gender Studies, the University of British Columbia. Her dissertation was titled "Perceptions and Deceptions: Perspectives on Adoptions from South Korea to North America." She is currently teaching courses in France on Cross Cultural Management and Geopolitics with a focus on Asia and globalization. Her ongoing projects include a research on the adoption trends in France and a comparison of adoption from India and South Korea in France/Europe.

Grace M. Cho is associate professor of Sociology and Women's Studies at the College of Staten Island - City University of New York and author of *Haunting the Korean Diaspora: Shame, Secrecy, and the Forgotten War* (University of Minnesota Press, 2008). She is currently working on a food memoir, pieces of which have been published in *Gastronomica: the Journal of Food and Culture* and *Meatpaper*.

Melinda Luisa de Jesús is associate professor of Diversity Studies and Critical Studies at the California College of the Arts. She writes and teaches about Asian American cultural production, girl cultures, and race/ethnicity in the United States. In 2011-2012 she was the Fulbright Visiting Scholar at the Centre for Women's Studies, University of York, UK. She edited *Pinay Power: Peminist Critical Theory*, the first anthology of Filipina/American feminisms (Routledge 2005). Her writing has appeared in *Approaches to Teaching Multicultural Comics*; *Ethnic Literary Traditions in Children's Literature*; *Challenging Homophobia*; *The Lion and the Unicorn*; *Meridians*; *MELUS*; *Radical Teacher*; *The Journal of Asian American Studies*; and *Delinquents and Debutantes: Twentieth Century American Girls' Culture*. She is a mezzo-soprano, a mom, an Aquarian, and a big Hello Kitty fan.

Patti Duncan is associate professor and Coordinator of Women, Gender, and Sexuality Studies at Oregon State University where she specializes in transnational feminisms, women of color feminisms, and feminist media studies. She is the author of *Tell This Silence: Asian American Women Writers and the Politics of Speech* (University of Iowa Press, 2004), and co-producer/director of *Finding Face*, an award-winning documentary film. Her writings have appeared in numerous anthologies and journals. Her current research focuses on narratives of rescue, migration, and illegitimate motherhood in representations of women in the global South.

Reshmi Dutt Ballerstadt is an associate professor of English and co-coordinates the Gender Studies program at Linfield College. She is the author of the monograph, *The Postcolonial Citizen: The Intellectual Migrant*, and her articles and creative works have been published in *The South Asian Review*, *The Journal of Asian-American Renaissance*, *Jouvert: Journal of Postcolonial Studies*, *Saranac Review* and others. She teaches in the area of postcolonial theory and literature, gender studies and creative writing.

Talia Esnard is an assistant professor of Sociology at the University of Trinidad and Tobago. Her core research interests include gender and entrepreneurship, mothering and entrepreneurship, entrepreneurial orientations, educational and entrepreneurial leadership. Her 2012 Taiwan Research Fellowship award facilitated an extension of this core research on mothering and entrepreneurship to East Asian societies.

Valerie Francisco is an assistant professor of Sociology at the University of Portland in Oregon. Francisco's forthcoming book examines the strategies of maintaining a transnational family from the perspectives of Filipino migrant women working as domestic workers in New York while their families live in the Philippines. Fundamentally, she interrogates the implications of neoliberal globalization on intimate relationships such as those of the family. Francisco's research is informed by the transnational activism of GABRIELA, an alliance of progressive Filipino women's organizations in the Philippines and in other countries internationally; and MIGRANTE International, an international alliance of Filipino migrant workers.

Kryn Freehling-Burton is an instructor and online advisor for the Women, Gender, and Sexualities Studies program at Oregon State University. Look for her co-edited Demeter book, *Performing Motherhood* (2014). She is also a playwright, actor, and director whose greatest role is mothering her four children with her partner, Eric.

Timothy Gitzen is a doctoral student of Anthropology at the University of Minnesota, Twin-Cities. His dissertation focuses on the everyday formations of national security in South Korea and the way marginalized populations are folded into the rubric of national security while simultaneously challenging its logic. In particular, he traces the peripheral populations of gay soldiers alongside proclaimed national security "experts," including decision makers, researchers, professors, and other consultants, all of whom construct a national security community. He is the author of "(Un) Conventional Investments: The Partnership of Avex and SM Entertainment" (PEAR 2009) and "Affective Resistance: Objects of Korean Popular Music" (IJAPS 2013).

Merose Hwang is an assistant professor of History and coordinator of the Asian Studies Program at Hiram College, near Cleveland, Ohio. She helped found the first Transpeople of Colour Collective in Toronto, Canada. Her writing has appeared in *Asian Journal of Women's Studies* and *Han Kut: Critical Art and Writing by Korean Canadian Women*. She teaches on

East Asian gender and sexuality, new imperialism, postcolonial discourse, and female labor in the global South. Her current research project compares modern discourses on indigenous spiritual practices and nation-building in Central and East Asia.

Hosu Kim is an assistant professor of Sociology at the College of Staten Island, City University of New York. She is currently working on a book manuscript, *Virtual Mothering: Korean Birthmothers in Transnational Adoption*. In addition to her academic work, Kim has been involved in Nodutdol, a Queens-based community organization for peace and economic justice since 2001. During 2005 and 2011, she was also a performance artist for *Still Present Pasts: Korean Americans and the 'Forgotten War'*, a collaborative art project based on the oral histories of Korean War survivors, shown at major cities in the U.S. and Seoul, Korea.

Hyojoung Kim is Associate Professor of Sociology and Director of the Center for Korean American and Korean Studies at California State University, Los Angeles. Kim specializes in political sociology, social movements and Korean and Korean American studies.

Fiona Tinwei Lam has authored two poetry books, *Intimate Distances* and *Enter the Chrysanthemum*, and the children's book, *The Rainbow Rocket*. Her poetry and prose appear in over twenty-two anthologies, including *The Best Canadian Poetry 2010*. She co-edited and contributed to the non-fiction anthology, *Double Lives: Writing and Motherhood*, and *The Bright Well: Contemporary Canadian Poetry about Facing Cancer*. www.fionalam.net

Victoria Law is a freelance writer and editor. She is the author of *Resistance Behind Bars: The Struggles of Incarcerated Women* and the co-editor of *Don't Leave Your Friends Behind: Concrete Ways to Support Families in Social Justice Movements and Communities*. Her writings on gender, incarceration and resistance have also appeared in *The Nation*, *Truthout*, *Bitchmedia* and *Salon*. She is also the editor of *Tenacious: Art and Writings by Women in Prison*.

Marie Lo is an associate professor of English at Portland State University. Her research focuses on Asian North American literature and culture and Critical Ethnic Studies. She is currently at work on a manuscript that examines Asian American cultural politics, U.S. Indian policies and the formation of the U.S. settler state.

Dmae Roberts is a writer/radio artist whose groundbreaking work has been heard on NPR and PRI. Her documentary projects have earned two Peabody awards: *Mei Mei, a Daughter's Song*, a harrowing account of her mother's childhood in Taiwan during WWII and *Crossing East*, the first Asian American history series on public radio. She is a 2006 inaugural United States Artists fellow. Her writing has been published by *Oregon Humanities Magazine*, *The Sun*, Temple University and UNC Press.

Eveline Shen is the Executive Director of Forward Together, a board member of the Movement Strategy Center, and a Bay Area Social Justice Funders Network advisory committee member. She served as PI for two NIH grants exploring the intersection between environmental and reproductive justice. Named a Women's eNews 21 Leader for the 21st Century, Eveline was also a Gerbode Fellow and holds a Masters in Public Health from U.C. Berkeley in Community Health Education.

June H. Sun is an Annenberg fellow and Sociology doctoral student at the University of Southern California specializing in family, demography, and economic and social institutions and organizations. She received her degrees in Sociology from the University of Notre Dame and California State University, Los Angeles.

Pamela Thoma is an associate professor in the Department of Critical Culture, Gender, and Race Studies at Washington State University. With teaching and research interests in Asian American literary and cultural studies, feminist theory, citizenship studies, and film and media studies, she has published articles in such journals as *Contemporary Women's Writing*, *Feminist Media Studies*, and *Genders*. She is the author of *Asian American Women's Popular Literature: Feminizing Genres and Neoliberal Belonging* (Temple University Press, 2014), and she is currently completing a book about fertility, family, and domesticity in postfeminist popular media culture.

Shu-Ju Wang was born and raised in Taiwan and trained as an engineer. She settled in Oregon after stays in Saudi Arabia, California, and New Jersey. In 2000, she left the high tech industry to become a full time studio artist working in painting, printmaking, and artist's books. With an immigrant's eye, Shu-Ju paints a portrait of her sometimes wonderful, sometimes unsettling, first generation American life. Shu-Ju has exhibited nationally and internationally and is represented in many public and private collections in North America. She has been profiled in local and national publications and is the recipient of several awards and grants.

Gina Wong is a Registered Psychologist and associate professor in the Graduate Centre for Applied Psychology at Athabasca University in Alberta, Canada. Gina has a program of research focused on maternal mental health and wellness. She publishes and presents widely on motherhood from feminist and cross-cultural perspectives. She edited *Moms Gone Mad* (Demeter Press, 2012) and received the President's Award for Research and Scholarly Excellence for this book at her university. She has contributed to numerous collections such as *Mothers, Mothering and Motherhood Across Cultural Differences: A Reader* edited by Andrea O'Reilly (Demeter Press, 2014).

Rita Wong is the author of three books of poetry: *sybil unrest* (co-written with Larissa Lai, Line Books, 2008), *forage* (Nightwood, 2007), and *monkeypuzzle* (Press Gang, 1998). She works as an Associate Professor at Emily Carr University of Art + Design, and her work investigates the relationships between contemporary poetics, social justice, ecology, and decolonization. She is currently researching the poetics of water: http://downstream.ecuad.ca